PERSPECTIVES

3

Hugh **DELLAR**

Andrew **WALKLEY**

Lewis **LANSFORD**

Daniel **BARBER**

Amanda **JEFFRIES**

NATIONAL GEOGRAPHIC
L E A R N I N G

Australia · Brazil · Mexico · Singapore · United Kingdom · United States

NATIONAL GEOGRAPHIC
L E A R N I N G

Perspectives 3b Combo Split
**Hugh Dellar, Andrew Walkley,
Lewis Lansford, Daniel Barber,
Amanda Jeffries**

Publisher: Sherrise Roehr

Executive Editor: Sarah Kenney

Publishing Consultant: Karen Spiller

Senior Development Editor: Lewis Thompson

Senior Development Editor: Brenden Layte

Editorial Assistant: Gabe Feldstein

Director of Global Marketing: Ian Martin

Product Marketing Manager: Anders Bylund

Director of Content and Media Production:
Michael Burggren

Production Manager: Daisy Sosa

Media Researcher: Leila Hishmeh

Manufacturing Customer Account Manager:
Mary Beth Hennebury

Art Director: Brenda Carmichael

Production Management, and Composition:
Lumina Datamatics, Inc.

Cover Image: The Hive at Kew Gardens,
London. ©Mark Hadden

For product information and technology assistance, contact us at
Cengage Learning Customer & Sales Support, cengage.com/contact

For permission to use material from this text or product,
submit all requests online at **cengage.com/permissions**
Further permissions questions can be emailed to
permissionrequest@cengage.com

Student Edition: Level 3 Combo Split B
ISBN: 978-1-337-29743-1

National Geographic Learning
20 Channel Center Street
Boston, MA 02210
USA

National Geographic Learning, a Cengage Learning Company, has a mission to bring the world to the classroom and the classroom to life. With our English language programs, students learn about their world by experiencing it. Through our partnerships with National Geographic and TED Talks, they develop the language and skills they need to be successful global citizens and leaders.

Locate your local office at **international.cengage.com/region**

Visit National Geographic Learning online at **NGL.Cengage.com/ELT**
Visit our corporate website at **www.cengage.com**

Printed in Mexico
Print Number: 2   Print Year: 2022

ACKNOWLEDGMENTS

Paulo Rogerio Rodrigues
Escola Móbile, São Paulo, Brazil

Claudia Colla de Amorim
Escola Móbile, São Paulo, Brazil

Antonio Oliveira
Escola Móbile, São Paulo, Brazil

Rory Ruddock
Atlantic International Language Center, Hanoi, Vietnam

Carmen Virginia Pérez Cervantes
La Salle, Mexico City, Mexico

Rossana Patricia Zuleta
CIPRODE, Guatemala City, Guatemala

Gloria Stella Quintero Riveros
Universidad Católica de Colombia, Bogotá, Colombia

Mónica Rodriguez Salvo
MAR English Services, Buenos Aires, Argentina

Itana de Almeida Lins
Grupo Educacional Anchieta, Salvador, Brazil

Alma Loya
Colegio de Chihuahua, Chihuahua, Mexico

María Trapero Dávila
Colegio Teresiano, Ciudad Obregon, Mexico

Silvia Kosaruk
Modern School, Lanús, Argentina

Florencia Adami
Dámaso Centeno, Caba, Argentina

Natan Galed Gomez Cartagena
Global English Teaching, Rionegro, Colombia

James Ubriaco
Colégio Santo Agostinho, Belo Horizonte, Brazil

Ryan Manley
The Chinese University of Hong Kong, Shenzhen, China

Silvia Teles
Colégio Cândido Portinari, Salvador, Brazil

María Camila Azuero Gutiérrez
Fundación Centro Electrónico de Idiomas, Bogotá, Colombia

Martha Ramirez
Colegio San Mateo Apostol, Bogotá, Colombia

Beata Polit
XXIII LO Warszawa, Poland

Beata Tomaszewska
V LO Toruń, Poland

Michał Szkudlarek
I LO Brzeg, Poland

Anna Buchowska
I LO Białystok, Poland

Natalia Maćkowiak
one2one, Kosakowo, Poland

Agnieszka Dończyk
one2one, Kosakowo, Poland

WELCOME TO *PERSPECTIVES!*

Perspectives teaches learners to think critically and to develop the language skills they need to find their own voice in English. The carefully-guided language lessons, real-world stories, and TED Talks motivate learners to think creatively and communicate effectively.

In *Perspectives*, learners develop:

● AN OPEN MIND

Every unit explores one idea from different perspectives, giving learners opportunities for practicing language as they look at the world in new ways.

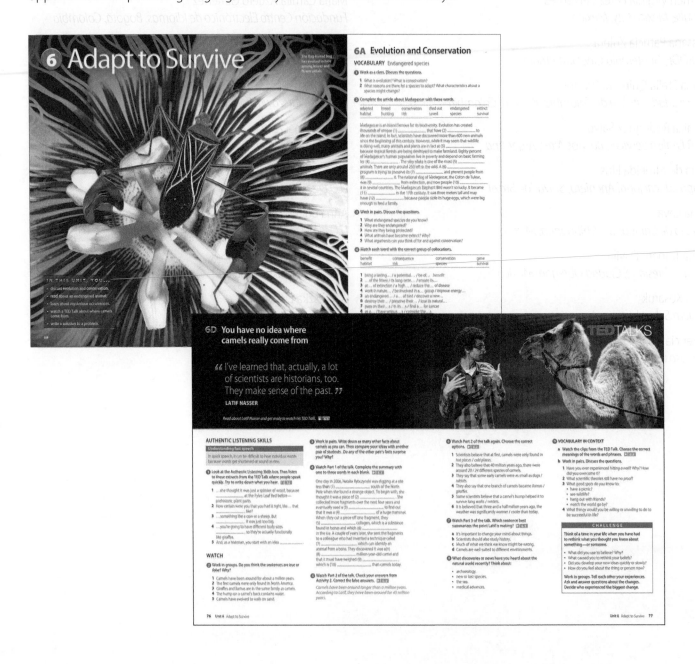

● A CRITICAL EYE

Students learn the critical thinking skills and strategies they need to evaluate new information and develop their own opinions and ideas to share.

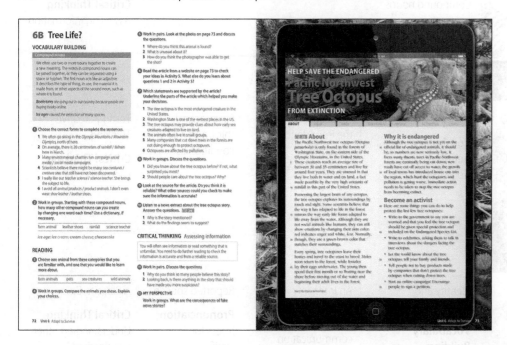

● A CLEAR VOICE

Students respond to the unit theme and express their own ideas confidently in English.

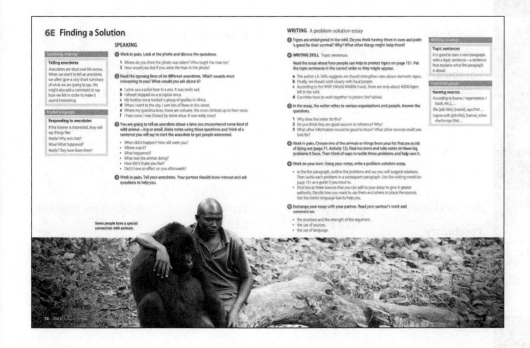

CONTENTS

6

GRAMMAR	TEDTALKS		SPEAKING	WRITING
Modals and infinitive forms **Pronunciation** Weak form of *have*	You have no idea where camels really come from	**LATIF NASSER** Latif Nasser's idea worth spreading is that in science, and in life, we are making surprising discoveries that force us to reexamine our assumptions. **Authentic Listening Skills** Understanding fast speech	Telling anecdotes	A problem-solution essay **Writing Skill** Topic sentences
Wish, if only, would rather **Pronunciation** Elision of final consonants *t* and *d*	Go ahead, make up new words!	**ERIN MCKEAN** Erin McKean's idea worth spreading is that making up new words will help us use language to express what we mean and will create new ways for us to understand one another. **Authentic Listening Skills** Speeding up and slowing down speech	Offering solutions	A report **Writing Skill** Cohesion
Patterns after reporting verbs	Why I keep speaking up, even when people mock my accent	**SAFWAT SALEEM** Safwat Saleem's idea worth spreading is that we all benefit when we use our work and our voices to question and enlarge our understanding of what is "normal." **Authentic Listening Skills** *Just*	Challenging ideas and assumptions	A complaint **Writing Skill** Using appropriate tone
Participle clauses **Pronunciation** *ing* forms	(Re)Touching Lives through Photos	**BECCI MANSON** Becci Manson's idea worth spreading is that photographs hold our memories and our histories, connecting us to each other and to the past. **Authentic Listening Skills** Intonation and completing a point	Countering opposition	A letter of application **Writing Skill** Structuring an application
Emphatic structures **Pronunciation** Adding emphasis	A Broken Body Isn't a Broken Person	**JANINE SHEPHERD** Janine Shepherd's idea worth spreading is that we have inner strength and spirit that is much more powerful than the physical capabilities of even the greatest athletes. **Authentic Listening Skills** Collaborative listening	Developing conversations	A success story **Writing Skill** Using descriptive verbs

6 Adapt to Survive

IN THIS UNIT, YOU...

- discuss evolution and conservation.
- read about an endangered animal.
- learn about mysterious occurrences.
- watch a TED Talk about where camels come from.
- write a solution to a problem.

The flag-footed bug has evolved to hide among leaves and flower petals.

6A Evolution and Conservation

VOCABULARY Endangered species

1 Work as a class. Discuss the questions.

1 What is evolution? What is conservation?
2 What reasons are there for a species to adapt? What characteristics about a species might change?

2 Complete the article about Madagascar with these words.

| adapted | breed | conservation | died out | endangered | extinct |
| habitat | hunting | risk | saved | species | survival |

Madagascar is an island famous for its biodiversity. Evolution has created thousands of unique (1) _____ that have (2) _____ to life on the island. In fact, scientists have discovered more than 600 new animals since the beginning of this century. However, while it may seem that wildlife is doing well, many animals and plants are in fact at (3) _____ because tropical forests are being destroyed to make farmland. Eighty percent of Madagascar's human population live in poverty and depend on basic farming for (4) _____ . The silky sifaka is one of the most (5) _____ animals. There are only around 250 left in the wild. A (6) _____ program is trying to preserve its (7) _____ and prevent people from (8) _____ it. The national dog of Madagascar, the Coton de Tulear, was (9) _____ from extinction, and now people (10) _____ it in several countries. The Madagascan Elephant Bird wasn't so lucky. It became (11) _____ in the 17th century. It was three meters tall and may have (12) _____ because people stole its huge eggs, which were big enough to feed a family.

3 Work in pairs. Discuss the questions.

1 What endangered species do you know?
2 Why are they endangered?
3 How are they being protected?
4 What animals have become extinct? Why?
5 What arguments can you think of for and against conservation?

4 Match each word with the correct group of collocations.

| benefit | consequence | conservation | gene |
| habitat | risk | species | survival |

1 bring a lasting… / a potential… / be of… *benefit*
2 …of the fittest / its long-term… / ensure its…
3 at… of extinction / a high… / reduce the… of disease
4 work in nature… / be involved in a… group / improve energy…
5 an endangered… / a… of bird / discover a new…
6 destroy their… / preserve their… / lose its natural…
7 pass on their…s / in its…s / find a… for cancer
8 as a… / have serious…s / consider the…s

5 Look through the collocations in Activity 4. Underline any phrases that are new to you. Write an example sentence for each of the new phrases.

LISTENING

6 Listen to the interview with a conservationist. Who mentions these points—the interviewer (I), the conservationist (C), or both (B)? 🎧 **27**

1 Most animals have died out.
2 Conservation goes against evolution.
3 Genetic changes through evolution do not make a species more perfect.
4 Animals can't choose to adapt to a new environment.
5 Human activity is increasing the number of extinctions.
6 We must protect endangered species because we can.
7 Conservation is expensive.
8 Humans may become extinct sooner rather than later.

7 What reasons for possible human extinction did you hear in the interview? Listen again and check. 🎧 **27**

8 Work in pairs. Discuss the questions.

1 Do you like television shows about the natural world? What was the last one you saw? What was it about?
2 Have you studied anything about conservation at school? What other things did you learn?
3 Would you like to be a conservationist? What might be good or bad about the job?
4 Have you ever taken action to protect something? What did you do?

GRAMMAR Modals and meaning

9 Look at the Grammar box. Then compare the first and second sentence in each item below. Notice the changes in the use of modals. What is the difference in meaning?

1 You might stop weak species from going extinct.
 You will stop weak species from going extinct.
2 Maybe we shouldn't interfere.
 We must not interfere.
3 "The survival of the fittest" can suggest evolution is a kind of competition.
 "The survival of the fittest" suggests evolution is a kind of competition.
4 If that habitat disappeared for whatever reason, they'd easily die out.
 When the habitat disappears, the animals die out.
5 Will you leave it there?
 Could you leave it there?

Modals and meaning

A modal (*would, will, may, might, could, can, should, shall, must*) adds a general meaning to another verb to show a speaker's attitude or intention.

*The first thing that **will strike** people is...*
= I am certain it strikes people.

*The first thing that **should strike** people is...*
= I believe it strikes people, but I'm not certain.

Other meanings are: certainty, uncertainty, obligation, permission, suggestion, possibility, and frequency (habit).

Check the Grammar Reference for more information and practice.

Baobab trees in Madagascar have adapted to survive in places where there is little rainfall. Their wide trunks can store large amounts of water.

10 Read about National Geographic explorer Cagan Sekercioglu. What similarities can you find with what you heard in the interview? Think about:

1 the rate of extinction.
2 the importance of conservation.
3 what happens to animals that adapt and then face a sudden change.

Growing up in Turkey, Cagan Sekercioglu was once taken to a child psychologist because he (1) <u>constantly brought</u> small animals and insects <u>back</u> to his house. Fortunately, it didn't end his interest in wildlife, and now he's a professor of biology working to protect birds in countries such as Costa Rica, Australia, Ethiopia, the United States, and Turkey. He says (2) <u>losing 25 percent of all bird species this century is a possibility</u>, and that whatever happens to birds (3) <u>is certain to happen</u> to other animals and even people. The question is not if (4) <u>it's better for us to do something</u> about it, but when (5) <u>are we going to decide to do something</u> and (6) <u>what are we going to decide to do</u>?

In Costa Rica, he's found that species (7) <u>sometimes become</u> endangered because the area of forest they live in shrinks as it becomes surrounded by agriculture. The birds are so well adapted to a certain part of the forest that they (8) <u>refuse to</u> move, even when bigger areas of forest (9) <u>are possibly</u> close by. Cagan says (10) <u>it's essential that conservationists work</u> with local people to improve the situation by explaining to farmers why (11) <u>they're better off encouraging</u> bird diversity. For example, if farmers encourage birds to live on their land, (12) <u>the birds will eat</u> insects that destroy their crops, which could possibly increase farmers' profits.

11 Rewrite the underlined parts in Activity 10 using modals. Use each modal in the Grammar box at least once.

12 Write nine sentences about yourself, using a different modal in each sentence. Your teacher will read the sentences to the class. Guess who the person is.

13 MY PERSPECTIVE

Make a list of animals, habitats, jobs, languages, customs, activities, or skills that are at risk of dying out. Would you try to preserve any of them? Why?

6B Tree Life?

VOCABULARY BUILDING

Compound nouns

We often use two or more nouns together to create a new meaning. The words in compound nouns can be joined together, or they can be separated using a space or hyphen. The first noun acts like an adjective. It describes the type of thing, its use, the material it is made from, or other aspects of the second noun, such as where it is found.

Bookstores are dying out in our country because people are buying books online.

Ice ages caused the extinction of many species.

1 Choose the correct forms to complete the sentences.

1 We often go skiing in the *Olympic Mountains / Mountain Olympics*, north of here.
2 On average, there is 20 centimeters of *rainfall / fallrain* here in March.
3 Many environmental charities run *campaign social media / social media campaigns*.
4 Scientists believe there might be many *sea creatures / creature seas* that still have not been discovered.
5 I really like our *teacher science / science teacher*. She brings the subject to life.
6 I avoid all *animal products / product animals*. I don't even wear *shoe leather / leather shoes*.

2 Work in groups. Starting with these compound nouns, how many other compound nouns can you create by changing one word each time? Use a dictionary, if necessary.

farm animal	leather shoes	rainfall	science teacher

ice age: ice cream; **cream** cheese; **cheese**cake

READING

3 Choose one animal from these categories that you are familiar with, and one that you would like to learn more about.

farm animals	pets	sea creatures	wild animals

4 Work in groups. Compare the animals you chose. Explain your choices.

5 Work in pairs. Look at the photo on page 73 and discuss the questions.

1 Where do you think this animal is found?
2 What is unusual about it?
3 How do you think the photographer was able to get the shot?

6 Read the article from a website on page 73 to check your ideas in Activity 5. What else do you learn about questions 1 and 2 in Activity 5?

7 Which statements are supported by the article? Underline the parts of the article which helped you make your decisions.

1 The tree octopus is the most endangered creature in the United States.
2 Washington State is one of the wettest places in the US.
3 The tree octopus may provide clues about how early sea creatures adapted to live on land.
4 The animals often live in small groups.
5 Many companies that cut down trees in the forests are not doing enough to protect octopuses.
6 Octopuses are affected by pollution.

8 Work in groups. Discuss the questions.

1 Did you know about the tree octopus before? If not, what surprised you most?
2 Should people care about the tree octopus? Why?

9 Look at the source for the article. Do you think it is reliable? What other sources could you check to make sure the information is accurate?

10 Listen to a news extract about the tree octopus story. Answer the questions. 🎧 29

1 Why is the story mentioned?
2 What do the findings seem to suggest?

CRITICAL THINKING Assessing information

You will often see information or read something that is unfamiliar. You need to do further reading to check the information is accurate and from a reliable source.

11 Work in pairs. Discuss the questions

1 Why do you think so many people believe this story?
2 Looking back, is there anything in the story that should have made you more suspicious?

12 MY PERSPECTIVE

Work in groups. What are the consequences of fake news stories?

HELP SAVE THE ENDANGERED
Pacific Northwest
Tree Octopus
FROM EXTINCTION

ABOUT   HELP   FAQs   SIGHTINGS   MEDIA   ACTIVITIES   LINKS

28 About

The Pacific Northwest tree octopus (*Octopus paxarbolis*) is only found in the forests of Washington State, on the eastern side of the Olympic Mountains, in the United States.
5 These creatures reach an average size of between 30 and 35 centimeters and live for around four years. They are unusual in that they live both in water and on land, a fact made possible by the very high amounts of
10 rainfall in this part of the United States.

Possessing the largest brain of any octopus, the tree octopus explores its surroundings by touch and sight. Some scientists believe that the way it has adapted to life in the forest
15 mirrors the way early life forms adapted to life away from the water. Although they are not social animals like humans, they can still show emotions by changing their skin color: red indicates anger and white, fear. Normally,
20 though, they are a green-brown color that matches their surroundings.

Every spring, tree octopuses leave their homes and travel to the coast to breed. Males soon return to the forest, while females
25 lay their eggs underwater. The young then spend their first month or so floating near the shore before moving out of the water and beginning their adult lives in the forest.

Source: http://zapatopi.net/treeoctopus/

Why it is endangered

Although the tree octopus is not yet on the
30 official list of endangered animals, it should be, as numbers are now seriously low. It faces many threats: trees in Pacific-Northwest forests are constantly being cut down; new roads have cut off access to water; the growth
35 of local towns has introduced house cats into the region, which hunt the octopuses; and pollution is getting worse. Immediate action needs to be taken to stop the tree octopus from becoming extinct.

Become an activist

40 Here are some things you can do to help protect the last few tree octopuses:

- Write to the government to say you are worried and that you feel the tree octopus should be given special protection and
45 included on the Endangered Species List.

- Write to celebrities, asking them to talk in interviews about the dangers facing the tree octopus.

- Let the world know about the tree
50 octopus: tell your family and friends.

- Tell people not to buy products made by companies that don't protect the tree octopus when cutting down trees.

- Start an online campaign! Encourage
55 people to sign a petition.

Mount Merapi erupts in Indonesia. Volcanic gases are made up of many different gases, including methane.

6C Mysterious Changes

GRAMMAR Modals and infinitive forms

1 Listen to three people. What did they change their minds about? Why? 🎧 **30**

2 Listen to the people again. Complete the sentences. 🎧 **30**

1a I _____ attention when I read about it.

1b All the links about the different kinds of tree octopuses go to the same page. I really _____ that.

1c Even my little brother _____ me that the photos were fake.

2a I mean, you _____ me how cruel it was, and I honestly _____ .

2b I don't know, but if it was that, it _____ an impact because I've been vegan for quite some time now.

3a I _____ touch one or pick one up if the chance had arisen.

3b I _____ certainly _____ about owning one, that's for sure.

3c Our favorite is a python called Monty. We _____ him for three years this November.

3 Look at the sentences in Activity 2. Answer the questions.

1 Which sentence describes a period leading up to a future point?

2 Are the other sentences about the past, the present, or the future?

3 Which modal emphasizes that an action was in progress at the same time as another?

Modals and infinitive forms

Modals can be followed by different kinds of infinitive forms.

*I **can't see** it.*
*We **should be doing** more to help.*
*It **wouldn't have made** any difference.*
*You **can't have been listening** properly.*
*More attention **must be paid** to this issue.*
*The eggs **must have been moved** from the nest.*

Check the Grammar Reference for more information and practice.

4 Work in groups. Look at the Grammar box. Does each pair of sentences have the same meaning? Discuss any differences.

1a They must not have been serious.

1b They must have been joking.

2a I should have helped him.

2b I would have helped him.

3a It must have been really interesting.

3b It was really interesting.

4a I guess that might have been the reason.

4b I guess that could have been the reason.

5a You shouldn't have texted me.

5b You shouldn't have been texting me.

6a It should have arrived by now.

6b It will have arrived by now.

5 PRONUNCIATION Weak form of *have*

When the sentences in Activity 4 are said slowly and carefully, *have* is often pronounced differently than how it is pronounced in fast speech.

a Listen to each sentence from Activity 4. Notice how *have* changes its sound in fast speech. Repeat what you hear. 🎧 31

b Work in pairs. Practice reading the sentences in Activity 4 slowly and quickly.

6 Complete the summary using the modals and the correct form of the verbs in parentheses. Make one modal negative.

Reported sightings of the Loch Ness Monster
(1) _____ soon _____ (will / go on) for a century! In 1933, a man named George Spicer reported seeing something that looked like a plesiosaur, a kind of long-necked marine dinosaur. Some people think such a creature (2) _____ very easily (could / survive) in the quiet Scottish waters, away from people, while others are convinced that Spicer (3) _____ (must / lie) or that he (4) _____ (might / see) a piece of wood covered in green water plants. Most scientists question the whole story and claim that a creature like this (5) _____ (can / live) in the loch* for so long without any real human contact. If it was real, they say, it (6) _____ (would / capture) by now—or at least caught on film. Others, though, suspect that the monster (7) _____ (might / develop) special skills that help it to hide from those hunting it. Even today, true believers can be found on the shores of the loch trying to spot a beast that (8) _____ (should / die out) 65 million years ago.

loch *a Scottish word for a lake.*

7 Work in pairs. Read the two paragraphs about mysteries of the natural world. Then discuss what you think happened. Use modals where necessary.

The Great Dying
Around 250 million years ago, long before dinosaurs roamed the Earth, about 95 percent of all species were suddenly wiped out. This was by far the biggest mass extinction the world has ever seen. The event—widely known as the Great Dying—came close to ending all life on the planet. Everything alive today comes from the five percent of species that survived back then.

The Bloop
The Bloop was an extremely low and very powerful underwater sound first detected at points across the vast Pacific Ocean by NOAA, the National Oceanic and

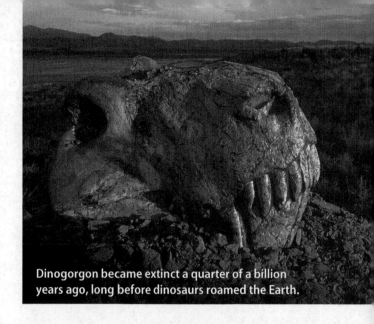

Dinogorgon became extinct a quarter of a billion years ago, long before dinosaurs roamed the Earth.

Atmospheric Administration. The Bloop was significantly different from other previously recorded sounds and many theories emerged to explain the mysterious noise.

8 Read about what really happened. Student A: read about the Great Dying; Student B: read about the Bloop. See if you guessed correctly. Then report back to your partner.

Student A: The Great Dying
Many theories to explain the Great Dying have been put forward—everything from asteroids from space hitting Earth to huge volcanic eruptions. Volcanoes did in fact play a part in the event. At the time, Siberian volcanoes were erupting almost constantly, sending out huge quantities of a gas called methane. This resulted in the oceans and the atmosphere being poisoned and so many species dying out.

Student B: The Bloop
Theories put forward to explain the Bloop ranged from the sensible to the strange. Some people thought the noise must be from an unknown deep-sea creature while others thought it could be mermaids or voices from a lost city. In the end, it turned out that the sound was actually made by an icequake. A large mass of ice in Antarctica was slowly breaking up and was picked up by NOAA.

9 CHOOSE

Choose one of the following activities.

- Work in groups. Prepare a short presentation about a mystery you have read about or know. Include at least four different modals.

- Write a story about something you regret doing—or not doing. Include at least four different modals.

- Work in pairs. Write a conversation between two people about an influential or inspiring person. Include at least four different modals.

AUTHENTIC LISTENING SKILLS

Understanding fast speech

In quick speech, it can be difficult to hear individual words because words get shortened or sound as one.

1 Look at the Authentic Listening Skills box. Then listen to these extracts from the TED Talk where people speak quickly. Try to write down what you hear. 🎧 32

1 … she thought it was just a splinter of wood, because _____ at the Fyles Leaf Bed before— prehistoric plant parts.

2 How certain were you that you had it right, like… that _____, like?

3 … something like a cow or a sheep. But _____. It was just too big.

4 … you're going to have different body sizes. _____, so they're actually functionally like giraffes.

5 And, as a historian, you start with an idea _____.

WATCH

2 Work in groups. Do you think the sentences are *true* or *false*? Why?

1 Camels have been around for about a million years.
2 The first camels were only found in North America.
3 Giraffes and llamas are in the same family as camels.
4 The hump on a camel's back contains water.
5 Camels have evolved to walk on sand.

3 Work in pairs. Write down as many other facts about camels as you can. Then compare your ideas with another pair of students . Do any of the other pair's facts surprise you? Why?

4 Watch Part 1 of the talk. Complete the summary with one to three words in each blank. ▶ 6.1

One day in 2006, Natalia Rybczynski was digging at a site less than (1) _____ south of the North Pole when she found a strange object. To begin with, she thought it was a piece of (2) _____ . She collected more fragments over the next four years and eventually used a (3) _____ to find out that it was a (4) _____ of a huge mammal. When they cut a piece off one fragment, they (5) _____ collagen, which is a substance found in bones and which (6) _____ in the ice. A couple of years later, she sent the fragments to a colleague who had invented a technique called (7) _____ , which can identify an animal from a bone. They discovered it was a(n) (8) _____ million-year-old camel and that it must have weighed (9) _____ , which is (10) _____ than camels today.

5 Watch Part 2 of the talk. Check your answers from Activity 2. Correct the false answers. ▶ 6.2

Camels have been around longer than a million years. According to Latif, they have been around for 45 million years.

6 Watch Part 2 of the talk again. Choose the correct options. ▶ 6.2

1 Scientists believe that at first, camels were only found in *hot places* / *cold places*.
2 They also believe that 40 million years ago, there were around *20* / *24* different species of camels.
3 They say that some early camels were as small as *dogs* / *rabbits*.
4 They also say that one branch of camels became *llamas* / *giraffes*.
5 Some scientists believe that a camel's hump helped it to survive long *walks* / *winters*.
6 It is believed that three and a half million years ago, the weather was significantly *warmer* / *cooler* than today.

7 Watch Part 3 of the talk. Which sentence best summarizes the point Latif is making? ▶ 6.3

a It's important to change your mind about things.
b Scientists should also study history.
c Much of what we think we know might be wrong.
d Camels are well suited to different environments.

8 What discoveries or news have you heard about the natural world recently? Think about:

• archaeology.
• new or lost species.
• the sea.
• medical advances.

9 VOCABULARY IN CONTEXT

a Watch the clips from the TED Talk. Choose the correct meanings of the words and phrases. ▶ 6.4

b Work in pairs. Discuss the questions.

1 Have you ever experienced *hitting a wall*? Why? How did you overcome it?
2 What scientific theories still have no *proof*?
3 What good *spots* do you know to:
   • have a picnic?
   • see wildlife?
   • hang out with friends?
   • watch the world go by?
4 What things would you be *willing* or *unwilling* to do to be successful in life?

CHALLENGE

Think of a time in your life when you have had to rethink what you thought you knew about something—or someone.

• What did you use to believe? Why?
• What caused you to rethink your beliefs?
• Did you develop your new ideas quickly or slowly?
• How do you feel about the thing or person now?

Work in groups. Tell each other your experiences. Ask and answer questions about the changes. Decide who experienced the biggest change.

Unit 6 Adapt to Survive **77**

6E Finding a Solution

SPEAKING

1 Work in pairs. Look at the photo and discuss the questions.

1 Where do you think the photo was taken? Who might the man be?

2 How would you feel if you were the man in the photo?

2 Read the opening lines of six different anecdotes. Which sounds most interesting to you? What would you ask about it?

a I once saw a polar bear in a zoo. It was really sad.

b I almost stepped on a scorpion once.

c My brother once tracked a group of gorillas in Africa.

d When I went to the city, I saw lots of foxes in the street.

e Where my grandma lives, there are vultures. We once climbed up to their nests.

f I hate cows. I was chased by some once. It was really scary!

3 You are going to tell an anecdote about a time you encountered some kind of wild animal—big or small. Make notes using these questions and think of a sentence you will say to start the anecdote to get people interested.

- When did it happen? How old were you?
- Where was it?
- What happened?
- What was the animal doing?
- How did it make you feel?
- Did it have an effect on you afterwards?

4 Work in pairs. Tell your anecdotes. Your partner should show interest and ask questions to help you.

Some people have a special connection with animals.

WRITING A problem-solution essay

5 Tigers are endangered in the wild. Do you think having them in zoos and parks is good for their survival? Why? What other things might help them?

6 WRITING SKILL Topic sentences

Read the essay about how people can help to protect tigers on page 151. Put the topic sentences in the correct order as they might appear.

a The author J.A. Mills suggests we should strengthen rules about domestic tigers.
b Finally, we should work closely with local people.
c According to the WWF (World Wildlife Fund), there are only about 4,000 tigers left in the wild.
d Countries have to work together to protect the habitat.

7 In the essay, the writer refers to various organizations and people. Answer the questions.

1 Why does the writer do this?
2 Do you think they are good sources to reference? Why?
3 What other information would be good to know? What other sources could you look for?

8 Work in pairs. Choose one of the animals or things from your list that are at risk of dying out (page 71, Activity 13). Find out more and take notes on three big problems it faces. Then think of ways to tackle these problems and help save it.

9 Work on your own. Using your notes, write a problem-solution essay.

- In the first paragraph, outline the problems and say you will suggest solutions. Then tackle each problem in a subsequent paragraph. Use the writing model on page 151 as a guide if you need to.
- Find two or three sources that you can add to your essay to give it greater authority. Decide how you want to use them and where to place the sources. Use the Useful language box to help you.

10 Exchange your essay with your partner. Read your partner's work and comment on:

- the structure and the strength of the argument.
- the use of sources.
- the use of language.

Writing strategy

Topic sentences
It is good to start a new paragraph with a topic sentence—a sentence that explains what the paragraph is about.

Useful language

Naming sources
According to [name / organization / book, etc.],...
The [job title], [name], *says that*...
I agree with [job title], [name], *when she/he says that*...

7 Outside the Box

IN THIS UNIT, YOU...

- discuss the importance of creativity.
- read about creativity tests.
- imagine alternative outcomes to situations.
- watch a TED Talk about making up new words.
- come up with creative approaches.

The members of the band A-WA are three Israeli sisters who mix traditional Yemenite music with modern electronic dance music.

7A Rules of Creativity

VOCABULARY Breaking the mold

1 Work in pairs. How many different words based on the root word *create* can you think of? Think of at least two collocations for each.

create   *create a group, create excitement*

2 Complete the sentences with words based on the root word *create*. You can use the same word more than once.

1 Everyone should learn a musical instrument in their spare time to encourage _____ .

2 Students have not needed to learn facts since the _____ of the internet.

3 You need to study a lot and copy other people before you can be _____ yourself.

4 There aren't many people who actually _____ something completely new.

5 Watching a lot of television kills people's _____ .

6 People who can think _____ do better in school.

3 Identify the collocations with the different forms of *create* from Activity 2. Were they the same as the ones you thought of in Activity 1?

4 Work in pairs. Do you agree with the sentences from Activity 2? Why?

5 Complete the phrases with these pairs of words. Use a dictionary, if necessary.

approaches + solution	comes up with + adapts
invents + follows	makes up + writes
obeys + breaks	writes + scores

1 someone who does what he is told and _____ the rules or someone who _____ them

2 someone who _____ a test or someone who _____ highly on a test

3 someone who _____ a new word or someone who _____ word definitions

4 someone who comes up with a wide variety of _____ to a problem or someone who analyzes things and comes up with a simple _____

5 someone who _____ something or someone who _____ a set of rules to make something

6 someone who _____ new ways of doing things or someone who _____ existing ways of doing things

6 MY PERSPECTIVE

Work in pairs. Which person in each phrase in Activity 5 do you think is more creative? Explain your ideas.

LISTENING

7 Listen to an extract from a podcast. Which sentence best summarizes the main point? 🎧 33

a You can only be truly creative if you think like a child.
b The best monsters are usually created by children.
c Schools could do more to encourage creativity.
d In the future, there will be lots of new kinds of jobs.

8 Listen again. Choose the correct options. 🎧 33

1 *The Monster Engine*:
  a exists across a range of different formats.
  b has only been around for a few years.
  c was created by Dave Devries and his children.

2 Dave Devries started working on *The Monster Engine*:
  a to make one of his relatives happy.
  b because he illustrates comic books.
  c after being inspired by a young child.

3 Sir Ken Robinson claimed that:
  a drawing cartoons makes you more creative.
  b if you're creative, you're more likely to do well in the future.
  c people will need to work harder in the next 20 or 30 years.

4 The speaker thinks that, at its heart, creativity is about:
  a playing games.
  b listening to young people more.
  c not giving up and learning from mistakes.

9 Work in groups. Discuss whether you agree with the statements.

1 It's sometimes useful to see the world like a child.
2 Jobs will be very different in the future.
3 Skills are more important than knowledge.
4 Trying and failing are important parts of the creative process.

GRAMMAR First, second, third, and mixed conditionals

10 Work in pairs. Look at the Grammar box. Discuss which forms you see in the *if* clauses and result clauses in each of the four sentences.

> ### First, second, third, and mixed conditionals
>
> **First conditionals**
> **a** *If you're in school today, you'll probably start working sometime in the 2020s.*
>
> **Second conditionals**
> **b** *If these drawings were painted more realistically, they would look amazing.*
>
> **Third conditionals**
> **c** *If Dave Devries hadn't spent a day with his niece back in 1998, The Monster Engine would never have happened.*
>
> **Mixed conditionals**
> **d** *If their schools had encouraged unusual ways of seeing the world, lots of adults would be more creative.*

Check the Grammar Reference for more information and practice.

11 Which kind of conditional sentences do we use to talk about:

1 an imaginary past situation and an imaginary present result?
2 an imaginary situation and result now or in the future?
3 an imaginary situation and result in the past?
4 a possible situation and result now or in the future?

Dave Devries applies color and shading to children's artwork (right) to bring their pictures to life.

12 Complete the conditional sentences by using the correct forms of the verbs in parentheses.

Many people think of creativity as chance Eureka moments.* The mathematician and inventor who coined the term *Eureka*, Archimedes, discovered that the weight of an object floating on water is the same as the amount of water it displaces. He made this discovery by chance. If he (1) _____ (pay) more attention to the amount of water in his bathtub, he (2) _____ (not step) into it and spilled water over the side. Apparently, we (3) _____ (not have) penicillin today if Alexander Fleming (4) _____ (be) a bit neater and washed his petri dishes before he went on vacation. On his return, he discovered the penicillin mold had killed bacteria on the dishes. What (5) _____ (our world / be) like now without these discoveries?

The book *Inside the Box* by Drew Boyd and Jacob Goldenberg suggests that such moments are rare and if we (6) _____ (rely) on these "methods," we would not get very far. In fact, the authors say, most inventions come from following a limited set of rules. The rules can help failing schools and companies; if they (7) _____ (integrate) the rules into their teaching and product development, they (8) _____ (become) more successful. The implication of their argument is that it's not all up to luck.

Eureka moment *sudden understanding of a previously unknown solution to something*

13 Work in pairs. Read the situations. How many conditional sentences can you come up with to talk about:

- the different outcomes and how the situations could have been avoided?
- what could be done next?

Situation 1

Some schoolchildren were waiting outside before lunch. There was snow on the ground. The teacher who usually supervises the children arrived late because of a meeting. The students were pushing each other and playing around. Two students slipped on the ice and one ended up in the hospital. The treatment cost a lot of money. The parents complained, but the school says that students have to wait outside because a health and safety report explained that there was not enough space inside. Therefore, it was dangerous to line up inside.

Situation 2

Last year, the teacher who usually helps students with study skills lost her job because the school was trying to save money. Since then, one of the best students in the school has gotten into trouble because she copied an essay from the internet. She is worried this will ruin her chances of going to a good college. She says she did it because she was under a lot of pressure from her parents and did not have anyone to go to for advice.

14 Work with another pair of students. Compare your ideas from Activity 13. Who thought of the most conditional sentences? Who has the main responsibility for the outcomes in both situations?

7B Testing Times

VOCABULARY BUILDING Noun forms

1 Look at these pairs of words. How are the nouns formed from verbs and adjectives?

Verb	Noun	Adjective	Noun
analyze	analysis	concerned	concern
assess	assessment	intelligent	intelligence
conclude	conclusion	flexible	flexibility
know	knowledge	fluent	fluency
publish	publication	logical	logic
vary	variety	useful	usefulness

2 Choose the correct words from Activity 1 to complete the sentences.

1 I know a lot of words in English, but I need to become more _____ in using them!

2 My main _____ when I do anything in English is not to make any mistakes.

3 I got a good grade in the last _____ I did for English.

4 I'd like to write a novel and _____ it myself.

5 I like to do things in a(n) _____ order, from A to B to C.

6 The _____ in my study schedule allows me to study when I feel most productive.

7 I don't think exams are a(n) _____ demonstration of how much people know.

3 Work in pairs. Which sentences in Activity 2 are true for you? What do you think they say about you? Which sentences do you think are signs of creativity? Why?

4 Work in groups. Think of other *verb / noun* and *adjective / noun* combinations that follow the patterns in Activity 1.

READING

5 Work in groups. Discuss the questions.

1 What do you think it means to be creative?

2 Do you think creativity is only connected to the arts?

3 How important is creativity these days? Why?

4 Do you think it is possible to assess levels of creativity?

5 Who is the most creative person you know? Why?

6 Read about a set of tests commonly used to assess creativity. Think about the questions as you read.

1 What do the tests involve?

2 Does the author think they are good tests of creativity?

7 Work in pairs. Answer the questions and discuss your ideas. Then read about the tests again to check.

1 When were the tests first published?

2 How are the tests scored?

3 How are divergent and convergent thinking different?

4 Why were people worried about children's test scores in the United States?

5 What are the possible causes for the drop in test scores?

6 How does problem-based learning encourage creativity?

8 Look at the four examples of divergent thinking tasks in lines 11–22. Work in groups to complete one.

9 Compare your results from Activity 8 with a partner. Use the questions to evaluate their creativity. What do you think the questions tell you about a person's creativity?

1 How many logical solutions are there to the task?

2 How original are the solutions?

3 How well can the solutions be explained?

CRITICAL THINKING Fact and opinion

> **Facts** are statements that are true. **Opinions** are statements showing what people believe.

10 Read the statements about Torrance's *Tests of Creative Thinking*. Do they present *facts* or *opinions*? Does each fact or opinion support the value of the tests as a test of creativity? Why?

1 Torrance found that people often scored very differently on the different parts of the tests.

2 Torrance believed you could teach creativity. The tests were originally teaching tools.

3 The tests give the idea that creativity is all one thing. Fail the tests and you are not creative.

4 Torrance collected information about adults' creative success by asking them to fill out a form to report what they had achieved creatively.

5 Learning to solve one problem rarely helps to solve another kind of problem.

6 It's difficult to see how the tests measure creativity in science or mathematics.

11 MY PERSPECTIVE

Work in pairs. Discuss the questions.

1 Would you like to use the problem-based way of learning? Why?

2 How is creativity encouraged in your school?

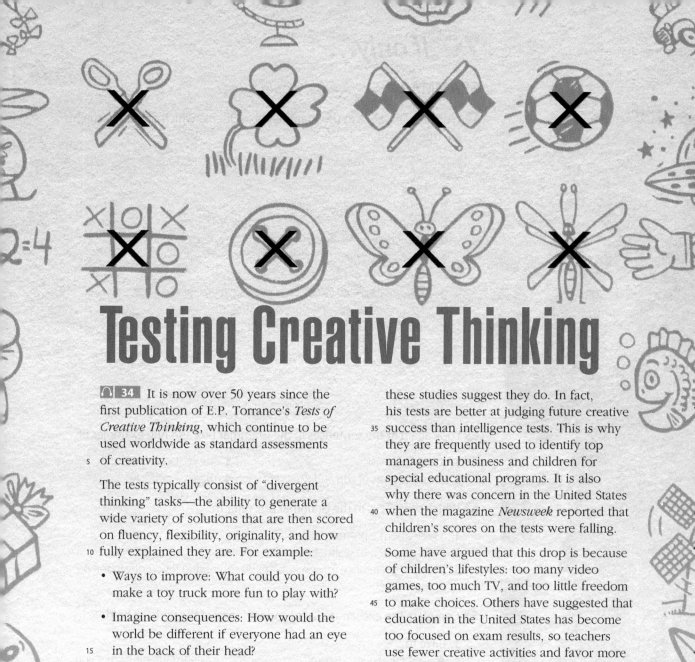

Testing Creative Thinking

🎧 34 It is now over 50 years since the first publication of E.P. Torrance's *Tests of Creative Thinking*, which continue to be used worldwide as standard assessments
5 of creativity.

The tests typically consist of "divergent thinking" tasks—the ability to generate a wide variety of solutions that are then scored on fluency, flexibility, originality, and how
10 fully explained they are. For example:

- Ways to improve: What could you do to make a toy truck more fun to play with?

- Imagine consequences: How would the world be different if everyone had an eye
15 in the back of their head?

- Alternative uses: How many unusual uses for a brick can you think of?

- Make drawings from a shape: Turn the Xs into pictures people might be surprised
20 by. The X can be in any part of the picture. Add details to tell complete stories and give each picture a title.

Some question if the tests fully assess creativity because they say creativity is about
25 originality and usefulness. Creativity not only requires divergent thinking but also "convergent thinking," where you find one single solution that you feel is the best for the problem you are trying to solve.

30 Torrance followed the lives of children who first took his tests to see if they predicted creative achievements as adults. Analyses of these studies suggest they do. In fact, his tests are better at judging future creative
35 success than intelligence tests. This is why they are frequently used to identify top managers in business and children for special educational programs. It is also why there was concern in the United States
40 when the magazine *Newsweek* reported that children's scores on the tests were falling.

Some have argued that this drop is because of children's lifestyles: too many video games, too much TV, and too little freedom
45 to make choices. Others have suggested that education in the United States has become too focused on exam results, so teachers use fewer creative activities and favor more traditional learning. This is in contrast to
50 countries with a history of more traditional activities, like China and its emphasis on memorization and drills. These countries are doing the opposite, and encouraging creativity through techniques such as
55 problem-based learning.

Problem-based learning involves setting a genuine problem, such as reducing noise in a school library or deciding on a week of meals for an athlete. In reaching
60 a conclusion, students have to do research across several subjects and be creative in the fullest sense. No doubt Torrance would have approved if he was still alive.

One of the tests for creative thinking involves making drawings from a shape.

Do you ever wish you were a better dancer?

7C *If only…*

GRAMMAR *Wish, if only, would rather*

1 Work in pairs. Look at the Grammar box. Discuss which of the statements are true for you.

> ### Wish, if only, would rather
>
> **a** *I wish I could draw better.*
> **b** *I wish I was a better dancer.*
> **c** *I wish my parents hadn't forced me to learn Latin.*
> **d** *I sometimes wish my classmates wouldn't make so much noise.*
> **e** *I wish I didn't have to take art classes.*
> **f** *I'd rather not get any homework.*
> **g** *My parents would rather I studied something else in college.*
> **h** *If only I had an eye in the back of my head!*
> **i** *I often say to myself, "If only I'd spent more time thinking about this before I started."*
> **j** *If only I wasn't sitting here now!*

Check the Grammar Reference for more information and practice.

2 Look again at the sentences in the Grammar box and find examples of:

1 the simple past.   **3** the past continuous.
2 the past forms of *can* and *will*.   **4** the past perfect.

3 Which sentences in the Grammar box refer to:

1 a wish about a present situation?
2 a wish about a past situation?
3 a wish or preference for someone to do something differently in the present or the future?

4 Complete the exchanges using correct forms of the verbs in bold.

1 have to
  A Don't you ever wish you _____ sleep? Imagine what you could do with all those extra hours.
  B Stop it! You're making me tired!

2 hear
  A I wish I _____ that song. I can't get it out of my head now.
  B I know. It's incredibly catchy, isn't it?

3 hate
  A With those grades, maybe you should study medicine.
  B Yeah, if only I _____ the sight of blood or needles! Honestly, I could never work as a doctor.

4 finish
  A Should we stop now and do the rest tomorrow?
  B I'd rather we _____ it today. It will bother me all night if we leave it.

5 have + be

A You four should start a band. You could be really big!

B Yeah, if only we _____ the money to buy equipment—and could come up with ideas!

A You have lots of good ideas! I wish I _____ as creative as you!

6 be + relax

A I wish you _____ there. You would've loved it.

B Yeah, I know. I wish my parents _____ and let me go out more.

A Well, maybe next time.

5 PRONUNCIATION Elision of consonants *t* and *d*

> When people talk fast, they often leave out the final consonant when the next word starts with a consonant.
>
> *I'd get bored* will often sound like *I-ge-bored.*

a Look at the phrases with *wish*, *if only*, and *I'd rather* in Activity 4. Which final consonants do you think might disappear?

b Listen to the phrases and repeat them. 🎧 **35**

6 We often add comments to statements with *wish*, *if only*, and *would rather*. Match the statements (1–5) with the pairs of follow-up comments (a–e). Does each comment refer to an imagined consequence (IC) or the actual situation (AS)?

1 I wish you'd told me earlier. *c*
2 If only he was taller.
3 I'd rather we didn't talk now.
4 I wish they would do more to help.
5 I wish I didn't have to go.

a People might hear.
I need to think more carefully about it.

b The place is a mess.
We could get things done a lot faster.

c It would've saved me a lot of effort. *IC*
I don't have time to do it now. *AS*

d I don't really like meetings.
Unfortunately, he's expecting me to be there.

e He could have become a model.
He probably would make the basketball team.

7 Work in pairs. Look again at the sentences that are true for you in Activity 1. Add comments, like in Activity 6.

8 Read the poem. What do you think happened?

Regrets

I wish I could tell you how I really feel
And say what's on my mind.
I wish I hadn't done what I did
Or had thought before I acted.
I wish I was spending my time with you
Instead of sitting here all alone.

9 CHOOSE Choose one of the following activities.

- Write a poem similar to the one in Activity 8 about regrets. Write it from the perspective of another person, such as a student, a teacher, or an athlete.

- Write a list of eight sentences like those in the Grammar box for your classmates to discuss.

- Write five things you would wish for if anything was possible. Discuss your ideas with a partner.

  I wish money grew on trees.

Do you ever wish you were taller?

7D Go ahead, make up new words!

" Everybody who speaks English decides together what's a word and what's not a word. "

ERIN MCKEAN

Read about Erin McKean and get ready to watch her TED Talk. ▶ 7.0

AUTHENTIC LISTENING SKILLS

Speeding up and slowing down speech

Speakers often vary the speed of their speech in order to maintain people's interest, as well as for other specific reasons. For example, they may speak more quickly when they are saying very common phrases, making jokes, or making comments that are not important. They may speak more slowy when they are starting their speech, emphasizing something important, or thinking of what to say next.

1 Look at the Authentic Listening Skills box. Then listen to the opening of Erin's talk. Identify where her speech slows down and speeds up. 🎧 36

I'm a lexicographer. I make dictionaries. And my job as a lexicographer is to try to put all the words possible into the dictionary. My job is not to decide what a word is; that is your job. Everybody who speaks English decides together what's a word and what's not a word. Every language is just a group of people who agree to understand each other. Now, sometimes when people are trying to decide whether a word is good or bad, they don't really have a good reason. So they say something like, "Because grammar!" I don't actually really care about grammar too much—don't tell anybody.

2 Work in pairs. Compare your answers from Activity 1. Practice reading the paragraph using the same kind of speech patterns as Erin.

WATCH

3 Work in pairs. Discuss the questions.

1 Which dictionaries do you use? Why?
2 Do you know how dictionaries are made? How?
3 Do you like learning new words in English? in your own language? Why?
4 Have you seen or heard any new words recently? Where? What do they mean?
5 Have you ever made up a new word? What was it? What does it mean?

4 Watch Part 1 of the talk. Match the excerpts from the talk (a–e) with these notes (1–3). ▶ 7.1

1 New words
2 The unconscious natural grammar rules that live inside our brains
3 The grammar of "manners," known as usage

a "Because grammar!"
b "This is a wug, right? It's a wug. Now… there are two…"
c "…take a hoodie, don't forget to obey the law of gravity."
d "Can you wear hats inside?"
e "No! No. Creativity stops right here, whippersnappers."

5 Work in pairs. Compare your ideas from Activity 4 and explain the point Erin was making in each excerpt.

6 Look at these notes about six ways to make new words. Watch Part 2 of the talk. Complete the notes. ▶ 7.2

Erin gives six ways to create new words in English:

1 _____ : using words from another language, e.g. *kumquat* and *caramel*.

2 Compounding: putting two words together, e.g. _____ .

3 _____ : putting parts of two words together, e.g. _____ .

4 Functional _____ : e.g. using a noun as a verb, e.g. _____ .

5 Back formation: _____ a part of the word to create a new one, e.g. _____ .

6 Acronym: taking the first letter of several words, e.g. _____ .

7 Watch Part 3 of the talk. The purpose of her talk is to: ▶ 7.3

a explain her job and what is important about it.

b argue that words are more important than grammar.

c encourage people to create words and contribute to her online dictionary.

d argue that it is important to break rules to be more creative.

e explain different ways new words are formed and disappear from use.

8 VOCABULARY IN CONTEXT

a Watch the clips from the TED Talk. Choose the correct meanings of the words. ▶ 7.4

b Work in pairs. Discuss the questions.

1 What did your parents teach you about *manners*? Do you think good *manners* are important?

2 Why might someone be *heartbroken*? What would you do or say for him or her?

3 What do you do to *edit* your essays before you hand them in? Do you get anyone else to help?

4 Give an example of a time when it was difficult to *get your meaning across*. Did you succeed?

5 What movies or books *grabbed* your attention right at the beginning? How? Did they keep your attention?

9 MY PERSPECTIVE

Work in groups. Discuss the questions.

1 Why do you think these groups of people might invent new words? Is it always to aid in communication?

poets	politicians	scientists	teenagers

2 Why do you think some words disappear from use?

3 If you are learning English, do you think it's OK to create new words? Why?

4 How might knowing how to make new words help you to develop your English?

CHALLENGE

Work in groups. How many examples of the six different ways of forming words can you think of?

- borrowing
- blending
- back formation
- compounding
- functional shift
- acronyms

7E Creative Solutions

Useful language

Raising concerns

I don't see how that would work.

The issue with that is…

If we did that, wouldn't…?

Suggesting a better approach

Wouldn't it be better to…?

If you ask me, I think we should…

Giving reasons

That way you could…

That allows / enables…

If we do that,…

SPEAKING

1 Work in groups. Look at the photo and discuss the questions.

1 In what ways is this class similar to and different from yours?

2 How many ways of improving your learning environment can you think of? Which two ways would make the biggest difference to the teacher and the learners? Why?

2 Read the situations (a–c). As a class, choose the situation you want to resolve. Then work in groups and:

1 discuss what additional facts you would like to find out about the situation.

2 use divergent thinking to make a list of as many different ways of approaching the situation as you can.

   a Your town or city wants to attract more tourists. It is planning to spend a lot of money on advertising, but no decisions have yet been made about how best to sell the town or city—or what kind of advertisements might work best.

   b This year, a lot less money is going to be available for your school. The school will need to continue offering a great education to students while spending up to 50 percent less. No decisions have yet been made on what changes will need to be made.

   c Your English class has been given some money to make an app or a website to help current and future students deal with their biggest problems. No decisions have yet been made about what should go on the app or website.

3 Exchange the list you made in Activity 2 with another group of students. Then use convergent thinking and the expressions in the Useful language box to:

* discuss the difficulties there might be with each of the ideas.
* decide what the best approach would be—and why.

4 Each group should now choose one person to present their approach to the class. Listen to each group and decide who has the best solution.

High school students in a robotics class build a robot to enter into a competition.

WRITING A report

5 Look at the report on page 152. Identify the two suggestions made by students for reducing external noise in the school library. Can you think of any other possible solution?

a Install two panes of glass in each window to stop 75 percent of the water coming in from outside.

b Install two panes of glass in 75 percent of the windows to reduce the noise coming in from outside.

c Install two panes of glass in each window to reduce the noise coming in from outside.

d Fill the space between two panes of glass with water to reduce the noise by 75 percent.

6 **WRITING SKILL** Cohesion

Look at the Writing strategy box. Find examples of how to structure reports in the model on page 152.

7 Work in pairs. Rewrite the sentences using the sentence starters in bold.

1 I guess we could invest in some new, heavier curtains.

We might consider _____ .

2 It would be much better if we moved the library to another room.

I would strongly recommend _____ .

3 Maybe we could play quiet music to cover the noise from outside.

We would suggest _____ .

4 If we put more plants in the library, they would stop some of the sound.

I propose _____ .

8 Write a short report about the situation your class chose in Activity 2.

- Follow the guidance in the Writing strategy box.
- Make your recommendations using some of the language in Activity 7.

8 Common Ground

A *kunik* is a traditional Inuit greeting between family members and loved ones.

8A Cultural Crossings

VOCABULARY Identity and communication

1 Work in groups. Look at the photo and discuss the questions.

1 Could this be a typical scene where you are from? Why?
2 How do you normally greet the people in the box? Does it vary at all? Does everyone in the group greet each other in the same way? Why?

friends	friends' parents	sales associates
teachers	visitors from another country	your parents

2 MY PERSPECTIVE

In addition to greetings, are there any rules you think it would be important for a foreign visitor to your country to know? Do you *always* follow these rules?

3 Complete the sentences with these pairs of words.

awkward + compliment	be offended + implied
conscious + discrimination	discourage + reaction
misunderstanding + work it out	response + negative comments

1 If my friends have a(n) _____ or a big argument, I'm good at helping them _____ .
2 I usually feel a bit _____ if someone pays me a(n) _____ or praises what I've done.
3 I would _____ if someone _____ that I looked older than I really am.
4 I think the best _____ to things like _____ is to challenge them.
5 If someone tries to _____ me from doing something, my initial _____ is to want to do it more!
6 I think I'm pretty _____ of how to avoid _____ .

4 Work in pairs. Read the sentences in Activity 3 aloud. Are they are true or false for you? Why?

5 Complete the collocations with the correct forms, based on the word families.

1 pay me a big **compliment** / _____ me on my work / be very **complimentary** about it
2 _____ against young people / fight **discrimination** / **discriminatory** rules
3 avoid _____ people / a negative _____ / a **stereotypical** person
4 took _____ at what he said / didn't mean to **offend** anyone / use _____ language
5 respond _____ to questions / an **awkward** silence / a sense of **awkwardness** in social settings
6 _____ the instructions / a silly **misunderstanding**

6 Choose five of the collocations from Activity 5. Write example sentences that are true for you.

LISTENING

7 Work as a class. Discuss the questions.

1 How might you define *intercultural communication*?
2 In what situations is it necessary to be considerate of other cultures?

8 Work in pairs. What can cause communication to break down in these situations? What might you do if this happens? How could you avoid it?

greeting people	making plans
ordering food	trying to get somebody's attention

9 Listen to an interview about travel and intercultural communication. What is normal for people from these countries that may be different elsewhere? 🎧 37

China	Germany	Russia	US

10 According to the conversation, are the sentences *true*, *false*, or *not stated*? Listen again and check your answers. 🎧 37

1 Stacey's parents are diplomats.
2 The German girl who Stacey spoke to was deliberately rude to her.
3 If a Russian person smiles at another Russian they don't know, they may be seen as untrustworthy.
4 Stacey's Korean friend was confused by people in the United States asking "How're you doing?"
5 In Chinese, a common greeting can be translated as *Have you eaten*?
6 Intercultural communication courses are effective.

GRAMMAR Reported speech

11 Look at the Grammar box. Try to complete the sentences. Listen again and check your ideas. 🎧 37

Reported speech

a *I asked a German girl from my class if she _____ the train station.*
b *And I thought, "That _____ rude."*
c *I said I _____ something and _____ go back to school.*
d *That evening I told my dad what had happened and he said that I _____ be so sensitive.*
e *A Russian friend told me their parents kind of _____ them from smiling at strangers. There _____ a Russian proverb that says, "Laughter for no reason is a sign of stupidity."*

Check the Grammar Reference for more information and practice.

12 Match the sentences in the grammar box to these points.

1 The sentence includes the actual words that were spoken or thought.
2 The sentence includes advice or instruction the speaker was given.
3 The sentence includes a question (or plan) about an action in progress at the time.
4 The sentence includes a statement about a previous action and consequence.
5 The sentence includes a statement about something which is still generally true.

13 Look at sentences a–c in the Grammar box. What happens to the tenses when we report speech? Why?

14 Complete the responses to the statements that are correcting misunderstandings.

1 A We're meeting on Tuesday.
B Really? I thought you said we _____ on Thursday!

2 A I got a B on my science essay.
B Oh, that's pretty good! I thought you said you _____ a D!

3 A I'm interested in seeing the new *Star Wars* movie.
B Really? I thought you told me you _____ interested!

4 A I'll bring you all the stuff you need next week.
B You don't have it? I thought you _____ it today.

5 A I'm going to my dance class later.
B I didn't know you _____ dancing. How long have you been doing that?

6 A We have to leave at 11 o'clock.
B I thought we _____ leave at 12 o'clock.

15 PRONUNCIATION Stress for clarification

a Work in pairs. Listen to the exchanges from Activity 14. Notice how we stress the corrections. Then practice the exchanges. 🎧 38

b Work in pairs. Take turns saying the sentences. Your partner should respond with something they had misunderstood.
1 Are you coming to my birthday party on Saturday?
2 We went to Mexico on vacation last summer.
3 My mom works at a hospital near here.
4 I can't stand that band.
5 Sorry, I can't come out tonight. I have to study.

16 Think of two situations when you might hear these expressions. How might they possibly have different meanings or interpretations?

1 I've been waiting here forever.
Someone in a line advising someone not to wait.
Someone you had arranged to meet being very annoyed because you were late.

2 Don't be silly!
3 Are you going to eat that?
4 What did you do that for?
5 You'll be sorry.

17 Use your ideas from Activity 16 to tell a short story. Report what was said, how you replied, and what you did next.

I went to buy tickets for a concert, but when I got to the theater there was a huge line. Someone there said they'd been waiting forever, so I decided to forget it and just went home.

18 MY PERSPECTIVE

Choose one of these situations. Spend a few minutes planning how to explain what happened. Include some reporting. Then work in pairs. Tell your partner your story.

- A compliment someone paid you or you paid someone else
- A misunderstanding or argument you once had or saw
- A conversation you wish you hadn't overheard

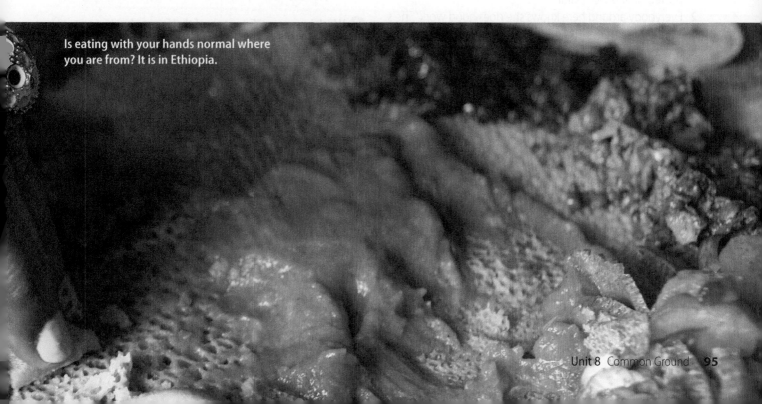

Is eating with your hands normal where you are from? It is in Ethiopia.

8B I Am Who I Am

VOCABULARY BUILDING

Compound adjectives

Compound adjectives are made up of more than one word. As with single-word adjectives, it is important to learn not only the meanings, but also the nouns that they most commonly describe.

1 Match these compound adjectives with their meanings.

cost-effective	deep-rooted
heartbroken	highly respected
like-minded	long-lasting
open-minded	two-faced
well-mannered	worldwide

1 sharing tastes, interests, and opinions
2 dishonest and not to be trusted
3 admired by lots of people because of qualities or achievements
4 willing to consider new ideas and ways of thinking
5 existing or happening everywhere
6 behaving in a polite way
7 firmly fixed; strong and hard to change
8 providing good value for the amount of money paid
9 continuing for a long period of time
10 extremely sad and upset

2 Complete the sentences with compound adjectives from Activity 1.

1 She achieved _____ fame when a video she posted online went viral.
2 Everybody around here knows she does good work. She's a _____ figure.
3 My little brother was absolutely _____ when his team lost the championship game!
4 The problems are too _____ for there to be any real hope of a quick fix.
5 If you only ever spend time talking to _____ people, you don't get to hear different points of view.

3 Work in groups. Use five of the adjectives in Activity 1 to describe people or things from your own experience.

My dog died last year, which left me heartbroken.

I bike almost everywhere. It's the most cost-effective way of getting around.

READING

4 Work in pairs. Look at the photo showing a subculture.* Predict:

1 where the subculture originated.
2 what members of the subculture have in common.
3 what kind of music—if any—is associated with this subculture.

subculture *a group of people within a larger cultural group who share the same interests*

5 Read the article and find the answers to the questions in Activity 4 for all of the subcultures mentioned.

6 What reasons for joining subcultures are mentioned in the article? What downside is mentioned?

7 Which of the four subcultures:

1 is more of a virtual than real-world phenomenon?
2 became known worldwide thanks to a music video?
3 is a combination of the ultra-modern and the old?
4 includes members who identify with animals?
5 can trace its origins back the furthest?
6 involves a form of recycling?
7 rejects a common belief about their characteristics?
8 involves regional rivalries?

CRITICAL THINKING Understanding other perspectives

Learning to think more critically sometimes requires us to suspend our own judgment and instead to try to see things from other points of view.

8 Work in groups. For each of the four subcultures mentioned in the article, decide:

1 what the appeal might be for those who get involved.
2 what common ground might exist with other groups.
3 what concerns parents might have.
4 which are common—or have some kind of local equivalents—where you live.

9 MY PERSPECTIVE

The article is written from the point of view of someone who is not involved in any of the subcultures mentioned. Do you think people who are part of the subcultures might want to change any of the details? Why?

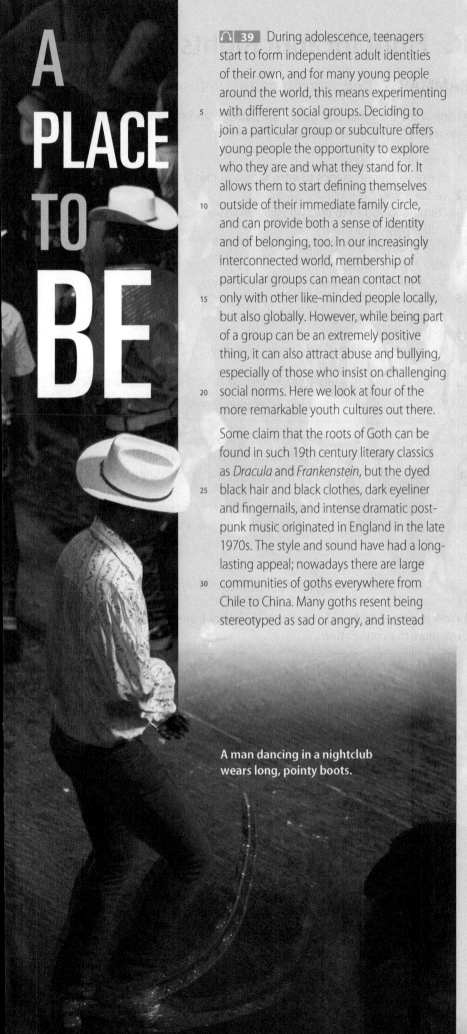

A PLACE TO BE

🎧 **39** During adolescence, teenagers start to form independent adult identities of their own, and for many young people around the world, this means experimenting
5 with different social groups. Deciding to join a particular group or subculture offers young people the opportunity to explore who they are and what they stand for. It allows them to start defining themselves
10 outside of their immediate family circle, and can provide both a sense of identity and of belonging, too. In our increasingly interconnected world, membership of particular groups can mean contact not
15 only with other like-minded people locally, but also globally. However, while being part of a group can be an extremely positive thing, it can also attract abuse and bullying, especially of those who insist on challenging
20 social norms. Here we look at four of the more remarkable youth cultures out there.

Some claim that the roots of Goth can be found in such 19th century literary classics as *Dracula* and *Frankenstein*, but the dyed
25 black hair and black clothes, dark eyeliner and fingernails, and intense dramatic post-punk music originated in England in the late 1970s. The style and sound have had a long-lasting appeal; nowadays there are large
30 communities of goths everywhere from Chile to China. Many goths resent being stereotyped as sad or angry, and instead

A man dancing in a nightclub wears long, pointy boots.

see themselves as romantic, creative, open-minded, and able to find beauty in
35 what others may see as dark or ugly.

Over recent years, a far more localized subculture has been developing in Mexico, where a style of music known as *Tribal Guarachero* has evolved, complete with its
40 own remarkable fashions. More commonly known just as *Trival*, the hugely popular sound mixes traditional regional folk music with electronic dance. Young fans often identify themselves by combining futuristic
45 elements with a basic farmworker look... and wearing extremely long, pointy boots when dancing, often competitively against groups from other local towns. Believe it or not, some items of footwear have apparently
50 reached five feet in length!

Of course, subcultures that develop in a particular area can spread like wildfire in a matter of moments these days, thanks to the internet. This is what's happened with
55 the Scraper Biker subculture. Originally the obsession of a small group of young people in the San Francisco Bay area, scraper bikes are simply ordinary bicycles that have been modified by their owners, typically
60 with decorated wheels and bright body colors. Much of the decoration is done very cheaply, using tinfoil, reused cardboard, candy wrappers, and paint! The craze went global after a hip-hop video featuring these
65 creations went viral. Scraper bikes can now be seen in cities all over the world.

If the internet helps some subcultures grow, for others it's their main home. Otherkin—people who identify to some degree as non-
70 human—have a massive online presence that's growing all the time. While some otherkin believe themselves to actually be, say, dragons or lions or witches or foxes, others simply feel special connections to
75 certain creatures—and have found a space within which to explore these feelings.

It seems that, whatever you're going through and whatever your own personal enthusiasms, there's a worldwide
80 community out there just waiting for you to find it—and to assure you that you belong!

Iceland was the first European country to elect a female president. Vigdis Finnbogadottir was elected in 1980.

8C Fight for Your Rights

GRAMMAR Patterns after reporting verbs

1 Look at the Grammar box. Match the patterns and sentences (1–6) with the examples (a–f) that have the same pattern.

1 verb + infinitive (with *to*)
The government **intends to introduce** new laws to tackle the problem.
2 verb + someone + infinitive (with *to*)
I **reminded you all to bring** in your permission slips.
3 verb + preposition + *-ing*
They **apologized for doing** what they did.
4 verb + (*that*) clause
She **argued (that)** things really need to change.
5 verb + *-ing*
He **denied answering** the question.
6 verb + someone + (*that*) clause
He **promised me (that)** he'd never do anything like that again.

Patterns after reporting verbs

a *Deciding to join a particular group offers young people the opportunity to explore who they are.*
b *Many goths resent being stereotyped as sad or angry.*
c *Some claim that the roots of Goth can be found in 19th century literary classics.*
d *There's a worldwide community out there just waiting to assure you that you belong!*
e *It allows them to start defining themselves outside of their immediate family circle.*
f *It can also attract abuse and bullying of those who insist on challenging social norms.*

Check the Grammar Reference for more information and practice.

2 Work in pairs. Decide which patterns in Activity 1 these verbs use. Some verbs use more than one pattern.

acknowledge	advise	agree	be accused
be blamed	convince	imagine	invite
persuade	pretend	state	suggest

3 Choose the correct options.

Many governments have been criticized (1) *of / in / for* turning a blind eye to racism. Some have even been accused (2) *of / for / from* encouraging it when it suits them. However, the Bolivian government recently announced (3) *to launch / launching / that it's launching* an app designed to encourage citizens (4) *that they should report / to report / reporting* any incidents of racism or discrimination that they encounter. The app is called No Racism. Reports can be submitted 24 hours a day. The government has promised (5) *responding / for responding / to respond* to all complaints and take legal action, where appropriate.

4 Complete the report with the correct forms of the verbs. Add prepositions where necessary.

It was recently announced that Iceland (1) _____ (be) now the best place in the world to be female. However, young Icelandic women have previous generations to thank (2) _____ (fight) for their rights. On October 24th, 1975, fed up with their status as second-class citizens, 90 percent of all women in the country refused (3) _____ (work). Their goal was to remind men that the success of the nation (4) _____ (depend) women and to urge them (5) _____ (accept) greater equality. They threatened (6) _____ (continue) their general strike until changes were made. Men listened, and within five years the country had become the first to elect a female president, Vigdis Finnbogadottir. Iceland can now claim (7) _____ (have) one of the highest proportions of female politicians—over 40 percent—in Europe. In the spring of 2017, a law was passed (8) _____ (require) employers to prove that their companies are free from gender-based salary discrimination.

5 Work in pairs. Look at the ideas for tackling gender inequality. Discuss:

- how they might change things.
- which you think are good ideas. Why?
- other ways in which things could be improved.

a Encourage stores to stop selling toys aimed at either boys or girls.

b Demand that companies employ an equal number of female and male bosses.

c Insist on mothers and fathers getting equal amounts of parental leave when they have children.

d Advise schools to ensure that both boys and girls do school subjects such as cooking and woodwork.

e Force schools to have equal numbers of men and women in photos on the walls.

f Persuade parents to discuss images of men and women in the media with their children.

6 Complete the short news article with the correct forms of these pairs of linked verbs.

accuse + discriminate	agree + examine	decide + make
deny + be	force + change	insist on + have

A 13-year-old girl in South Africa has been (1) _____ schools three times because of her hair. Zulaikha Patel has (2) _____ her current school, Pretoria High School for Girls, of _____ against black students through its uniform policies that (3) _____ students _____ a "neat, conservative appearance." Angry that this was being interpreted as meaning that she couldn't wear her hair in her natural afro style, she launched a silent protest, which attracted the attention of the national media. The school (4) _____ discriminatory in any way, but (5) _____ its policies before (6) _____ whether or not _____ any significant changes.

7 CHOOSE

Choose one of the following activities.

- Think of conversations you have had—or heard—recently. Use some of the reporting verbs from pages 98 and 99 to describe what they were about.

- Work in pairs. Write a news report about one of these topics. Use at least four reporting verbs.
  - an incident of discrimination
  - a protest
  - a new project that's trying to change things

- Work in groups. Tell each other about a time that:
  - you intended to do something, but then didn't. Explain why you didn't do it.
  - you refused to do something. Why?
  - someone famous was accused of doing something bad.
  - you had to apologize for doing something.
  - someone powerful acknowledged they'd done something wrong.

Zulaikha Patel and her classmates are fighting for rights that go beyond the style of their hair. They are standing up against racism.

> ❝ Normal is simply a construction of what we've been exposed to, and how visible it is around us. ❞

SAFWAT SALEEM

Read about Safwat Saleem and get ready to watch his TED Talk. ▶ 8.0

AUTHENTIC LISTENING SKILLS

Just

Just has several meanings—*only, simply, exactly, soon, recently*—and is also used to emphasize a statement or soften a request, to make it sound smaller or more polite.

1 Look at the Authentic Listening Skills box. Listen to these extracts from the TED Talk and add *just* in the correct place. 🎧 40

1 I had to grunt a lot for that one.
2 I sat there on the computer, hitting "refresh."
3 This was the first of a two-part video.
4 I could not do it.
5 If I stutter along the way, I go back in and fix it.
6 And the year before, that number was about eight percent.
7 Like the color blue for Ancient Greeks, minorities are not a part of what we consider "normal."

2 Work in pairs. Discuss each meaning of *just* in Activity 1. Then practice saying the sentences.

WATCH

3 Work in pairs. Discuss the questions.

1 In what ways do people make fun of others?
2 In what ways might people react to being made fun of?
3 Why do you think people make fun of others?

4 Watch Part 1 of the talk. Are the sentences *true* or *false*? ▶ 8.1

1 People have sometimes joked, "Have you forgotten your name?" because of Safwat's stutter.
2 Safwat is interested in video games.
3 The video Safwat posted only got negative feedback.
4 The negative comments were mainly about Safwat's stutter.
5 The incident led Safwat to do more voice-overs in order to prove his critics wrong.
6 In the past, Safwat used video and voice-overs to become more confident in speaking.
7 Safwat practiced to improve his voice and accent to sound more normal.

5 Work as a class. Read the conclusion of Safwat's talk. Discuss the questions.

The Ancient Greeks didn't just wake up one day and realize that the sky was blue. It took centuries, even, for humans to realize what we had been ignoring for so long. And so we must continuously challenge our notion of normal, because doing so is going to allow us as a society to finally see the sky for what it is.

1 How do you think the Ancient Greeks and the color of the sky might be related to what you have talked about and seen so far?
2 What do you think Safwat means by "the sky," with regard to society today?

6 Put the sentences in order. The first one is given. Then watch Part 2 of the talk and check your answers. ▶ 8.2

1 Few colors are mentioned in ancient literature. Why?

a In the same way, narrators with strong accents are not part of people's "normal."

b People discriminate because they don't "see" or relate to people who are different from themselves.

c Should Safwat accept or challenge ideas of normality?

d Blue was "invisible" and not part of ancient people's "normal," unlike red.

e Minorities are not part of society's "normal," like the color blue wasn't for the Greeks.

f One theory is that colors weren't named or "seen" until people could make them.

g This is why Safwat has gone back to using his voice in his work.

h People learn not to relate to minorities because there are few images of minorities in books.

i People's ideas of "normal" can lead to discrimination, such as offering fewer interviews to people with black-sounding names.

7 MY PERSPECTIVE

How do you feel about your own accent in English? Would you like to change it at all? What would be a "normal" accent for you?

8 VOCABULARY IN CONTEXT

a Watch the clips from the TED Talk. Choose the correct meanings of the words and phrases. ▶ 8.3

b Work in pairs. Tell each other about:
- something *humorous* you have seen or read recently.
- a time you felt a bit *self-conscious*.
- a time you took *a big step*.

CHALLENGE

Work in groups. You are going to discuss a video you could make about ONE of these topics. Choose a topic and follow the steps (1–5).

- Challenge the idea of what is "normal."
- Raise awareness of discrimination.
- Discourage bullying.
- Show how different groups share experiences, likes, and dreams.
- Encourage people to do activities with different groups of people.

1 Decide on one aspect of the topic to focus on.
2 Think of two or three different messages for the campaign.
3 Brainstorm some ideas to illustrate these messages.
4 Choose the best idea and develop it further.
5 Share your idea with the rest of the class.

8E Teenage Kicks

Useful language

Identify yourself

As a… / someone who…

Speaking as…

If you look at it from… point of view…

Agree or disagree

I totally support it.

I'm in favor.

I'm (totally) for / against the idea.

It's crazy.

I don't get it.

Challenge ideas and assumptions

Just because…, (it) doesn't mean…

…are we supposed to…?

Give examples

I mean, …

SPEAKING

1 Work in pairs. Look at the photo and discuss the questions.

1 Where was the photo taken?
2 What are the people doing? What else might they do?
3 How do you think others might react to these people? Why?

2 Listen to five people giving opinions about a policy. What do you think the policy is about? 🎧 41

3 Listen to the five people again. 🎧 41

1 Who is speaking in each case?
2 Are they for or against the policy? Why?

4 Complete the sentences by adding two words in each blank—contractions count as one word. Then listen again and check your answers. 🎧 41

1 We've lost some stock recently, which I think might be _____ .
2 I mean, where else are we _____ go? Or are we just _____ to hang out at all?
3 As _____ goes there pretty often, I _____ the idea.
4 _____ one or two misbehave _____ they all do. _____ , adults shoplift and cause problems, too.
5 If I look _____ from my grandpa's _____ view, I can kind of understand it.

5 Work in pairs. Look at the statements. Which ones are normal in your country? Which ones do you agree or disagree with? Why? Use some of the expressions in the Useful language box to discuss them.

1 Teenagers shouldn't hang out without a responsible adult around.
2 Everyone should wear a school uniform.
3 Boys and girls should be educated separately.
4 Men are better at certain subjects or in certain jobs than women.
5 You can only get a good job if you go to college.
6 Students need to do lots of homework to succeed.

6 Work in groups. Choose a role. Discuss the statements in Activity 5 in your role. Then think about the statements from a different perspective.

businessperson	parent	politician	teacher

Just hanging out?

WRITING A complaint

7 One of the speakers in Activity 2 mentioned negative stereotypes about teenagers in the media. What stereotypes do you think you fit? How does that make you feel? Why?

8 Do you think there are any stereotypes in the media about these groups of people? Are they positive, negative, or neither?

boys	businesspeople	girls
old people	people from your country	students

9 Read the complaint on page 152 and answer the questions.

1 Who is the person writing to and why?
2 How does she feel? Why?
3 What does she want to happen? Why?

10 WRITING SKILL Using appropriate tone

Work in pairs. Read the complaint on page 152 again. Discuss the questions.

1 Does the writer follow the advice in the Writing strategy box?
2 What other details could the writer give, if any?
3 Do you think complaints are worth writing? Why?

11 Work in groups. Think of reports, policies, rules, TV programs, or movies you know about. Discuss the questions.

1 Have you read or seen anything that you thought was untrue, unfair, or stereotyped people?
2 What was the problem?
3 Who was responsible?
4 How could it have been changed?

12 Write a complaint about one of the ideas you discussed in Activity 11. Follow the structure of the writing model on page 152. Try to use some of the language from this unit.

Read the complaint on page 152 and answer the questions.
Read the complaint on page 152 again.
Follow the structure of the writing model on page 152.

Writing strategy

When we write to complain about something, we:

- say what the general problem is in the first sentence.
- give details of the problem (including times and examples).
- explain more about how the problem has affected us.
- ask for some kind of action.
- sometimes say what we will do next if we are unsatisfied with the response.

The writing is more effective if it:

- is polite.
- is fairly formal.
- uses linking words such as *however* and *while*.

9 Lend a Helping Hand

Rescuers evacuate local people from their homes in China.

9A In Times of Crisis

VOCABULARY Dealing with disaster

1 Work in pairs. Look at the photo and discuss the questions.

1 What do you think has happened?
2 What do you think the three main challenges in this area would be at this time?
3 What would be needed to help people overcome these challenges?

2 Check that you understand these pairs of words. Use a dictionary, if necessary. Then complete the series of events following an earthquake.

appealed + aid	blocked + supplies
debris + task	earthquake + devastation
infrastructure + flee	launched + evacuate
rise + crisis	shortages + limited

1 The _____ struck coastal areas just after midnight and caused widespread _____ .
2 Much of the _____ was damaged or destroyed, and thousands of people started to _____ the worst-affected areas.
3 As the number of injuries continued to _____ , it became clear that a humanitarian _____ was starting to unfold.
4 There were food _____ and a _____ amount of clean drinking water.
5 The government _____ to the international community for _____ .
6 The roads were _____ , so they had to use helicopters to drop _____ to people.
7 They _____ a relief effort and started to _____ people from the disaster zones.
8 They finally managed to clear the _____ and started the huge _____ of rebuilding.

3 Work in pairs. Discuss the questions.

1 In addition to earthquakes, what else can cause **widespread devastation**?
2 What kind of systems form the **infrastructure** of a town or city?
3 What else might there be **shortages of** after a disaster?
4 What else might **rise** after a natural disaster?
5 What kind of **aid** can the international community provide in crises?
6 How is **debris** usually cleared?
7 How are people usually **evacuated from disaster zones**?
8 What other reasons are there that roads may be **blocked**?

4 Think about a natural disaster you know about and prepare to discuss it. Write notes on:

• what happened, where, and when.
• the immediate impact of the disaster.
• the relief effort involved—and how effective it was.
• the biggest challenges.

5 Work in groups. Discuss your notes from Activity 4. Try to use some of the language from Activity 2.

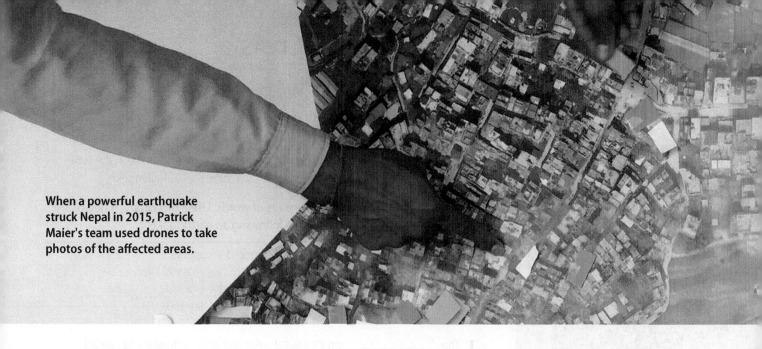

When a powerful earthquake struck Nepal in 2015, Patrick Maier's team used drones to take photos of the affected areas.

LISTENING

6 Listen to the first part of a radio program. Find out:
🎧 42

1 what the disaster was, where it happened, and when.
2 what the impact of the disaster was.

7 Work in groups. Discuss the questions.

- Had you heard about the disaster described in Exercise 6 before? Do you know anything more about it and how the country is now?
- How do you think social media, maps, and photographs, such as the one above, could help in this situation?

8 Listen to the second part of the radio program about how Patrick Maier first used an online mapping technology called Ushahidi in Haiti. Answer the questions. 🎧 43

1 How did he get information to update the online maps on Ushahidi?
2 How did this information help the people affected by the disaster?
3 How else has Ushahidi helped people elsewhere in the world?

9 Work in pairs. Try to remember what was said about the following. Then listen again and check your ideas.
🎧 43

1 Christine Martin
2 Kenya
3 Haitian roots
4 one million
5 helicopters
6 world attention
7 Russia
8 a smartphone

10 Patrick Maier calls the work he does *crisis mapping*. In recent years, crisis mappers have started using more technological tools in their work. How might these tools be useful to them? Can you think of anything else that might help?

3D modeling technology	artificial intelligence
drones	GPS
hashtags	satellites

Hashtags might be useful for crisis mappers because they can use social media to see where the most requests for aid are coming from.

GRAMMAR Relative clauses

11 Look at the Grammar box. Answer the questions.

1 What are the relative pronouns in each sentence?
2 When do you think each one is used?
3 Defining relative clauses qualify nouns and tell us exactly which thing, person, or place is being referred to. Which sentences include them?
4 What is the difference between the defining relative clauses in the sentences you just identified and the others?
5 In which sentence can the relative pronoun be left out? Why?
6 Look at sentence *d*. Where does the preposition go in relation to the verb? How else could you write this clause?

Relative clauses

a *The earthquake that struck Haiti measured seven on the Richter scale.**

b *The devastation which it caused was simply staggering!*

c *The country, which has long been one of the poorest in the world, struggled to cope.*

d *The seaport, which supplies would normally have been delivered to, was also unusable.*

e *Watching all of this in his Boston home was Patrick Maier, who decided that he had to do something to help.*

f *Maier, whose girlfriend was doing research in Haiti at the time, came up with the idea of using technology to create an interactive online map.*

g *He had to reach out for volunteers, many of whom had Haitian roots and were very happy to help.*

h *Helicopters were able to drop tents and food to desperate people whose homes had been destroyed and evacuate people who were trapped or injured.*

Richter scale *a scale for measuring the size of an earthquake*

Check the Grammar Reference for more information and practice.

12 Complete the summary with a relative pronoun in each blank. Can any of the blanks contain a different word or be left blank? If so, which ones? Explain your choices.

The year 1945 was an important one for Europe. Some people see it as the year (1) _____ the modern world started. Europe was in a mess, the kind of mess (2) _____ is almost impossible for people today to imagine. Six years of war had devastated the continent. Tens of millions had died; millions more had been forced to move from the places (3) _____ they had previously lived—and life was unbelievably hard for those (4) _____ had survived. The majority of the survivors were women and children (5) _____ husbands and fathers had been killed or imprisoned. Nobody had anything (6) _____ they could sell, and men with weapons wandered the land, taking whatever they wanted. How was the task of rebuilding achieved?

Well, most importantly, Harry Truman, (7) _____ was then President of the United States, put into place systems (8) _____ were intended to help all states regarded as allies. In 1947, the US Secretary of State, General George Marshall, (9) _____ name was given to the plan, announced massive amounts of aid for war-torn countries, much of which was to be used for reconstruction. The Marshall Plan ran for over ten years and paid for the rebuilding of infrastructure, (10) _____ provided employment and sped up the return of normal life.

13 Work in pairs. Add relative clauses to the sentences.

1 Crisis mapping has been used in many countries.
2 At 4:35 AM local time, the hurricane hit the coastal town.
3 The International Red Cross and Red Crescent have over 50 million volunteers.
4 Donations have now topped ten million dollars.
5 People are taking shelter in the local school.

14 MY PERSPECTIVE

Work in groups. Discuss the questions.

1 Have any disasters affected your country? In what way?
2 Did there need to be any rebuilding after the disaster(s)? How was this done?

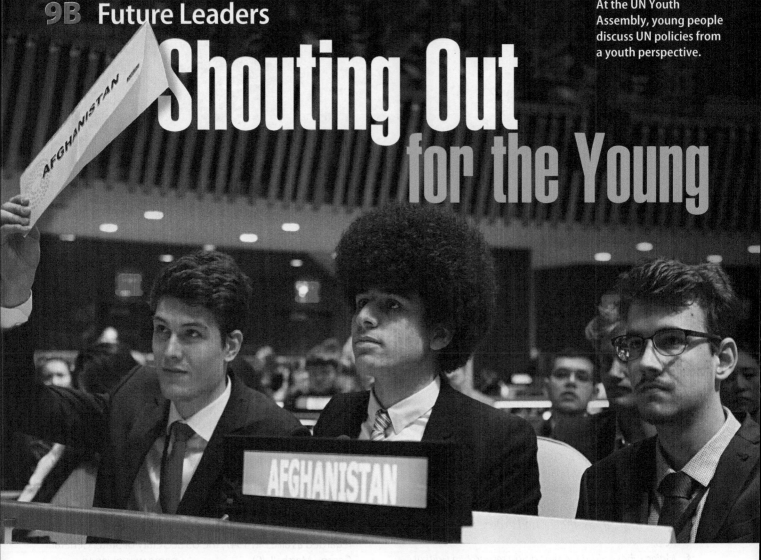

9B Future Leaders

Shouting Out for the Young

At the UN Youth Assembly, young people discuss UN policies from a youth perspective.

VOCABULARY BUILDING

the + adjective

We sometimes talk generally about groups of people using *the* + adjective.

*These days, **the young** face many challenges that didn't exist in the past.*

1 Work in pairs. Discuss whether you agree or disagree with the sentences.

1 The old need to listen to the young more.
2 There is one set of rules for the rich and another for the poor.
3 The loud and outgoing get too much attention.
4 Only the brave or the stupid would believe they could change the world.
5 Only the best get to the top.

2 Write your own sentence starting *Only the*. Then share your idea with the class and discuss what it means.

READING

3 Look at the photo and discuss the questions.

1 Who do you think the people are?
2 Would you like to take part in something like this?
3 Do you think young people can change policies in these areas? Why?

| the world | your country | your school | your town |

4 Read the article quickly. Write a one-sentence summary. Then work in pairs and discuss your summaries.

5 Read the article again. Find:

1 someone who started a trend.
2 an organization that provides aid.
3 someone who created a record.
4 someone who showed determination.
5 someone who founded an organization.
6 a country that has changed a law to benefit children.

44 Almost half of the world's seven billion citizens are under the age of 25, and they have huge potential to shape the countries they live in. A few countries, such as Argentina, have tried to empower their youth by giving them the right to vote at the age of 16, but it still seems that in many places young people's opinions are often overlooked or simply not heard. However, one organization that has a long history of giving a voice to young people is the United Nations (UN).

In 1946, the UN created a fund called UNICEF to support the millions of children affected by World War II, thanks to the leadership of the Polish medical scientist Ludwik Rajchman. The fund distributed aid without discrimination because, as its director Maurice Pate said, "There are no enemy children." One of those helped by the fund was seven-year-old Dzitka Samkova from Czechoslovakia, as it was known then. She painted a picture of five dancing girls as a thank you and it was turned into a greeting card, the first of many such cards sold to raise money for millions more children.

Having campaigned on behalf of young people, UNICEF also had a key part in the creation of the UN's Convention on the Rights of the Child (CRC) in 1989, now signed by more countries than any other convention. The 54 articles of the CRC declare different rights connected to housing, health, the economy, culture, and politics, including such things as the right to a safe home, the right to play and rest, and a child's right to choose their own friends.

In recent years, the UN has opened up new ways to address Article 12 of the CRC, which states that children have the right to give their views, and for adults to listen and take them seriously. UNICEF's Voices of Youth website brings together young bloggers and activists working on development issues to share their ideas and successful projects for change in a huge range of countries, from Sierra Leone to the Philippines. Using online discussion boards as a "meeting place," the initiative provides a space for youngsters who care.

The UN also established the Youth Assembly in 2002 and a network of Youth Observers. Since starting, the assembly has brought around 20,000 people between the ages of 16 and 28 from over 100 countries to its headquarters in New York. Through workshops, panel discussions, and networking events, these young people discuss UN policies from a youth perspective. The assembly also helps to build friendships across different cultures and give political experience to those who can bring change for children. One of its graduates, Ahmad Alhendawi of Jordan, became the UN Secretary General's first ever representative for youth and the youngest ever senior official in the UN.

Of course, the Youth Assembly and its delegates are only a tiny number of those three and a half billion young people, but they are important role models. It can be easy to find reasons not to act, but as Nicol Perez, a youth observer to the UN General Assembly says, "I have a voice, and I'm going to use it. I'm going to shout it out till somebody hears me."

7 an online initiative that brings together politically active people.
8 a place where young people help to decide how things are done in the world.
9 a document that states the rights of children.

6 In your opinion, how influential were these people from the article? Put them in order from most influential to least influential. Then work in small groups. Compare your answers and discuss your choices.

Ahmad Alhendawi	Dzitka Samkova
Ludwik Rajchman	Maurice Pate
Nicol Perez	Voices of Youth bloggers

CRITICAL THINKING Detecting bias

Even though articles give a lot of factual details, the way that the arguments are organized and the vocabulary that is used can show if the writer has an underlying opinion.

7 What do you think the author's general opinion is about the UN and young people? Why?

8 Identify the words and phrases in the opening paragraph which reveal the author's opinion. How does the structure of the paragraph reinforce these opinions?

9 Rewrite the first paragraph so that it is neutral. Change words and the structure of the paragraph. Remove words or phrases as necessary.

10 Work in groups. Discuss ideas you have to achieve these UN 2030 goals. Then share your ideas as a class.

- End poverty in all its forms everywhere.
- Ensure inclusivity and equality for all and promote lifelong learning.
- Achieve gender equality.
- Make cities inclusive, safe, resilient, and sustainable.

Malala Yousafzai is a young activist for female education. She spoke at the United Nations on her 16th birthday.

9C Community Service

GRAMMAR Participle clauses

1 Identify all the relative clauses that are correct and could have the same meaning as the corresponding reduced clause in the Grammar box.

1 The UN created a fund
  a who is called UNICEF.
  b which was called UNICEF.
  c that is called UNICEF.

2 The fund supported millions of children
  a who were affected by World War II.
  b which affected World War II.
  c that had been affected by World War II.

3 The CRC declares different rights
  a where connected to housing, health, the economy and politics.
  b which the UN connected to housing, health, the economy and politics.
  c which are connected to housing, health, the economy and politics.

4 The Voices of Youth website brings together young bloggers and activists
  a who work on development issues.
  b who have been working on development issues.
  c that are working on development issues.

Reduced relative clauses

a In 1946, the UN created a fund (1) *called UNICEF* to support the millions of children (2) *affected by World War II.*

b The 54 articles of the CRC declare different rights (3) *connected to housing, health, the economy, culture, and politics,* (4) *including such things as the right to a safe home and the right to play.*

c The Voices of Youth website brings together young bloggers and activists (5) *working on development issues* to share their ideas.

Check the Grammar Reference for more information and practice.

2 When do we use an *-ing* participle and when do we use an *-ed* participle to shorten a relative clause?

3 Read about some research findings and projects available to young people. Fill in the blanks with the correct participle of each verb.

Research has found that the number of young people (1) _____ (involve) in dangerous behavior has fallen greatly over recent years. In fact, youths are actually far more likely to be victims of crime rather than criminals. Yet most people think that the amount of youth crime and antisocial behavior is getting worse. The suggestion is that this may be because media reports still focus on youngsters (2) _____ (misbehave), (3) _____ (ignore) the many community projects (4) _____ (reduce) crime. These community projects involve such things as cafes (5) _____ (set up) for teenagers to meet after school, community gardens (6) _____ (teach) teens about sustainability, and a "time bank" (7) _____ (design) by young people (8) _____ (allow) them to earn rewards for doing volunteer work.

4 Work in pairs. Discuss the questions.

1 Do you think the research explained in Activity 3 would produce similar results in your country? Why?
2 How are community projects successful in reducing crime and antisocial behavior?

5 PRONUNCIATION *-ing* forms

a Listen to the statements. Note the pronunciation of the /ŋ/ sound. 🎧 **45**
b Practice repeating the statements. 🎧 **45**

> **Adverbial participle clauses**
>
> **a** *Having campaigned on behalf of young people, UNICEF also had a key part in the creation of the UN's Convention on the Rights of the Child (CRC) in 1989.*
>
> **b** *Using online discussion boards as a "meeting place," the initiative provides a space for youngsters who care.*

Check the Grammar Reference for more information and practice.

6 Look at the sentences in the Grammar box. Choose the correct options.

1 The subject of the participle clause is *the same as / different from* the subject of the verb in the main clause.
2 The present participle (*Using*) shows the action happened *at the same time as / before* the action in the main clause.
3 A perfect participle (*Having campaigned*) shows the action happened *at the same time as / before* the action in the main clause.

7 Complete this story about a foolish criminal by choosing the correct options.

(1) *Having walking / Walking* home from school one day with a friend, we came across a man on his bike. He started asking us where we were going and what phones we had. We just ignored him, but then he blocked us, (2) *shouted / shouting* at us to give him our phones. (3) *Not wanting / Wanting* to

get into a fight, we handed them over and he biked off. (4) *Returned / Having returned* home, I told my mom what had happened and we reported the incident to the police.

A week or so later, (5) *arresting / having arrested* someone, the police asked us to go and see if we could identify him. Unfortunately, it wasn't the man who had robbed us. We left kind of frustrated. But then, two days later, my friend's mom got a WhatsApp message from my friend's stolen phone! The robber had actually sent her a message, (6) *thinking / thought* it was his own mom—and he had his picture on the account he was using!

Even after (7) *having seen / seeing* the evidence against him, the robber still tried to tell the police he was innocent! I think he was hoping we wouldn't go to court, but (8) *faced / facing* with us actually giving evidence, he changed his mind and pleaded guilty.

8 Do the participle clauses in Activity 7 add information about time, reason, or method? Can you rewrite them with words like *because, after, while,* etc.?

9 MY PERSPECTIVE

What other stories about failed crimes or foolish criminals have you heard?

10 CHOOSE

Choose one of the following activities.

- On your own, write a story about a failed crime or a foolish criminal.
- Work in pairs. Think of six different ways you could promote young people and their issues.
- Work in pairs. Using participle clauses, describe four other trends using similar patterns to the examples in Activity 5. Then, in groups, discuss why these trends are happening.

The number of young people playing sports has fallen a lot.

Young people volunteer to serve food to less fortunate people in their community.

9D (Re)touching Lives through Photos

> " We take photos constantly. A photo is a reminder of someone or something, a place, a relationship, a loved one. "

BECCI MANSON

Read about Becci Manson and get ready to watch her TED Talk. ▶ 9.0

AUTHENTIC LISTENING SKILLS

Intonation and completing a point

We often use a rising intonation to show we are going to add an idea and a falling intonation to show that our point is complete. This pattern is common in lists and contrasts.

1 Look at the Authentic Listening Skills box. Then listen to Becci. Practice saying the extract yourself. 🎧 46

A photo is a reminder of someone or something, a place, a relationship, a loved one. They're our memory-keepers and our histories, the last thing we would grab and the first thing you'd go back to look for.

2 Decide where you might use a rising intonation and where you might use a falling intonation in these extracts from the TED Talk. Practice saying them.

1 We make skinny models skinnier, perfect skin more perfect, and the impossible possible.

2 We pulled debris from canals and ditches. We cleaned schools. We de-mudded and gutted homes.

WATCH

3 Work in groups. Tell each other about—and show each other, if you can—photos that remind you of special people, places, or times in your life.

4 Watch Part 1 of the talk. Find an example of where Becci: ▶ 9.1

1 makes a joke about her profession.
2 defends her profession.
3 gives an example of an unpleasant job she did.
4 had an initial moment of realization.
5 felt a sense of pride.
6 had a positive reaction from her contacts.

5 Work in pairs. Tell each other about:

• things you've lost or broken and wish you still had.
• things you're good at repairing.

6 Watch Part 2 of the talk. Are these statements *true, false,* or *not stated*? ▶ 9.2

1 The little girl in the first photo didn't survive the tsunami.
2 Before long, Becci and her team were scanning photos every other day.
3 Some of the people who brought photos were unfamiliar with the technology Becci was using.
4 The kimono in the photo took months to retouch.
5 Photos would only get retouched once their owners had come forward.
6 The lady who brought the family portraits already had extra copies.
7 Both of the lady's children were caught in the waves when the tsunami reached land.
8 All of the photos Becci and her team retouched were returned to their owners.
9 Becci and her team needed new printers.

TEDTALKS

7 MY PERSPECTIVE

Work in pairs. Discuss the questions.

1 Why do you think the response to Becci's request for help on social media was so high?
2 What other causes do you think might receive a high response on social media? Why?

8 Watch Part 3 of the talk. Which sentence is the best summary of the main point Becci makes? ▶ 9.3

a Everyone loves taking photos.
b Photographs are the most important things most people own.
c Both survivors and volunteers involved in the project benefited in a major way.
d Without photos, we wouldn't be able to remember our past that well.

9 Work in pairs. Which of these statements do you think are lessons from the talk? Do you agree with them?

1 Our differences matter, but our common humanity matters more.
2 In times of crisis, individuals can make a difference in ways that governments cannot.
3 We don't think enough about the psychological and emotional side of recovery after disasters.
4 It's important to feel that the work you do has a positive impact on society.
5 Some people volunteer because they feel guilty about how lucky they've been.
6 Countries shouldn't be expected to deal with large-scale disasters on their own.

10 VOCABULARY IN CONTEXT

a Watch the clips from the TED Talk. Choose the correct meanings of the words and phrases. ▶ 9.4
b Work in pairs. Tell each other about:
• a film, book, photo, or piece of art that *struck a chord* with you.
• three places around *the globe* you'd love to visit.
• a time you remember watching a major news story *unfold*.

CHALLENGE

Work in groups. Look at the situations (1–3). Thinking about both the immediate and the longer-term future, list what you think are the most important things that could be done in each situation by:

• the local government.
• other governments around the world.
• NGOs (Non-Governmental Organizations).
• volunteers on the ground.
• individuals in other places around the world.
• you.

1 A remote Pacific island has been hit very badly by flooding caused by global warming. Whole villages have been washed away and land has been lost to the sea.

2 A humanitarian crisis is developing in a country that has been devastated. There's a shortage of food and medicine, with children and old people being particularly at risk.

3 A big fire has destroyed dozens of homes in a town near you, leaving over a hundred people homeless and causing serious environmental damage.

9E Give It a Try

SPEAKING

1 Work in pairs. Look at these jobs. Discuss how they might be useful in a crisis or disaster. How might they generally be good for society?

actor	banker	chemistry teacher
computer programmer	photo retoucher	plastic surgeon
politician	street cleaner	

2 Work in pairs. Which job in Activity 1 do you think each sentence describes? Do you agree?

1 They are often criticized for creating fake images, but they can also help restore things that are very precious to people.
2 Some people say they're only motivated by greed and self-interest, but they generate jobs, and businesses couldn't work without them.
3 Without them, we'd be surrounded by piles of trash and dirt.
4 They can bring a huge amount of joy to millions of people.
5 They can transform the lives of people who have been injured.
6 They are fundamental to the technological world.
7 Yes, they can be corrupt and lie, but they can also be a huge force for good.
8 They don't just have knowledge, they have the ability to pass it on.

3 Listen to a student explain a job she thinks is important for society. Answer the questions. 🎧 47

1 What job is she talking about?
2 What reasons does she give?

4 Work in pairs. Answer the questions.

1 What did the student mention before listing positive aspects of the job? Why?
2 Which aspects of her argument do you agree and disagree with? Explain why.

5 Work in groups. Discuss which person or job in Activity 1 is best suited to help in a crisis. Follow these steps.

1 Give each person in the group a job to defend.
2 Spend some time preparing what you'll say. Use the Useful language box.
3 Take turns presenting your arguments.
4 Discuss who is the best person to help in the crisis.
5 Vote to choose the best person for the job.

After an oil spill, people volunteer to help with the clean-up operation which can involve helping wildlife.

WRITING A letter of application

6 Read the advertisement. Discuss the questions.

> Spend your winter vacation this year doing something different. We're looking for volunteers between the ages of 16 and 21 to rebuild a school in Belize that was destroyed in a hurricane last year. You will learn traditional building methods to provide a great space where learning can take place. For more details, write and tell us who you are and what you would bring to the project.

1 What do you think daily life for volunteers on this project would involve?
2 What problems might they face?
3 What kind of skills do you think would be required to do this work?
4 How do you think any volunteers who take part might benefit?
5 Would you be interested in doing something like this? Why?

7 **WRITING** Structuring an application

If you were writing in response to an advertisement, decide how you would order each of these features. Compare your ideas with a partner.

a Refer to the ad that you saw
b List the skills and abilities you have
c Describe who you are and where you are from
d Outline your plans for the future
e Explain why you are writing

8 Work in pairs. Read the letter of application on page 153. Which order did the writer choose? Do you think this person would be a suitable volunteer? Why?

9 Complete the sentences by adding the correct prepositions from the letter.

1 I'm writing _____ response to your recent letter.
2 Please send me more information _____ the post.
3 Please send details _____ how to apply.
4 I'm currently _____ my last year of high school.
5 _____ terms of my experience, I have a part-time job.
6 _____ addition, I have experience working with animals.
7 I feel that I would be suitable _____ the post.
8 I look forward _____ hearing from you soon.

10 Look at the advertisement. List the skills and abilities you have that might make you a suitable volunteer.

> Spend your summer in Mexico helping to preserve some of the world's most endangered species by participating in wildlife volunteer projects. Depending on where you're placed, you may care for animals, conduct research, or help with community programs. You may also be asked to teach basic English to local guides. You may find yourself working with dolphins or even jaguars. Contact us for details and to let us know why you'd be a great fit for our team.

11 Write letter of application in response to the advertisement in Activity 10. Use the Useful language box to help you.

Life-changing

IN THIS UNIT, YOU...

- talk about recovering from illnesses and accidents.

- read about the fight against superbugs.

- learn how medical advances have changed lives.

- watch a TED Talk about redefining yourself after a life-changing moment.

- write a story about overcoming something.

The da Vinci surgical system allows surgeons to carry out difficult procedures by looking at a screen.

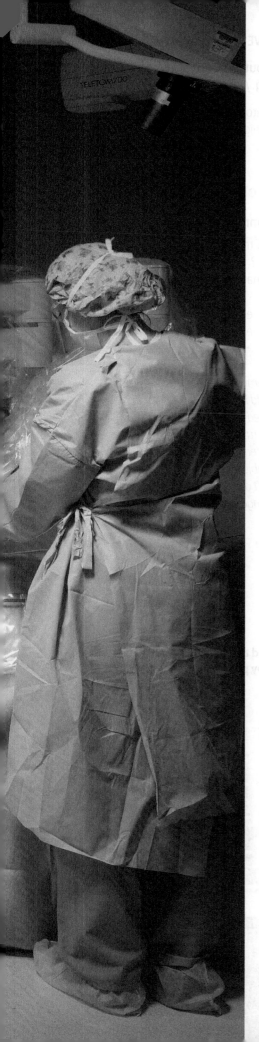

10A Road to Recovery

VOCABULARY Illness and injury

1 Look at the photo. Discuss the questions.

1 What do you think is happening?
2 What do you think has happened to the patient?
3 How might an operation like this have been carried out in the past?

2 Complete the sentences with the words in bold.

1 action / health / leg
I slipped on the stairs and broke my *leg*, so I was out of *action* for a while, but I'm back to full *health* now.

2 cure / drugs / symptoms
There's no for it, but she takes to control the, and she leads a fairly normal life.

3 injury / operation / physical therapy
It was quite a serious wrist, but thanks to the and all the I had, it's almost as good as new.

4 detected / made / spread
Luckily, they the cancer early before it to his lungs, and he a full recovery.

5 bleeding / damage / intensive care
They managed to stop the, but he was in for days. Thankfully, it didn't leave any permanent brain.

6 normal / therapy / stroke
He couldn't really speak after the, but he had a lot of speech, and he's more or less back to now.

7 lost / think / slammed
I the tip of my finger after I it in a car door. To be honest, I hardly about it now.

8 car accident / waist / wheelchair
He started playing basketball after he was left paralyzed from the down in a.

9 antibiotics / chest / prescribed
She said I just had a infection and nothing life-threatening! She me some, and it cleared up after a week.

10 feel / had / keep down
I an upset stomach, and I could hardly any food. It was horrible, but I a lot better now.

3 Work in groups. Look at your completed sentences in Activity 2. Find:

1 eight parts of the body.
2 at least five nouns that are medical problems.
3 four adjectives describing illnesses or injuries.
4 at least five phrases which show that someone has recovered from something.

4 Work in pairs. Discuss the questions.

1 Have you ever broken any bones? What happened?
2 When was the last time you had a day off of school due to illness? Why?
3 What do you do to recover from an illness? Are you a good patient?
4 What stories have you heard of people recovering from illnesses or injuries? What happened?

LISTENING

5 Listen to Jaime and Clara talking about movies. Answer the questions. 🎧 48

1 What four movies do they talk about?
2 What is the connection between the movies?
3 What doubts do they have about recommending the first three movies?

6 Work in pairs. Complete the sentences with three words in each blank. Listen again and check your answers. 🎧 48

1 He was in the _____ and no one could help because he hadn't told anyone where he was going.
2 It is horrible, but they managed to film it in a way which isn't _____.
3 It's the same with that film about the guy who had a stroke and was left completely paralyzed and _____ .
4 It's based on his book which he actually _____ by only moving his eye.
5 Yeah, it is incredible, but, sorry the movie didn't _____ me.
6 This is about Frida Kahlo, the Mexican artist who _____ all her life after a terrible bus accident.

7 Work in pairs. Discuss the questions.

1 Have you seen any of the movies Jaime and Clara talked about? If yes, what did you think of them? If not, would you like to see them? Why?
2 Can you think of any other movies that could fit the same category as those discussed? Are they based on true stories? What happened?

8 MY PERSPECTIVE

Think again about what you do when you are recovering from something. Answer the questions.

1 Would these stories inspire you to act differently? Why?
2 What things might you do to overcome challenges you face?

GRAMMAR Expressing past ability

9 Look at the Grammar box and answer the questions.

1 What forms of the verb follow *could*, *manage*, *able*, and *succeed in*?
2 How do you make negatives in the past with *could*, *able*, and *manage*?
3 Which sentences describe a general ability / inability?
4 Which sentences describe success in a task in the past?

Expressing past ability
a *He couldn't move his arm.*
b *No one could help.*
c *She managed to deal with that pain in the end and was able to turn it into incredible art.*
d *She succeeded in becoming a world-renowned artist.*
e *He was unable to speak.*
f *They weren't able to do anything about it.*
g *I didn't manage to see it when it was playing in theaters.*

Check the Grammar Reference for more information and practice.

Frida Khalo managed to deal with her pain and turn it into art that is admired by people all around the world.

10 Work in pairs. Are all the sentence endings in 1–3 correct? Explain those that are incorrect.

1 After I recovered from the illness,
  a I could see perfectly well in front of me, but I couldn't see anything to the side.
  b I was able to see perfectly well in front of me, but I wasn't able to see anything to the side.
  c I managed to see things perfectly well in front of me, but I didn't succeed to see anything to the side.

2 Following the accident,
  a she couldn't walk to begin with, but she could learn again since then.
  b she was unable to walk to begin with, but she's been able to learn again since then.
  c she wasn't able to walk, but she's managed to learn again since then.

3 He wrote a book about his experiences
  a and managed to get it published.
  b and succeeded in getting it published.
  c and could get it published.

11 Discuss how you think the paralyzed man Clara and Jaime talk about managed to dictate his book. Then read the summary and find out what happened.

Although his mind was working perfectly, his thoughts were locked inside him. He (1) *couldn't move* a muscle in his body. He (2) *couldn't make* a sound or even see clearly. So how did the ex-actor and magazine editor Jean-Dominique Bauby write a whole book? Well, first the nurses started communicating with him by asking a question and saying "yes" or "no." Bauby (3) *was able to indicate* his answer by blinking the only part of his body he (4) *could move*—his left eye. Then his speech therapist invented a way of arranging the alphabet in the order of the most frequent letters in French. She pointed to each letter, and Bauby blinked at

the correct one so (5) *she was able to spell* the word. Claude Mendible, an editor, then took up the job of writing with Bauby. Together, they (6) *managed to complete* a 120-page book about Jean-Dominique's life and his experience of "locked in" syndrome. After its publication, Bauby's memoir became a bestseller.

12 Rewrite the italicized words in Activity 11 using these words at least once.

able	could	managed	succeeded	unable

13 PRONUNCIATION Stress on auxiliaries

> Stress is sometimes added to the verbs *be* or *have* to emphasize that something is true—especially when clarifying or contrasting with another viewpoint.

a Listen and repeat the sentences. 🎧 **49**

b Complete these sentences with your own ideas. Then work in pairs. Practice saying the sentences.
  1 It is an amazing story, but _____ .
  2 I have heard of the story, but _____ .
  3 I am happy to be here. It's just _____ .
  4 It was a difficult situation, but _____ .

14 Work in pairs. Think of an inspiring story about someone who survived an accident or managed to deal with an illness. Think about:

- who it happened to and how old they were.
- how the accident happened or the person got sick.
- what the consequences were.
- how they survived and recovered.
- what the lessons from the story are.

15 Tell your stories to each other in groups or as a class.

10B The Battle against Bacteria

VOCABULARY BUILDING

Dependent prepositions

Certain verbs, adjectives, and nouns are often followed by specific prepositions, which we call *dependent*, because their choice depends on the particular word and its meaning. There are no fixed rules about which dependent prepositions go with which words, so it is important to pay attention to them as you learn them.

She was **diagnosed with** a rare eye disease.

I'm **allergic to** nuts.

The drug offers at least some **protection from** disease.

1 Complete the sentences with the correct prepositions. Use a dictionary, if necessary.

1 I would love it if more time was **devoted** _____ physical education at school.

2 I would be very **capable** _____ living on my own on a desert island.

3 Most fast food advertising is **aimed** _____ children.

4 We're all **exposed** _____ far too much air pollution.

5 A lot is done to raise **awareness** _____ health issues—especially among young people.

6 Any **investment** _____ health care has to be a good thing.

7 I think I have a good **chance** _____ living until I am 100.

8 It's natural for people to be **resistant** _____ change.

9 I can't remember the last time I needed a **prescription** _____ anything.

2 Work in pairs. Do you agree or disagree with the sentences in Activity 1? Why?

READING

3 Work in groups. Look at the title of the article you are going to read. Then discuss:

- how you think some of the words in bold in Activity 1 might be connected to the story.
- what, if anything, you know about the discovery of antibiotics.
- why antibiotics are important and how you think they may have changed medicine.
- what you think antibiotics are generally used for.
- what the "apocalypse" in the title might refer to—and how it might be avoided.

4 Read the article. Find out what the "antibiotic apocalypse" is and how it can be avoided.

5 Read the article again. Which of the points below are not made?

a Airplane cabins provide perfect conditions for bacteria to multiply.

b New forms of old diseases are now proving fatal.

c The WHO doubts that the worst-case scenario will happen.

d The possibility of resistant bacteria has been known since the early days of antibiotics.

e Technology is contributing to the overuse of antibiotics.

f Agricultural uses of antibiotics increase the likelihood that deadly superbugs will develop.

g Hosam Zowawi is developing a way of treating bacterial infections faster.

h The slower the recognition of resistant bacteria, the greater the risk of superbugs spreading.

6 MY PERSPECTIVE

Work in pairs. Discuss the questions.

1 Had you heard about the battle against bacteria before? If yes, did you learn anything new?

2 How does the article make you feel? Scared? Optimistic? Determined to change things? Or something else? Why?

CRITICAL THINKING Thinking through the consequences

The consequences of an action are the results or effects that the action produces. One element of reading critically is being able to see possible consequences of actions mentioned in a text.

7 Work in groups. How many possible consequences of these actions can you think of?

1 Drug-resistant diseases spread as a result of international air travel.

2 Antibiotics can no longer be used in hospitals.

3 Online sites selling antibiotics are closed down.

4 The use of antibiotics in farming is banned.

5 The government decides to greatly increase investment in medical research.

Avoiding the Antibiotic Apocalypse

🎧 **50** This may sound like the stuff of nightmares or of terrifying science-fiction movies, but according to the World Health Organization (WHO) the threat of an "antibiotic apocalypse" is very real, and many experts
5 fear that it's only a matter of time before we see the emergence of a superbug—a very powerful type of bacteria that normal drugs cannot kill—capable of wiping out huge numbers of people.

Perhaps most disturbing of all is the fact that this
10 potential disaster has been predicted for many decades. In fact, the earliest warnings came from Sir Alexander Fleming, the Scottish doctor and bacteriologist who in 1928 discovered the world's first antibiotic substance—penicillin.

15 Like many groundbreaking scientific finds, the discovery of penicillin was largely accidental. Its importance wasn't realized for at least another ten years, and mass production didn't start until the 1940s. However, there's no doubting the fact that it changed
20 medical practices beyond all recognition. Infections that had previously been fatal were now treatable.

In the speech he made when accepting the Nobel Prize for his work, Fleming warned that bacteria could easily become resistant to antibiotics if regularly exposed to
25 concentrations insufficient to kill them. He went on to express his fears that penicillin would end up being so widely used that such changes were inevitable. Worryingly, this is precisely what happened!

Antibiotics are now regularly prescribed for such
30 non-life-threatening illnesses as sore throats, colds, and ear infections, and if doctors refuse their requests, many patients turn to the internet for their desired medication. On top of this, a large percentage of all antibiotics sold are now being used in farming. They
35 are, for instance, often given to healthy animals to ensure rapid weight gain. Given all of this, it's no surprise that more and more bacteria are evolving a resistance.

One man determined to overcome this challenge is
40 the Saudi microbiologist Hosam Zowawi, who has devoted a considerable portion of his time to developing a test that's able to identify bacteria in hours rather than days, allowing doctors to act more quickly and efficiently, and slowing the potential
45 spread of any deadly infections. Zowawi is also very actively involved in campaigns designed to raise public awareness of the risks of antibiotic overuse.

In addition to reducing the use of antibiotics, there are many other ways that the situation is now being
50 addressed. For instance, in the Netherlands, the government has started putting pressure on farmers to reduce the amount of antibiotics given to animals. Elsewhere, there's a growing understanding of the need to address the underlying conditions that allow
55 new diseases to spread, which, in turn, leads to better trash collection, better drainage, and better housing. Finally, we're starting to see increased investment in research aimed at finding the new antibiotics that could be the penicillin of tomorrow.

E. coli infections make up a large percentage of antibiotic-resistant infections.

New technology is helping people to recover their sight and see for the first time.

10C Medical Advances

1 Work in groups. The photos show different ways that technology is helping to improve vision. Discuss what you think each picture shows and how it might work.

2 Listen to an extract from a radio program. Find out: 🎧 **51**

  1 which of the photos is being discussed.
  2 if the technology is expensive.

3 Work in pairs. Can you explain how the technology works using these words? Listen again and check your answers. 🎧 **51**

| camera | cells | chip | electrical signals |

4 MY PERSPECTIVE

Work in pairs. Think of as many different ways to fund medical research and treatments as you can. Then discuss these questions with another pair of students.

  1 What is the best way to fund medical research and treatment?
  2 How might a health service decide when a treatment is too expensive?
  3 How might a health service decide between two very expensive treatments?

GRAMMAR Emphatic structures

5 As well as pronunciation grammar can also be used to add emphasis. Look at the Grammar box and answer the questions.

  1 How is emphasis added in sentences *a* and *b*?
  2 What adverbs are used in sentences *c* and *d* to introduce the point being emphasized?
  3 What happens to the order of the words that follow these adverbs?

Emphatic structures

a *While surgical options did exist before, none were nearly as effective.*
b *While each bionic eye does cost a lot, reports from users have been incredibly positive.*
c *We're all used to hearing news about terrible things, but rarely do we hear much about exciting new developments.*
d *When Second Sight started experimenting, little did they know that they were on their way to revolutionizing the treatment of blindness!*

Check the Grammar Reference for more information and practice.

6 Rewrite the sentences in a more emphatic style, using the words in parentheses.

  1 Some doctors read research about new medicine, but too many just accept what big drug companies tell them. (do)
  2 While caffeine increases energy levels, in large doses it can actually prove fatal. (does)

3 In the old days, doctors sometimes removed arms or legs without using any painkillers! (did)

4 When the patient started having terrible headaches, she didn't know it was because a spider was living in her ear. (little)

5 No research suggests that there is anything unhealthy about a vegetarian diet. (in no way)

6 Doctors didn't often cut people open in the days before penicillin. (rarely)

7 You don't fully become an adult until the age of 24. (only after)

8 In the Middle Ages, doctors were never in doubt that releasing blood from the body kept people healthy. (at no time)

9 Plastic surgery didn't become very popular until the 1980s, despite having been around for over 200 years before then. (not until)

10 People in the United States do less exercise than anyone else in the world. (nowhere)

7 **PRONUNCIATION** Adding emphasis

> *Do / Does / Did* is usually stressed in sentences where it has been added for emphasis. Negative adverbs are also usually stressed when they introduce a point to be emphasized.

a Listen and check your answers in Activity 6. Then listen again and note the way stress is used to add emphasis. 🎧 52

b Practice saying each sentence in an emphatic way. Which of the ideas most and least surprised you? Why?

8 Complete the short article by adding one word in each blank.

There are 39 million blind people in the world. But (1) _____ do people realize that perhaps half of those affected by blindness could be cured, simply by removing the cataract* which causes it. Many people (2) _____ already have surgery to remove cataracts. In fact, it is a very common operation in many countries, and only very (3) _____ does the patient fail to recover good sight. However, until recently the procedure (4) _____ cost quite a lot and was too expensive for sufferers in developing countries. That was until Dr. Sanduk Ruit, a doctor from Nepal, created a new system for conducting cataract surgery. (5) _____ only did he manage to reduce the cost of the operation to around 25 dollars per patient, he reduced the time it took and developed a production-line approach. In fact, (6) _____ in the world do they conduct the operation more efficiently and successfully than in Nepal. The result makes a huge difference to thousands of lives. Not only (7) _____ the operation bring sight back, it (8) _____ brings back the ability to farm and do similar work, which in turn helps to reduce poverty.

cataract *a medical condition which causes the lens of the eye to become cloudy, resulting in blurred vision*

9 **CHOOSE** Choose one of the following activities.

- On your own, find out about an amazing development in medical history. Write a summary of your findings, explaining what happened, when, and why it was important.

- Work in pairs. Decide what you think the biggest health risk facing your country is. Think of five ways it could be tackled.

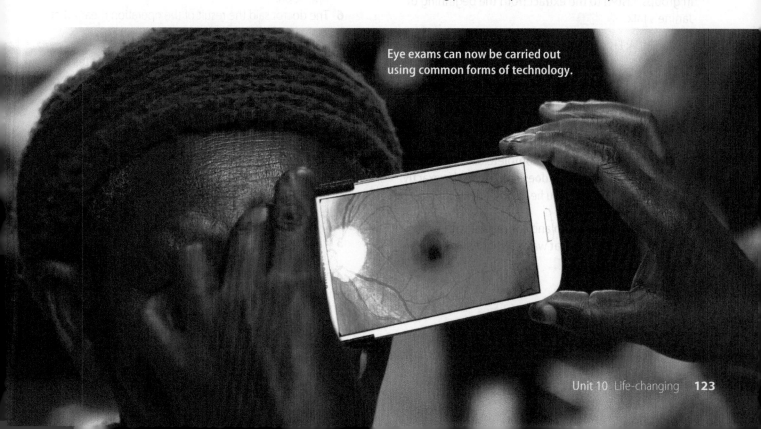

Eye exams can now be carried out using common forms of technology.

AUTHENTIC LISTENING SKILLS

Collaborative listening

Fast speech can be difficult to understand. Focus on what you did hear. Think about the context and what you know about the subject or situation to guess what might have been said. If you are with someone, compare what you heard; you may have heard different things.

1 Look at the Authentic Listening Skills box. Then work in groups. Listen to the extract from the beginning of Janine's talk. ∩ 53

- Student A: Listen and note the nouns and things you hear.
- Student B: Listen and note the verbs and actions you hear.
- Student C: Listen and note whatever you want.
- Student D: Listen carefully without taking notes.

2 Work in your groups. Write a complete text based on your combined notes. Your text does not have to be exactly the same as the extract you heard in Activity 1.

3 Listen to the extract again and compare it with what you wrote in Activity 2. In what ways is your text different from the extract? ∩ 53

WATCH

4 Watch Part 1 of the talk. Are the sentences *true* or *false*? ▶ 10.1

1 The accident took place at the time of the Olympics.
2 The vehicle that hit Janine was going fast.
3 Janine's bike helmet protected her head from any damage.
4 Janine had an out-of-body experience as she was fighting for her life.
5 Janine had no movement below her waist after the operation.
6 The doctor said the result of the operation meant that Janine would eventually be as good as new.

5 Work in pairs. Watch Part 2 of the talk. Take notes on what you hear and compare. ▶ 10.2

6 Work in pairs. Complete the sentences together. Then watch Part 2 of the talk again and check your answers. ▶ 10.2

1 Janine did not know what the other people in the spinal ward _____ .
2 Janine felt the friendships she made there were unusual because they were _____ .
3 The other people in the ward shared their hopes and _____ rather than have _____ .
4 When Janine left the ward and first saw the sun again, she felt _____ for her life.
5 The head nurse had told Janine she would _____ , but she did not believe her.
6 Janine wanted to give up because she was in _____ .

7 Look at these phrases. How do you think they are connected? What new activity and job do you think Janine took up?

buttons and dials	get a license
learn to navigate	pass a medical
sense of freedom	slide up on the wing
take the controls	teach other people

8 Watch Part 3 of the talk. Was your answer to Activity 7 correct? ▶ 10.3

9 Work in pairs. Explain what happened to Janine using the phrases in Activity 7.

10 Watch Part 4 of the talk. What do you think Janine's message is? Discuss your idea with a partner. ▶ 10.4

11 VOCABULARY IN CONTEXT

a Watch the clips from the TED Talk. Choose the correct meaning of the words and phrases. ▶ 10.5

b Work in pairs. Discuss the questions.
   1 What might be something that is difficult to *grasp*? Have you ever experienced this?
   2 Do you think it is good to get *out of your comfort zone*? Why? Have you ever been in that situation? What happened?
   3 Do any of your friends or family have a *nickname* you like? Why do they have it?

12 Work in pairs. Discuss the questions.
   1 Did you enjoy Janine's talk? Why?
   2 Do you think you could have overcome something like Janine's experience? Why?
   3 What judgments do people make when they meet people for the first time?
   4 Have your friends ever helped you overcome a problem or difficulty? How?
   5 Is there something you would like to do but have not? What's stopping you?

CHALLENGE

Work in pairs. Discuss what challenges these situations might create for a person and what opportunities might be created. Then work with another pair of students and put your challenges in order from the most difficult to the easiest. Discuss your reasons.
- Having a serious accident like Janine's.
- Moving to a new country because of a parent's job.
- Failing your final exams at school.
- Going to college in a new city.

10E Getting Better

SPEAKING

1 Work in pairs. What would you say or ask if you heard that someone you knew:

- got good grades on their exams?
- had been kicked out of school?
- was moving from where they live?
- was sick or had an accident?

2 Listen to two conversations between friends. Answer the questions. 🎧 54

1 Who are they talking about? Why?
2 What happened to the person they are talking about?

3 Which of the phrases in the Useful language box did you hear in each conversation? Listen again and check. 🎧 54

4 Work in pairs. Take turns saying the sentences below. Your partner should respond and add a follow-up question or comment.

1 Apparently, he'll have to have an operation.
2 Her mom said she was grounded.*
3 I saw him yesterday and he said he was feeling a lot better.
4 Apparently, it's a really bad cold. He's going to be out all week.
5 Did I tell you? My older sister's going to have a baby!

grounded *not allowed to go out as a punishment for doing something wrong*

5 Practice having conversations based on your ideas in Activity 1. Use the Useful language box to help you.

WRITING   A success story

6 Work in groups. Can you think of a time you overcame one of the following? Tell each other your success stories.

a difficulty	disgust	a fear
an illness	an inability	an opponent

7 Work in pairs. Student A: read the story on this page. Student B: read the story on page 153. Then tell each other:

1 which of the things mentioned in Activity 6 each writer overcame.

2 what the writer finally managed to do.

I looked down at the water and the waves crashing against the rocks. My legs immediately started to shake. Someone shouted "Come on Yasine, you can do it!" I was on an adventure vacation. This is what I had wanted to do—walking, climbing, camping—and now here I was doing these things and I couldn't move. I wanted to be anywhere else but here. We were doing a walk along a narrow coastal path, but it had become less and less like a path and more like a cliff we had to climb along. We finally came to a point where we had to hold on to a rock and jump over a small gap to get to the rest of the path. Everyone else had done it and I was the last one. It wasn't far—not much more than a few feet. But I just couldn't do it. I was sure I was going to fall. I was stuck. The rest of the group then started to shout together, "You can do it! You can do it!" I grabbed the rock and leapt to the other side. I made it! Everyone cheered. I had finally managed to do it and it felt like I was champion of the world.

8 Read the story that you did not read in Activity 7. Can you find these features in either text? Compare your findings.

1 An interesting opening sentence that grabs the reader's attention

2 Inversion to make part of the story more emphatic

3 Examples of direct speech

4 Descriptive verbs that make the story more exciting

9 **WRITING SKILL** Using descriptive verbs

Complete each sentence with the correct form of these descriptive verbs.

creep	grab	leap	peer
rush	scream	slam	stare

1 They _____ me to the hospital and we got there just in time!

2 I _____ the top of the table and pulled myself up.

3 "Watch out!" she _____ as the motorcycle came speeding towards me.

4 I could hear a strange noise, but as I _____ into the darkness, I couldn't see anything!

5 When I heard the scream, I _____ out of my chair and ran into the kitchen to see what the problem was.

6 I _____ at the letter in complete amazement! I just couldn't believe my eyes!

10 Write a story of between 200 and 250 words about overcoming something. Use the phrase *I finally managed to...* somewhere in the story.

Explaining how you felt before you succeeded

I was absolutely terrified.

I was sure I was going to fall / fail / lose!

I'd tried absolutely everything.

I was ready to just give up.

Explaining how you felt in the end

It was the best day / one of the best days of my life.

It was a moment I'll never forget.

It was a truly memorable experience.

It was a day that changed my life.

Have you ever overcome a fear?

MODALS AND MEANING

Modals never change their form. They go with normal verbs and are followed by the infinitive without *to* form of those verbs. Modals add meaning to verbs. A phrase or normal verb can sometimes be used instead of a modal.

Will/would

Will is used to express that something is certain or sure to happen, and to express promises, offers, habits, and refusals.

*The first thing that **will** strike people…*

Would is used to express that something is theoretically certain to happen, to report as the past form of *will*, and to express a habit in the past.

*If the habitat disappeared, they**'d** die out.*

Should/shall

Should is used to express a good or better idea, or if something is expected to happen in the future.

***Should** we be trying to conserve these species?*

Shall is used to ask for and give suggestions, or to make offers about a current or future situation.

*What **shall** we do about it?*

Can/could

Can expresses ability and permission. It is also used if something is only possible sometimes and factually possible (or not, in the negative).

*They **can** be difficult to see in the wild.*

Could is used to express past ability / inability, if something happened sometimes, or is theoretically possible. *Could* is also used in polite requests.

*I **couldn't** swim until I was in my twenties.*

may/might/must

Might is used if something is uncertain but possible.

*You **might** stop weak species from going extinct.*

May is also used if something is uncertain but possible, and for permission.

*These changes **may** bring benefits.*

Must is used if something is necessary and if the speaker is sure of something based on experience.

*These changes **must** bring benefits.*

Have can sometimes behave as a modal.

*You **have** to go to school.*

MODALS AND INFINITIVE FORMS

Modals can be followed by different kinds of infinitive forms.

To talk about actions generally, use a modal + the infinitive without *to* form.

*As you **can see**, it does look quite professional.*

To talk about actions in progress or extended over time, use a modal + *be* + *-ing* (the continuous infinitive without *to*).

*We **should be doing** more to protect them.*

To talk about the past in general, use a modal + *have* + past participle (the perfect infinitive without *to*).

*You **could have (could've) told** me how cruel it was and I honestly **wouldn't have cared**.*

To emphasize that an action was in progress when another thing happened, use a modal + *have been* + *-ing* (the perfect continuous infinitive without *to*).

*I **can't have been paying** attention when I read about it.*

Modals can also be used with passive forms.

*More **should be done** to reduce the suffering of animals.* (= generally)

*I got really sick after eating that meat. It **can't have been** cooked properly.* (= in the past)

1 Choose the correct option.

Juliana Machado Ferreira is a conservation biologist who is trying to stop illegal wildlife trade in Brazil. People in Brazil (1) *will / shall* often keep wild birds as pets, but Machado says they (2) *shouldn't / couldn't*. Taking animals from nature (3) *can / should* have a terrible impact on the habitat and other animals there. For example, if a large proportion of the wild birds that are captured are female, this (4) *might / will* inevitably reduce future populations. The birds (5) *may / would* also be predators for other animals or consume particular plants, so a reduction in the bird numbers (6) *can / can't* have an impact on the rest of the ecosytem. She believes the public (7) *must / might* be educated about these effects. In the past, she has worked with the police to help return birds to their original habitat. The problem is that they (8) *could / shall* be from any number of different places, so Machado used a genetic test to determine where the birds (9) *might / will* be from. She developed her ideas at the US Fish and Wildlife Service Forensics Laboratory. She got an internship there because she (10) *would / could* write regularly to them asking if she (11) *would / could* become a volunteer until eventually they said yes! And now Juliana shows the same determination in her work. She has a very varied work life but, in the next few years, she (12) *may / can* spend more time in her home office. She also says that if she (13) *can / could* talk to her younger self, she (14) *would / should* tell herself to learn something about finance and marketing. This is because she is now in a management position, and students aren't taught how to deal with money in biology classes.

2 Choose the best self-follow-up comment to each question.

1 Would I ever do it?
   a Only if I had no other option.
   b Of course I can.

2 Shall I do it for you?
   a I still haven't decided.
   b It's no trouble.

3 Must I do it?
   a It'll be fun.
   b Can't someone else?

4 Should I really do it?
   a There's no other option.
   b I'm not sure it'll improve things.

5 Will I do it at some point?
   a I still haven't decided.
   b I don't mind if you don't want to.

6 Can I do it?
   a I'd really like to try.
   b I might not.

3 Choose the correct option.

1 New research has shown that there *can't / might* once have been a creature similar to a unicorn.

2 I can't believe how little he ate. He *can't be feeling / can't have been feeling* very hungry.

3 I can't believe you thought that story was true. You *should / must* have checked it on some other sites!

4 I'm not surprised his parents were angry. He *shouldn't have had / shouldn't have been having* snakes without telling them!

5 Surely there *would / will* have been more in the papers about the tree octopus if it were true.

6 I'm guessing that you *might / should* have heard about the tree octopus, right?

7 We promise that any cat you buy from us *will have been being / will have been* thoroughly checked by a vet.

8 You *shouldn't have scared / shouldn't scare* the dog. He *wouldn't / couldn't* have barked at you otherwise.

4 Complete the rewrite for each sentence. Use the best modal and two or three other words in each space.

1 It's just not possible for the Loch Ness monster to have survived that long without being found.
The Loch Ness monster _____ that long without being found. It's impossible.

2 It's possible that Loch Ness was once connected to the ocean.
Loch Ness _____ connected to the ocean.

3 I can't believe I didn't realize the movie was a fake.
I'm so stupid. I really _____ the movie was a fake.

4 If there really was a monster, why aren't there more photos of it?
People _____ more photos of the monster if it really existed!

5 It's impossible to get near the loch now without being filmed by security cameras.
By the time you get to the edge of the loch, you _____ by security cameras.

6 There's no way he was telling the truth about what he saw.
If you ask me, he _____ about what he saw.

7 Loch Ness is only 10,000 years old. Plesiosaurs died out 60 million years ago.
Loch Ness _____ around when plesiosaurs still existed.

8 I swear I saw something. Honestly, if only I'd had my camera with me!
I _____ my camera with me. I _____ what I saw if I'd had it.

FIRST, SECOND, THIRD, AND MIXED CONDITIONALS

First conditional

First conditionals describe possible results of real situations now or in the future.

If you're in school today, **you'll** *probably start working sometime in the 2020s.*

I'm going to take *the test again* **if I fail.**

Second conditional

Second conditionals describe imaginary situations and results now or in the future.

If these drawings **were painted** *more realistically, they* **would look** *amazing.*

I wouldn't joke *about it* **if I were you.**

Third conditional

Third conditionals describe imaginary situations and results in the past.

If she'd wanted *pictures,* **she'd have told** *us.*

If he hadn't spent *that day with his niece, the Monster Engine* **would never have happened.**

Mixed conditional

Mixed conditionals describe imaginary past situations and imaginary present results.

If their schools had encouraged *unusual ways of seeing the world, lots of adults* **would be** *more creative.*

I wouldn't be *here now* **if she hadn't helped** *me.*

Other modals can also be used in the result clauses of conditional sentences.

If I do OK on my exams, I **might / may try** *to study fine art in college.*
= Maybe I will study fine art.

If I get really good grades, I **can go** *and study abroad.*
= It will be possible for me to study abroad.

If he had been a little taller, he **could have become** *a really great basketball player.*
= It would have been possible for him to become a great player.

WISH, IF ONLY, WOULD RATHER

Wish, if only, and *would rather* all introduce hypothetical ideas—things that a speaker wants to be true, but sees as impossible. As with conditional sentences, past forms of verbs are used to talk about hypothetical events.

The simple past, the past continuous, *could,* and *would* are used to hypothesize about present situations.

The simple past is used when hypothesizing about general situations or states.

I wish I **was** *better with words.*

I wish I **was** *as creative as her / him.*

I wish I **didn't have** *to take art classes.*

If only I **had** *an extra eye in the back of my head!*

I'd rather the teacher **didn't give** *homework.*

The past continuous is used to hypothesize about an action or specific situation happening now.

If only I **wasn't sitting** *here now!*

I wish I **was doing** *something else. This is boring.*

Could is used to hypothesize about an ability we want.

I wish I **could draw** *better.*

I wish I **could help** *you, but I just can't.*

Would is used to hypothesize about a habit or behavior we want to stop (or start).

I sometimes wish my classmates **wouldn't make** *so much noise.*

I wish she **would speak** *slower. I can't understand anything she says.*

The past perfect is used to hypothesize about the past and express regrets.

I wish my parents **hadn't forced** *me to learn an instrument.*

I often say to myself, "If only I'd spent more time thinking about this before I started."

Note that, where the subject of *would rather* is the same as the verb that follows it, an infinitive without *to* is used.

I'd rather **you did** *it.*

I'd rather **do it** *myself.*

1 Choose the correct option.

1 If you *will want / want* to study abroad, you'll need to save some money first.

2 I wouldn't play this instrument well if my dad *hadn't helped / doesn't help* me when I first started.

3 If I *would have / had* more time, I'd love to learn how to paint with watercolors.

4 It's your fault! If you hadn't been late, everything *would've been / was* fine.

5 The test's next week and you *don't / are not going to* do well if you don't work more!

6 If we hadn't changed things when we did, the situation *would / will* be worse now.

7 It might not have worked if we *tried / had tried* it that way.

8 If I spoke to my mother like that, she really *won't / wouldn't* be happy!

2 Complete the sentences with the correct form of the verbs in parentheses.

1 If I _____ (not ask) lots of questions when I was at school, I wouldn't be a scientist now.

2 If you _____ (create) a culture that encourages creativity, people will be happier.

3 I don't think I _____ (start) painting if my parents hadn't encouraged me.

4 If I _____ (be) fluent in English, life would be so much easier!

5 Just think! Things _____ (be) very different today if ways of writing hadn't developed.

6 If you don't practice, you _____ (never get) better at it.

7 I _____ (not do) that if I was you.

8 If it _____ (not be) so noisy in the exam room, I would've done better.

3 Make conditional sentences based on the information below.

1 They only realized how talented she was after giving all the children tests to assess creativity levels.

They wouldn't have realized how talented she was if they hadn't given all the children tests to assess creativity levels.

2 Follow the rules or fail the course. It's your choice!

3 I can't really play this. I haven't practiced recently.

4 Some colleges don't value creativity. That's why they don't really help students develop it.

5 She didn't obey the rules when she started her business. That's why she's successful today.

6 Creativity in children is like anything else: encourage it or be prepared for it not to grow.

4 Choose the correct options.

1 A This is taking too long to do.
B Yeah, sorry. I thought it was a good idea at the time, but I wish I *hadn't suggested / didn't suggest* it now.

2 A Shall I ask my mom or dad if they can take us there?
B I'd rather we *go / went* on our own.

3 A I'd like to study abroad somewhere.
B Me too. If only I *can / could* speak Chinese! I'd love to go to Shanghai.

4 A I wish the teacher *would / wouldn't* make us copy everything from the book.
B I know. It's a little boring, isn't it?

5 A Did you go to the gig yesterday?
B No, but I wish I *had / did*. I heard it was great.

6 A If only I *didn't have to / wouldn't have to* leave. I'd love to talk more.
B Don't worry. I need to be home before 12, anyway.

5 Complete each second sentence so that it has a similar meaning to the first sentence, using the word given and three extra words.

1 I'm afraid we can't do anything more to help. **only**
If _____ more to help.

2 My brother is so negative. It's really annoying. **would**
I wish my brother _____ about things.

3 I wanted to walk here, but we took the car. **rather**
I _____ the car at home.

4 We should have done a better analysis of the problem. **wish**
I _____ the problem better.

6 Complete each sentence with one word. Contractions count as one word.

1 A Is it OK if I put some music on?
B I'd rather you _____ . I'm trying to study.

2 A Do you want to go to the mall?
B I'd rather _____ somewhere else. I don't like the stores there.

3 A I wish we _____ asked someone to help us.
B Really? I'd rather _____ to do it myself first, even if I make a mistake.

4 A I'd rather you _____ this a secret between us. It's a bit embarrassing.
B Don't worry. I'd rather _____ knew what happened! If _____ I could forget it myself!

REPORTED SPEECH

When an anecdote or story is told, what people said is often reported. This can be done with:

- direct speech.

She said, "I love you," and then he said, "Will you marry me?"

- indirect speech.

She said she loved him, and he then asked (her) if she'd marry him.

- a mixture of the two.

She said, "I love you," and then he asked if she'd marry him.

When reporting with indirect speech, follow the normal rules of tenses within a story. This often involves a tense backshift from direct speech. Look at the direct and indirect speech used to report statements about:

- a situation or action at the time it was said / thought.

I said, "I need to go back to school."
I said I needed to go back to school.

- an action in progress at the time it was said.

She said, "I'm going to the station."
She said she was going to the station.

- an action further back in time before it was said.

He said, "I've forgotten my money."
He told me he'd forgotten his money.

- a plan or prediction for the future at the time it was said.

I asked and they said, "We'll try!"
They said they would try.

When the statement being reported is still true, present and other tenses can be used, as they apply to now.

Miriam told me to tell you she'll be late.
= She's not here yet, so she still will be late.
He told me he's never had tea.
= As far as I know, he still hasn't had tea.

When correcting a misunderstanding, the backshift is preferred because the misunderstanding is no longer true, but it is not essential.

A: We are meeting at 10.
B: I thought we were meeting at 11.

In indirect reporting of questions the normal word order of a statement is used.

I said, "What are you doing here?"
I asked her what she was doing there.
I thought, "Why did you ask that?"
I wondered why she'd asked me that.
She said, "Do you need any help?"
She asked if I needed any help.

Remember that when what was said is reported, different words must be used for times or places if what is being reported has finished, is no longer true, and / or was in a different place.

They said, "Can we wait until tomorrow?"
They asked if they could wait until the next day.
He said, "I talked to her yesterday."
He said he'd talked to you the day before.
I told them, "I was here last Tuesday!"
I told them I'd been there the previous Tuesday.

Other useful time phrases for reporting:

today	that day
now / immediately	at that moment / right away
tomorrow	the next day
next week	the next week / the following week
last week	the week before / the previous week

PATTERNS AFTER REPORTING VERBS

Notice the patterns that often go with particular verbs.

verb + infinitive (with *to*): agree; arrange; claim; decide; intend; offer; pretend; promise; refuse; threaten

verb + *-ing*: admit; avoid; consider; continue; deny; imagine; resent; recommend; suggest

verb + (*that*) clause: acknowledge; announce; argue; claim; confess; declare; deny; insist; recommend; state

verb + someone + (*that*) clause: assure; convince; notify; persuade; promise; remind; tell; warn

verb + someone + infinitive (with *to*): advise; ask; encourage; force; invite; persuade; remind; tell; urge; warn

verb + preposition + *-ing*: accuse somebody of; admit / confess to; apologize for; blame somebody for; criticize somebody for; forgive somebody for; insist on; thank somebody for

1 Choose the correct option.

A few years ago, a Chinese friend of my parents asked if I (1) *want / wanted* to visit (2) *the following summer / this summer* to spend time with their daughter, who was my age. It was a great opportunity, so I agreed to go. I had to fill out a long visa application. My father and I took it to the Chinese embassy, and they told us to come back (3) *next week / the next week* to pick up the visa. When we went back, there was a long line for some reason. My dad explained to the security people that we had been (4) *here / there* (5) *the previous week / last week* and we were just picking up a visa, but he was told that we (6) *have to / had to* line up like everyone else. So we stood there and started chatting with the man in front of us. He asked my dad where (7) *I was / was I* going, and it turned out it was the same place where he lived. "What (8) *were / are* you doing there?" he asked. My dad told him I (9) *was going to / will* stay with a friend of his from college. Then the man asked, "What college?" When my dad told him, the man said one of his best friends (10) *had been / be* at the same college a few years before. He said his friend's name, and it was actually my dad's friend, too! It was an amazing coincidence!

2 Complete the story with the verbs in parentheses and the correct modals, verb forms, or tenses.

Yesterday, I was trying to get to sleep when I heard my dog barking. I got up and my dog was there with some paper in his mouth. I told him (1) _____ (let) it go. I pulled, and the piece of paper tore. I suddenly realized it was my math homework and asked my mom (2) _____ (come) and take a look. When she saw what had happened, she just laughed. I said it (3) _____ (be not) funny and I (4) _____ (have to) do it all over again, but my mom said it (5) _____ (be) too late. She promised she (6) _____ (write) a note to the teacher in the morning and said I (7) _____ (not worry). However, the next morning my mom got a call from work before I got up. They told her someone (8) _____ (call) in sick and asked her if she (9) _____ (go) in early. She completely forgot about the note. So of course, in my math class, when the teacher asked why I (10) _____ (not do) my homework and I explained, he didn't believe me! His exact words were, "Do you (11) _____ (think) I was born yesterday?" But I swear that (12) _____ (be) exactly what happened!

3 Complete the second sentences so they have a similar meaning to the first. Use two to five words, including the correct form of the verb in bold.

1 My mom said I should write to the TV company and complain about it.
My mom *suggested writing* to the TV company to tell them how I felt. **suggest**

2 They said that they'd meet me to explain their decision.
After I complained, they _____ me and explain their decision. **agree**

3 I felt terrible for what I said, so I wrote to say sorry.
I wrote them a letter _____ for such awful things. **apologize**

4 Of course, they reject all accusations and claim that they're in the right.
Naturally, they _____ anything wrong. **deny**

5 The goal of the rule was prevention of discrimination.
The rule _____ discrimination. **intend**

6 There has been a lot of pressure on the school to change its dress code.
The school _____ its dress code. **urge**

7 He knew what the rules were, but he decided to ignore them!
He basically just _____ the rules! **refuse**

8 They have an employment policy that prioritizes total gender equality.
The school _____ an equal number of male and female teachers. **insist**

4 Which two options are possible in each sentence?

1 My parents *advised / recommended / urged* my sister to complain to her boss about it.

2 He's been *blamed / accused / criticized* for not employing enough staff from minority backgrounds.

3 We've been trying to *tell / warn / state* them that there will be problems if things don't change!

4 I read online that she'd *admitted / apologized / denied* sending racist emails.

5 They've *avoided / promised / refused* to tackle the problem.

6 He was *arguing / telling / insisting* that nothing will change unless people take direct action.

5 Rewrite each sentence in Activity 4 using one of the verbs with a different verb pattern.

1 *My parents **recommended** that my sister complain to her boss about it.*

RELATIVE CLAUSES

Relative clauses add information after nouns. Different relative pronouns are used depending on the nouns being qualified or on the information that follows.

Defining and non-defining clauses

Some relative clauses explain exactly what the thing or person is (defining), and some just add extra information that may be of interest (non-defining).

With defining relative clauses:

- commas are not used.
- the relative pronoun can be left out when it is the object of the relative clause.

*The devastation **(which) it caused** was simply staggering!*

With non-defining relative clauses:

- the clause is separated from the rest of the sentence by commas.
- *that* isn't used as a relative pronoun.
- the relative pronoun is never left out.

*The country, **which has long been one of the poorest in the world,** descended into chaos.*

A relative clause can start with a preposition + *which / whom*. However, this is rather formal in English and the preposition is usually placed at the end of the clause.

Where or *when* can also replace a preposition + *which*.

*Crisis mapping brought about change in the place **in which / where** I was born.*

PARTICIPLE CLAUSES

A relative clause is often reduced by using a participle construction.

Past participle clauses reduce relative clauses which use a passive verb, whichever tense is used.

*The UN created a fund **called** UNICEF.*
*= The UN created a fund **which was called** UNICEF.*

Present participle clauses reduce relative clauses which use an active verb, whichever tense is used.

*The CRC declares different rights **including** things such as the right to a safe home.*
*= The CRC declares different rights, **which include** things such as the right to a safe home.*

Adding *not* to the participle can make a negative.

*Students **not wearing** the correct uniform will be punished.*

Adverbial participle clauses

Participle clauses add information about the time or reason / method connected to the main clause. The subject of both clauses must be the same.

***Having campaigned** on behalf of young people, **UNICEF** also had a key part in the creation of the UN's Convention on the Rights of the Child (CRC) in 1989.*
*= **After UNICEF had campaigned** on behalf of young people, **UNICEF** also had a key part in the creation of the UN's Convention on the Rights of the Child (CRC) in 1989.*

***Using** online discussion boards as a "meeting place," **the initiative** provides a space for youngsters who care.*
*= **The initiative uses** online discussion boards as a "meeting place" through which **the initiative** provides a space for youngsters who care.*

***Having seen** the robbery, I had to go to court to give evidence.*
*= **Because I had seen the robbery** I had to go to court to give evidence.*

-ing participles are more common in this kind of clause, but *-ed* participles can also be used with passives.

***Faced** with a robber in the street, I would give them whatever they wanted.*
= If I was faced with a robber in the street, I would give them whatever they wanted.

The present participle shows that an action happens or happened more or less at the same time as the action in the main clause.

***Working** as a policeman, my dad sees a lot of really scary things.*
= My dad is a policeman and while he's at work, he sees a lot of really scary things.

A perfect participle (*having + -ed*) shows that the action happened before the action in the main clause.

***Having just closed** the door, I realized I didn't have my keys.*
= I had just closed the door when I realized I didn't have my keys.

1 Complete the sentences with these relative pronouns.

none of whom	most of which	that	where
which	which is when	who	whose

1 One of the first major events to utilize crisis mapping was the 2010 Haiti earthquake, _____ killed and injured hundreds of thousands of people.

2 Technology is particularly relevant in places _____ official government is limited, or no longer fully functions.

3 More than 40 percent of the population now receives some form of international aid, _____ is food assistance.

4 Many local people, _____ lands have been ruined by illegal mining, are now turning to technology to tackle the problem.

5 The plane crashed in thick fog with 87 people on board, _____ is thought to have survived.

6 The volunteers, _____ come from all across the region, quite literally put roads, buildings, and highways onto the map.

7 The amount of data available via social media increased dramatically in October, _____ the flooding reached the capital.

8 Online mapping _____ relies on volunteers with varying skills to interpret satellite images obviously has its limitations.

2 Rewrite the sentences in a more informal manner with the prepositions at the end of the clauses. Leave out the relative pronouns where appropriate.

1 The town in which we were staying narrowly missed being hit by the hurricane.

The town we were staying in narrowly missed being hit by the hurricane.

2 It's an achievement of which we are all very proud.

3 The following day, a second, smaller earthquake hit the town from which the aid was being distributed.

4 As we fled the city, we encountered an elderly man with whom my son insisted we share our food.

5 The roads out of the west of the city, from where many thousands fled, were largely blocked by debris.

6 The experience varies wildly, depending on the charity with which we're working.

7 On her arrival, Ms. Kuti, with whose approach I totally agreed, took control of the situation.

8 The book to which you're referring was the very first on the subject to be published.

3 Rewrite the following sentences using a participle clause.

1 The policeman who dealt with my case was very helpful.
The policeman _____ my case was very helpful.

2 The man who was arrested after the incident last night has not been charged.
Police have not charged the man _____ the incident last night.

3 The number of young people who are not working or in school is rising.
There has been a rise in the number of young people _____ or in school.

4 The number of people who have personally experienced a crime has actually gone down.
The number of people _____ a crime has actually gone down.

5 I think that children who are exposed to lots of violent movies often become violent themselves.
I think that children _____ lots of violent movies often become violent themselves.

6 Anyone that the train strike tomorrow will seriously affect can stay home.
Anyone seriously _____ by the train strike tomorrow can stay at home.

4 Reduce the underlined clauses.

Police are searching for a man (1) who has been accused of attempting to rob a bank in Vienna today. A man wearing a bright red scarf (2) which was wrapped around his face approached a cashier and told her he wanted money. (3) Because she didn't realize that the man was actually demanding money, the clerk simply said that she didn't deal with cash transactions, (4) and at the same time directed him to the next counter. Apparently, (5) because he was put off by the long line at the next counter and the clerk's calm reply, the man dropped the box he was carrying and ran off. (6) After she had seen the man run off, the cashier suddenly realized what had happened. (7) Because they were concerned that the box looked suspicious, the bank called the police and evacuated the building. The package was found to be harmless and the robber pretty useless.

EXPRESSING PAST ABILITY

Could, be able to, and *managed to* describe ability or inability to do something when talking about specific situations or telling stories.

Could expresses that something was possible in a specific situation. *Couldn't* shows it wasn't possible to do something in a specific situation.

*He **couldn't move** his arm because it was trapped by a rock.*

Could can also be used with other words related to negatives.

***No one could** send for help.*
***All** he **could** do was wait.*
*I was so nervous I **could hardly** say a word.*

To talk about a specific ability to do something at a particular time in the past, use *was / were able to* rather than *could.*

*She managed to deal with the pain, and in the end, **was able** to turn it into great art.*

Negatives can be made with *not able to, unable to,* or *couldn't.*

I wasn't able to / was unable to / couldn't feel or say anything, I was in such shock.

Be able to is also used with other tenses and modals, where *could* is not possible.

*At least ~~we've could~~ **we've been able to** agree on one movie.*

Could usually describes a general ability in the past while *manage to* emphasizes an ability to do something that was difficult. It isn't usually used to talk about general ideas or senses.

*When it rained, he ~~could catch~~ **managed to catch** some water to drink.*

Manage to often goes with words and phrases such as *finally / in the end / eventually.*

Manage to can be used in a negative sentence in a similar way to *couldn't.*

*I looked for a long time, but I **didn't manage to / couldn't** find it.*

Sometimes *succeed in + -ing* is used instead of *manage to,* but *manage to* is far more common.

*She **succeeded in making** it as a professional.*
*= She **managed to make** it as a professional.*

EMPHATIC STRUCTURES

Stressing an auxiliary verb like *is* or *have* adds emphasis. When there is no auxiliary verb available to stress, as with verbs in the simple present and simple past, emphasis can be added by putting *do / does / did* before an infinitive.

*It **did make** a huge difference to my quality of life, having the implant.*

Emphasis is often added in this way to contradict what someone has said, or to contrast two opposing ideas.

*While **surgical options did exist before**, none were nearly as effective.*

Emphasis can also be added by starting a clause with a negative adverb or phrase (*rarely, not only,* etc.) and then using inversion (changing the order of the subject and verb, as in questions).

*We're all used to hearing news about terrible things, but **rarely do we hear** much about exciting new developments.*

*When Second Sight started experimenting, **little did they know** that they were on their way to revolutionizing the treatment of blindness!*

***Only after** the Second World War **were antibiotics** more widely available to the general public.*

Note that inversion is far more common in academic, literary, or journalistic writing, though it is also used in more formal speech or to make stories more dramatic.

1 Complete the article about Aron Ralston with one word in each space.

If the story of Aron Ralston's escape from a canyon was remarkable, what happened next is no less so. Immediately after freeing himself, he still had to return to safety. With only one arm and still bleeding, he (1) _____ to get down a 65-foot cliff and then walk several miles in the burning sun. Luckily, he met a family walking in the valley who (2) _____ able to give him something to eat and drink and then look for help. Then, a helicopter which was out searching for him was (3) _____ to pick him up. This all happened within four hours and saved his life. Following the accident, the park authorities (4) _____ only remove the rock that had trapped Aron's arm by using a machine and several men. While medics were (5) _____ to save Aron's arm, he otherwise made a full recovery and returned to full fitness. Amazingly, since then he's (6) _____ able to do pretty much all the things he did before the accident. He has since rafted down the Grand Canyon, skied down a volcano in Ecuador and, in 2011, (7) _____ in climbing all the mountains in Colorado that are over 14 thousand feet. He also now works as a motivational speaker.

2 Correct the error underlined in each sentence. You may need to change, add, and remove words.

1 I twisted my ankle very badly, but I still <u>manage walk</u> home. It was really painful, though.
I twisted my ankle very badly, but I still *managed to walk* home. It was really painful, though.

2 Following physical therapy, Janine Shepherd <u>were able walk</u> again with the help of a stick.

3 Doctors have been looking for a cure for motor neuron disease, but they <u>couldn't find</u> one yet.

4 After years of research, scientists believe they have finally <u>succeeded the development</u> a treatment for diabetes which avoids the need to inject insulin.

5 I wish I <u>could meet</u> my grandfather before he died. He sounded like an amazing person.

3 Rewrite the second sentences using the word in bold and the correct form of *could, be able to, manage to,* or *succeed in.*

1 Bethany Hamilton became a world champion surfer despite losing her arm in an accident. **becoming**
Bethany Hamilton lost her arm in an accident but still _____ a world champion surfer.

2 Luckily, we stopped the bleeding and he was fine. **stop**
We _____ the bleeding and he was fine.

3 After the accident, it was only because of the surgery that he didn't lose his eyesight. **save**
He damaged his eye in the accident, but the surgeon _____ his eyesight.

4 She lost most of her hearing after the accident, but she seems to be back to normal now. **hear**
She's recovered really well, considering she _____ a thing after the accident.

4 Make complete sentences by matching the halves.

1 While they **do** remove the immediate pain,
2 I **do** think that medical research is incredibly important,
3 Don't get me wrong. The operation **did** help,
4 Only after several tests **did they**
5 At no time during my stay in the hospital **did I**
6 Nowhere else in the world **do you**
7 Let's be clear about this. In no way **does this development**
8 We read a lot about medical developments, but rarely **do we**

a think I wouldn't make a complete recovery.
b hear about the psychological advances in managing disease.
c but I don't see why it can't all be privately funded.
d diagnose the problem.
e find so many 100-year-olds as in Okinawa, Japan.
f drugs are not the only solution and can create problems of their own.
g mean the disease has been cured, but it's a step in the right direction.
h just not as much as I was hoping it would.

5 Complete the sentences with these words.

at no time	little	not only
not until	only	rarely

1 What made things even worse was the fact that _____ did doctors ever admit they'd made a mistake.

2 In the days before antibiotics, only very _____ did children survive serious lung infections.

3 _____ after the Second World War did penicillin become widely available.

4 When the doctor first suggested it, _____ did I realize that the treatment was actually centuries old.

5 _____ do we need a massive increase in investment, but we also need to rethink the way we educate the young about physical and mental well-being.

6 _____ in this country do people go bankrupt from trying to pay their medical bills!

IRREGULAR VERB LIST

INFINITIVE	SIMPLE PAST	PAST PARTICIPLE
arise	arose	arisen
beat	beat	beaten
become	became	become
bend	bent	bent
bet	bet	bet
bite	bit	bitten
blow	blew	blown
break	broke	broken
breed	bred	bred
bring	brought	brought
broadcast	broadcast	broadcast
build	built	built
burn	burned	burned
burst	burst	burst
cost	cost	cost
cut	cut	cut
deal	dealt	dealt
dig	dug	dug
dream	dreamed	dreamed
fall	fell	fallen
feed	fed	fed
fight	fought	fought
flee	fled	fled
forget	forgot	forgotten
forgive	forgave	forgiven
freeze	froze	frozen
grow	grew	grown
hang	hanged/hung	hanged/hung
hide	hid	hidden
hit	hit	hit
hold	held	held
hurt	hurt	hurt
keep	kept	kept
kneel	knelt	knelt
lay	laid	laid
lead	led	led
lend	lent	lent
let	let	let
lie	lay	lain
light	lit	lit
lose	lost	lost
mean	meant	meant

INFINITIVE	SIMPLE PAST	PAST PARTICIPLE
misunderstand	misunderstood	misunderstood
must	had to	had to
overcome	overcame	overcome
rethink	rethought	rethought
ring	rang	rung
rise	rose	risen
sell	sold	sold
set	set	set
shake	shook	shaken
shine	shone/shined	shone/shined
shoot	shot	shot
shrink	shrank	shrunk
shut	shut	shut
sink	sank	sunk
slide	slid	slid
smell	smelled	smelled
spell	spelled	spelled
spend	spent	spent
spill	spilled	spilled
split	split	split
spoil	spoiled	spoiled
spread	spread	spread
stand	stood	stood
steal	stole	stolen
stick	stuck	stuck
strike	struck	struck
swear	swore	sworn
tear	tore	torn
throw	threw	thrown
upset	upset	upset
wake	woke	woken
win	won	won

UNIT 6 A problem-solution essay

Use topic sentences to start each paragraph. These sentences introduce and express the main idea of the paragraph.

How can we help save tigers?

(1) _____ Tigers are hunted and sold for their fur and other parts. They are losing the habitats they live in and they are shot by local people because they kill farm animals. In this essay, I will suggest solutions to these three problems.

(2) _____ In the US, there may be over 9,000 tigers that are kept as pets, for example. They are sold easily, and Mills says that can encourage the trade of wild tigers because people want "the real thing."

Refer to sources to strengthen your argument.

(3) _____ Tigers do not recognize borders, so the area they live in can be in more than one country. According to takepart.com, several countries met and agreed to take action together to save tigers. It has had some success, but they could do more.

(4) _____ National Geographic Explorer Krithi Karanth says that sometimes farmers cannot earn enough money to survive because of wildlife destroying their crops and animals. We need to compensate them so they do not take revenge on endangered species like tigers.

UNIT 7 A report

Improving Learning in the Library

Use the title to show what the report is about.

Purpose
The purpose of this report is to find out why so much external noise can be heard in the school library. The report will also make recommendations on how to reduce noise and create a better atmosphere to study in.

Explain the purpose of the report in the introduction.

Background
Students frequently complain about the noise in the school library and many choose not to use the space at all.

Subheadings are added to each paragraph.

Methods of Investigation
In order to better understand the issues, we visited the library twice and read about how sound travels through different materials. We then explored a range of possible solutions before making our own models, which we used to test our ideas.

Findings
The library windows face a public space and, even when closed, let too much noise through. This problem is made worse by the fact that the curtains in the room are made from a thin material that does not stop sound in any way.

Finish a report by making recommendations, if necessary.

Recommendations
To solve this problem, we would recommend installing two panes of glass in each window. Perhaps we could also consider filling the space between the glass with water. This would prevent up to 75 percent of the outside noise from entering the room.

UNIT 8 A complaint

Say what the general problem is in the first sentence and give details about the problem—including examples—in the first paragraph.

Dear Sir or Madam,

I am writing to complain about the recent reporting on the issue of immigration in your paper. In your reports, you frequently suggest that migrants who come to this country are looking for benefits and are involved in crime. While there are obviously unemployed people or criminals among the migrant population, official statistics show that there is a larger percentage among people who were born here. You have also used language such as "swarm" and "flood," which suggests migrants are not human and are a dangerous problem.

Explain how the problem has affected you.

As the granddaughter of an immigrant, I find use of this language very upsetting and I think that if a paper uses it, it often makes other people feel they can say similar things. My grandfather worked hard to make a home here. And for me it *is* my home, but your reporting makes me feel I am not a normal citizen.

Complete a complaint by asking for some kind of action.

I am not saying you should stop campaigning for immigration controls. Everyone has a right to their point of view. However, I would like you to stop using these stereotypes and generalizations to make your point. Migrants are all individuals like us—just born in a different place.

Sincerely,

Maria Asare

UNIT 9 A letter of application

Start a letter of application by referring to the advertisement or posting that you saw.

Dear Sir or Madam,

I am writing in response to your advertisement looking for volunteers to rebuild a school in Belize. I would be very grateful if you could send me more information about this opportunity and details of how to apply.

Explain why you are writing.

Explain who you are, where you are from and your plans for the future.

My name is Melanie Gleich and I am 17 years old. I am from Aachen in Germany. I am currently in my last year of high school and will be taking my final exams next spring. I hope to then go on to study Spanish and Latin American Studies in college.

In terms of what I would bring to the project, I already have a good level of both Spanish and English, and having traveled widely, I am used to being around people from other cultures. I am also prepared to get my hands dirty and help out in any way I can. I do a lot of sports and would say I have a good level of fitness, so I feel confident that I would be able to cope with the manual labor.

Explain any skills and abilities you have which would make you suitable for the job.

In addition, I have some experience in both gardening and farming because my grandparents live on a farm and I usually spend the summers helping out there. I am also an excellent team player and like to think I possess good social skills.

I hope you feel I am suitable for the post and look forward to hearing from you soon.

Yours sincerely,

Melanie Gleich

UNIT 10 A success story

When writing success stories, it is customary to explain how you felt before you succeeded.

"Stop!" my teacher whispered loudly. "Look over there." I had been dreading this moment—almost hoping we wouldn't find one. But there it was—a python lying in the grass. I hated snakes. I'd never even touched one. My usual reaction would have been to run away screaming, but I had no choice this time. It was a field trip for my biology class, and not only did we have to look for them, we had to catch one too!

There was a group of us. I had to put a special stick at the back of its head while my teacher and other students got hold of it. At least this way I wouldn't have to touch it. We had practiced lots of times with a plastic snake at school. We crept nearer. My hands started to sweat; my heart started beating like a drum. The snake didn't move. And then it all happened in a flash! I put the stick behind its neck and the others leapt over and grabbed it.

Use descriptive verbs to make the story more exciting.

Explain how you felt after succeeding.

As the others held the snake down and measured it, I forced myself to touch it. I finally managed to do it! Little did I know how nice they actually felt! That day changed my life. Rather than being disgusted by snakes, I became fascinated by them, and now I plan to do lots of research on them.

UNIT 6

administration (n)	/əd,mınə'streıʃən/
agriculture (n)	/'ægrı,kʌltʃər/
alarming (adj)	/ə'lɑrmıŋ/
anger (n)	/'æŋgər/
animal product (n)	/'ænəməl ,prɒdəkt/
arise (v)	/ə'raız/
assess (v)	/ə'sɛs/
breed (v)	/brid/
camp (n)	/kæmp/
capture (v)	/'kæptʃər/
catch on (phr v)	/'kætʃ 'ɒn/
characteristic (n)	/,kærıktə'rıstık/
chase (v)	/tʃeıs/
clue (n)	/klu/
compensate (v)	/'kɒmpən,seıt/
concern (n)	/kən'sɜrn/
consequence (n)	/'kɒnsı,kwɛns/
conservation (n)	/,kɒnsər'veıʃən/
constantly (adv)	/'kɒnstəntli/
cure (n)	/kjʊər/
die out (v)	/'daı 'aʊt/
diversity (n)	/dı'vɜrsıti/
domestic (adj)	/də'mɛstık/
emotion (n)	/ı'moʊʃən/
endanger (adj)	/ɛn'deındʒər/
ensure (v)	/ɛn'ʃʊər/
equivalent (adj)	/ı'kwıvələnt/
extinct (adj)	/ık'stıŋkt/
fake (adj)	/feık/
feature (n)	/'fitʃər/
fox (n)	/fɒks/
gene (n)	/dʒin/
genetic (adj)	/dʒə'nɛtık/
growth (n)	/groʊθ/
habitat (n)	/'hæbı,tæt/
historian (n)	/hı'stɔriən/
hit a wall (idiom)	/'hıt ə 'wɔl/
hunt (v)	/hʌnt/
indicate (v)	/'ındı,keıt/
influential (adj)	/,ınflu'ɛnʃəl/
inspire (v)	/ın'spaıər/
interfere (v)	/,ıntər'fıər/
mammal (n)	/'mæməl/
mass (adj)	/mæs/
misunderstanding (n)	/,mısʌndər'stændıŋ/
mysterious (adj)	/mı'stıəriəs/
overcome (v)	/,oʊvər'kʌm/
polar bear (n)	/'poʊlər ,bɛər/
proof (n)	/pruf/
psychologist (n)	/saı'kɒlədʒıst/
purely (adv)	/'pjʊərli/
put forward (phr v)	/,pʊt 'fɔrwərd/
rainfall (n)	/'reın,fɔl/
rate (n)	/reıt/
rethink (v)	/ri'θıŋk/
reveal (v)	/rı'vil/
revenge (n)	/rı'vɛndʒ/

save (v)	/seıv/
science teacher (n)	/'saıəns ,titʃər/
sea creature (n)	/'si ,kritʃər/
short-term (adj)	/'ʃɔrt'tɜrm/
shorten (v)	/'ʃɔrtn/
significantly (adv)	/sıg'nıfıkəntli/
social media campaign (n)	/'soʊʃəl 'midiə kæm,peın/
species (n)	/'spiʃiz/
sponsor (v)	/'spɒnsər/
spot (n)	/spɒt/
strengthen (v)	/'strɛŋkθən/
sudden (adj)	/'sʌdn/
surroundings (n)	/sə'raʊndıŋz/
survival (n)	/sər'vaıvəl/
survive (v)	/sər'vaıv/
suspect (v)	/sə'spɛkt/
suspicious (adj)	/sə'spıʃəs/
take to (phr v)	/'teık tu/
unique (adj)	/ju'nik/
unwilling (adj)	/ʌn'wılıŋ/
willingness (n)	/'wılıŋnıs/
wipe out (phr v)	/'waıp 'aʊt/

UNIT 7

additional (adj)	/ə'dıʃənl/
alternative (adj)	/ɔl'tɜrnətıv/
analysis (n)	/ə'næləsıs/
analyze (v)	/'ænə,laız/
approach (n)	/ə'proʊtʃ/
assessment (n)	/ə'sɛsmənt/
bacteria (n)	/bæk'tıəriə/
break (v)	/breık/
brick (n)	/brık/
combination (n)	/,kɒmbı'neıʃən/
come up with (phr v)	/'kʌm 'ʌp ,wıð/
commonly (adv)	/'kɒmənli/
concerned (adj)	/kən'sɜrnd/
conclude (v)	/kən'klud/
conclusion (n)	/kən'kluʒən/
contribute (v)	/kən'trıbjut/
create (v)	/kri'eıt/
creative (adj)	/kri'eıtıv/
creatively (adv)	/kri'eıtıvli/
demonstration (n)	/,dɛmən'streıʃən/
desire (v)	/dı'zaıər/
detailed (adj)	/'diteıld/
displace (v)	/dıs'pleıs/
electrocute (v)	/ı'lɛktrə,kjut/
external (adj)	/ık'stɜrnəl/
extreme (adj)	/ık'strim/
flexibility (n)	/,flɛksə'bılıti/
flexible (adj)	/'flɛksəbəl/
fluency (n)	/'fluənsi/
follow (v)	/'fɒloʊ/
format (n)	/'fɔrmæt/
freedom (n)	/'fridəm/

functional (adj)	/'fʌŋkʃənl/
genuine (adj)	/'dʒɛnjuın/
get (your) meaning across (phrase)	/'gɛt (jər) 'minıŋ ə,krɔs/
grab (v)	/græb/
heartbroken (adj)	/'hɑrt,broʊkən/
imaginary (adj)	/ı'mædʒə,nɛri/
implication (n)	/,ımplı'keıʃən/
integrate (v)	/'ıntı,greıt/
intelligent (adj)	/ın'tɛlıdʒənt/
know (v)	/noʊ/
knowledge (n)	/'nɒlıdʒ/
learner (n)	/'lɜrnər/
lifestyle (n)	/'laıf,staıl/
logic (n)	/'lɒdʒık/
logical (adj)	/'lɒdʒıkəl/
make up (phr v)	/'meık 'ʌp/
manners (n)	/'mænərz/
measure (v)	/'mɛʒər/
needle (n)	/'nidl/
obey (v)	/oʊ'beı/
original (n)	/ə'rıdʒənl/
outcome (n)	/'aʊt,kʌm/
preference (n)	/'prɛfərəns/
publication (n)	/,pʌblı'keıʃən/
publish (v)	/'pʌblıʃ/
realistically (adv)	/,rıə'lıstıkli/
recommendation (n)	/,rɛkəmɛn'deıʃən/
rely on (phr v)	/rı'laı ɒn/
resolve (v)	/rı'zɒlv/
safety (n)	/'seıfti/
score (v)	/skɔr/
sketch (n)	/skɛtʃ/
solution (n)	/sə'luʃən/
stimulate (v)	/'stımjʊ,leıt/
supervise (v)	/'supər,vaız/
task (n)	/tæsk/
treatment (n)	/'tritmənt/
truly (adv)	/'truli/
usage (n)	/'jusıdʒ/
usefulness (n)	/'jusfəlnıs/
variety (n)	/və'raıəti/

UNIT 8

abuse (n)	/ə'bjus/
accuse (v)	/ə'kjuz/
acknowledge (v)	/æk'nɒlıdʒ/
apparently (adv)	/ə'pærəntli/
appropriate (adj)	/ə'proʊpriıt/
associate with (phr v)	/ə'soʊʃi,eıt ,wıð/
assumption (n)	/ə'sʌmpʃən/
assure (v)	/ə'ʃʊər/
awkward (adj)	/'ɔkwərd/
awkwardness (n)	/'ɔkwərdnıs/
belong (v)	/bı'lɔŋ/
breakdown (n)	/'breık,daʊn/
bully (v)	/'bʊli/

campaign (v)	/kæmˈpeɪn/
cardboard (n)	/ˈkɑrdˌbɔrd/
citizen (n)	/ˈsɪtəzən/
classic (n)	/ˈklæsɪk/
combine (v)	/kəmˈbaɪn/
compliment (v)	/ˈkɒmpləˌmɛnt/
conscious (adj)	/ˈkɒnʃəs/
conservative (adj)	/kənˈsɜrvətɪv/
cost-effective (adj)	/ˈkɔst ɪˌfɛktɪv/
criticize (v)	/ˈkrɪtɪˌsaɪz/
decoration (n)	/ˌdɛkəˈreɪʃən/
deep-rooted (adj)	/ˈdip ˈrutɪd/
define (v)	/dɪˈfaɪn/
deliberately (adv)	/dɪˈlɪbərɪtli/
deny (v)	/dɪˈnaɪ/
diplomat (n)	/ˈdɪpləˌmæt/
discriminate (v)	/dɪˈskrɪməˌneɪt/
dishonest (adj)	/dɪsˈɒnɪst/
elect (v)	/ɪˈlɛkt/
element (n)	/ˈɛləmənt/
elsewhere (adv)	/ɛlsˈwɛər/
encounter (v)	/ɛnˈkaʊntər/
enthusiasm (n)	/ɪnˈθuziˌæzəm/
equality (n)	/ɪˈkwɒliti/
experiment (v)	/ɛkˈspɛrəˌmɛnt/
fed up (phr v)	/ˈfɛd ˈʌp/
fingernail (n)	/ˈfɪŋgərˌneɪl/
firmly (adv)	/ˈfɜrmli/
forget (v)	/fərˈgɛt/
generalization (n)	/ˌdʒɛnərələˈzeɪʃən/
global (adj)	/ˈgloʊbəl/
highly-respected (adj)	/ˈhaɪli rɪsˈpɛktɪd/
humorous (adj)	/ˈhjumərəs/
identity (n)	/aɪˈdɛntɪti/
ignore (v)	/ɪgˈnɔr/
immigrant (n)	/ˈɪmɪgrənt/
incident (n)	/ˈɪnsɪdənt/
insist on (v)	/ɪnˈsɪst ˌɒn/
intense (adj)	/ɪnˈtɛns/
interpret (v)	/ɪnˈtɜrprɪt/
invisible (n)	/ɪnˈvɪzəbəl/
like-minded (adj)	/ˈlaɪkˈmaɪndɪd/
long-lasting (adj)	/ˈlɒŋˈlæstɪŋ/
make fun (phr v)	/ˈmeɪk ˈfʌn/
massive (adj)	/ˈmæsɪv/
misbehave (v)	/ˌmɪsbɪˈheɪv/
misunderstand (v)	/ˌmɪsʌndərˈstænd/
modify (v)	/ˈmɒdɪˌfaɪ/
norm (n)	/nɔrm/
notion (n)	/ˈnoʊʃən/
obsession (n)	/əbˈsɛʃən/
offended (adj)	/əˈfɛndɪd/
open-minded (adj)	/ˈoʊpənˈmaɪndɪd/
phenomenon (n)	/fəˈnɒmɪˌnɒn/
policy (n)	/ˈpɒləsi/
praise (v)	/preɪz/
presence (n)	/ˈprɛzəns/
pretend (v)	/prɪˈtɛnd/
proportion (n)	/prəˈpɔrʃən/
protest (n)	/ˈproʊtɛst/

racism (n)	/ˈreɪsɪzəm/
react (v)	/riˈækt/
refresh (v)	/rɪˈfrɛʃ/
regional (adj)	/ˈridʒənl/
response (n)	/rɪˈspɒns/
self-conscious (adj)	/ˈsɛlfˈkɒnʃəs/
shopkeeper (n)	/ˈʃɒpˌkipər/
sort (it) out (phr v)	/ˈsɔrt (ɪt) ˈaʊt/
statistic (n)	/stəˈtɪstɪk/
stereotype (n)	/ˈstɛriəˌtaɪp/
stock (n)	/stɒk/
two-faced (adj)	/ˈtuˌfeɪst/
well-mannered (adj)	/ˈwɛlˈmænərd/

UNIT 9

absence (n)	/ˈæbsəns/
affect (v)	/əˈfɛkt/
aid (n)	/eɪd/
ally (n)	/ˈælaɪ/
appeal (v)	/əˈpil/
assistance (n)	/əˈsɪstəns/
block (v)	/blɒk/
care for (phr v)	/ˈkɛər ˌfɔr/
coastal (adj)	/ˈkoʊstl/
convention (n)	/kənˈvɛnʃən/
cope (v)	/koʊp/
corrupt (adj)	/kəˈrʌpt/
crisis (n)	/ˈkraɪsɪs/
debris (n)	/dəˈbri/
delegate (n)	/ˈdɛlɪgɪt/
devastation (n)	/ˌdɛvəˈsteɪʃən/
disaster (n)	/dɪˈzæstər/
donation (n)	/doʊˈneɪʃən/
earthquake (n)	/ˈɜrθˌkweɪk/
edit (n)	/ˈɛdɪt/
evacuate (v)	/ɪˈvækjuˌeɪt/
flee (v)	/fli/
frustrate (v)	/ˈfrʌstreɪt/
give (sth) a go (phr v)	/ˈgɪv ə ˈgoʊ/
global warming (n)	/ˈgloʊbəl ˈwɔrmɪŋ/
globe (n)	/gloʊb/
graduate (n)	/ˈgrædʒuɪt/
greed (n)	/grid/
headquarters (n)	/ˈhɛdˌkwɔrtərz/
homeless (adj)	/ˈhoʊmlɪs/
housing (n)	/ˈhaʊzɪŋ/
humanity (n)	/hjuˈmænɪti/
imprison (v)	/ɪmˈprɪzən/
inclusive (adj)	/ɪnˈklusɪv/
infrastructure (n)	/ˈɪnfrəˌstrʌktʃər/
initiative (n)	/ɪˈnɪʃətɪv/
interactive (adj)	/ˌɪntərˈæktɪv/
joy (n)	/dʒɔɪ/
launch (v)	/lɔntʃ/
limited (adj)	/ˈlɪmɪtɪd/
neutral (adj)	/ˈnutrəl/
on behalf of (phr v)	/ˌɒn bɪˈhæf əv/

on the ground (phrase)	/ˈɒn ðə ˈgraʊnd/
overlook (v)	/ˌoʊvərˈlʊk/
panel (n)	/ˈpænl/
portrait (n)	/ˈpɔrtrɪt/
precious (adj)	/ˈprɛʃəs/
programmer (n)	/ˈproʊgræmər/
psychological (adj) /	/ˌsaɪkəˈlɒdʒɪkəl
realization (n)	/ˌrɪələˈzeɪʃən/
reconstruction (n)	/ˌrikənˈstrʌkʃən/
recovery (n)	/rɪˈkʌvəri/
relief (n)	/rɪˈlif/
reminder (n)	/rɪˈmaɪndər/
remote (adj)	/rɪˈmoʊt/
representative (n)	/ˌrɛprɪˈzɛntətɪv/
restore (v)	/rɪˈstɔr/
right (n)	/raɪt/
rise (v)	/raɪz/
satellite (n)	/ˈsætlˌaɪt/
scale (n)	/skeɪl/
senior (adj)	/ˈsinjər/
shelter (n)	/ˈʃɛltər/
shortage (n)	/ˈʃɔrtɪdʒ/
skip (v)	/skɪp/
staggering (adj)	/ˈstægərɪŋ/
strike a chord (phr v)	/ˈstraɪk ə ˈkɔrd/
supply (n)	/səˈplaɪ/
survivor (n)	/sərˈvaɪvər/
sustainable (n)	/səˈsteɪnəbəl/
the best (n)	/ðə ˈbɛst/
the brave (n)	/ðə ˈbreɪv/
the loud (n)	/ðə ˈlaʊd/
the old (n)	/ði ˈoʊld/
the outgoing (n)	/ði ˈaʊtˌgoʊɪŋ/
the poor (n)	/ðə ˈpʊər/
the rich (n)	/ðə ˈrɪtʃ/
the stupid (n)	/ðə ˈstupɪd/
trap (v)	/træp/
unfamiliar (adj)	/ˌʌnfəˈmɪljər/
unfold (v)	/ʌnˈfoʊld/

UNIT 10

actively (adj)	/ˈæktɪvli/
address (v)	/əˈdrɛs/
aim (v)	/eɪm/
allergic (adj)	/əˈlɜrdʒɪk/
amazement (n)	/əˈmeɪzmənt/
antibiotics (n)	/ˌæntibaɪˈɒtɪks/
apocalypse (n)	/əˈpɒkəˌlɪps/
award (v)	/əˈwɔrd/
bench (n)	/bɛntʃ/
bestseller (n)	/ˈbɛstˈsɛlər/
blindness (n)	/ˈblaɪndnɪs/
blink (v)	/blɪŋk/
cast (n)	/kæst/
category (n)	/ˈkætɪˌgɔri/
cell (n)	/sɛl/
chance (n)	/tʃæns/

cheer (v)	/tʃɪər/
chest (n)	/tʃɛst/
clarify (v)	/ˈklærəˌfaɪ/
clear up (phr v)	/ˈklɪər ˈʌp/
close down (v)	/ˈcloʊz ˈdaʊn/
combine (v)	/kəmˈbaɪn/
comfort zone (n)	/ˈkʌmfərt ˌzoʊn /
concentration (n)	/ˌkɒnsənˈtreɪʃən/
consciousness (n)	/ˈkɒnʃəsnɪs/
considerable (adj)	/kənˈsɪdərəbəl/
contribute (v)	/kənˈtrɪbjut/
convert (v)	/kənˈvɜrt/
darkness (n)	/ˈdɑrknɪs/
deadly (adj)	/ˈdɛdli/
dependent (adj)	/dɪˈpɛndənt/
design (v)	/dɪˈzaɪn/
determined (adj)	/dɪˈtɜrmɪnd/
device (n)	/dɪˈvaɪs/
devote (v)	/dɪˈvoʊt/
diagnose (v)	/ˈdaɪəgˌnoʊs/
dictate (v)	/ˈdɪkteɪt/
disgust (n)	/dɪsˈgʌst/
disturbing (adj)	/dɪˈstɜrbɪŋ/
dose (n)	/doʊs/
drug (n)	/drʌg/
editor (n)	/ˈɛdɪtər/
efficiently (adv)	/ɪˈfɪʃəntli/
expose (v)	/ɪkˈspoʊz/
express (v)	/ɪkˈsprɛs/
extract (n)	/ɪkˈstrækt/
fascinated (adj)	/ˈfæsəˌneɪtɪd/
flash (n)	/flæʃ/
force (v)	/fɔrs/
get out (phr v)	/ˈgɛt ˈaʊt/
gripping (adj)	/ˈgrɪpɪŋ/
heath care (n)	/ˈhɛlθ ˌkɛər/
helmet (n)	/ˈhɛlmɪt/
honor (n)	/ˈɒnər/
house (v)	/haʊz/
inability (n)	/ˌɪnəˈbɪlɪti/
inevitable (adj)	/ɪnˈɛvɪtəbəl/
infection (n)	/ɪnˈfɛkʃən/
insufficient (adj)	/ˌɪnsəˈfɪʃənt/
intensive (adj)	/ɪnˈtɛnsɪv/
keep down (phr v)	/ˈkip ˈdaʊn/
lead (v)	/lid/
lung (n)	/lʌŋ/
make the most of (phrase)	/ˈmeɪk ðə ˈmoʊst əv/
misery (n)	/ˈmɪzəri/
nickname (n)	/ˈnɪkˌneɪm/
optimistic (adj)	/ˌɒptəˈmɪstɪk/
partial (adj)	/ˈpɑrʃəl/
peer (v)	/pɪər/
portion (n)	/ˈpɔrʃən/
precisely (adv)	/prɪˈsaɪsli/
prescribe (v)	/prɪˈskraɪb/
prescription (n)	/prɪˈskrɪpʃən/
procedure (n)	/prəˈsidʒər/
punishment (n)	/ˈpʌnɪʃmənt/

rapid (adj)	/ˈræpɪd/
resistant (adj)	/rɪˈzɪstənt/
respond (v)	/rɪˈspɒnd/
risk (n)	/rɪsk/
run away (v)	/ˈrʌn əˈweɪ/
slam (v)	/slæm/
slide (v)	/slaɪd/
slow (v)	/sloʊ/
stroke (n)	/stroʊk/
sweat (n)	/swɛt/
symptom (n)	/ˈsɪmptəm/
thankfully (adv)	/ˈθæŋkfəli/
therapist (n)	/ˈθɛrəpɪst/
therapy (n)	/ˈθɛrəpi/
think through (phr v)	/ˈθɪŋk ˈθru/
threatening (adj)	/ˈθrɛtnɪŋ/
treat (v)	/trit/
turn to (phr v)	/ˈtɜrn tu/
vision (n)	/ˈvɪʒən/
visual (adj)	/ˈvɪʒuəl/
waist (n)	/weɪst/
ward (n)	/wɔrd/
watch out (phr v)	/ˈwɒtʃ ˈaʊt/

PERSPECTIVES
3

Workbook

NATIONAL GEOGRAPHIC
L E A R N I N G

Perspectives 3

Publisher: Sherrise Roehr

Executive Editor: Sarah Kenney

Project Manager: Katherine Carroll

Senior Technology Product Manager:
  Lauren Krolick

Director of Global Marketing: Ian Martin

Senior Product Marketing Manager:
  Caitlin Thomas

Sr. Director, ELT & World Languages:
  Michael Burggren

Production Manager: Daisy Sosa

Senior Print Buyer: Mary Beth Hennebury

Composition: Lumina Datamatics, Inc.

Cover/Text Design: Brenda Carmichael

Art Director: Brenda Carmichael

Cover Image: The Hive at Kew Gardens,
  London. ©Mark Hadden

For product information and technology assistance, contact us at
Cengage Learning Customer & Sales Support, cengage.com/contact
For permission to use material from this text or product,
submit all requests online at **cengage.com/permissions**
Further permissions questions can be emailed to
permissionrequest@cengage.com

Perspectives 3 Workbook

ISBN: 978-1-337-29730-1

National Geographic Learning
20 Channel Center Street
Boston, MA 02210
USA

National Geographic Learning, a Cengage Learning Company, has a mission to bring the world to the classroom and the classroom to life. With our English language programs, students learn about their world by experiencing it. Through our partnerships with National Geographic and TED Talks, they develop the language and skills they need to be successful global citizens and leaders.

Locate your local office at **international.cengage.com/region**

Visit National Geographic Learning online at **NGL.Cengage.com/ELT**
Visit our corporate website at **www.cengage.com**

Photo Credits:
2 Lutz Jaekel/laif/Redux, 4 emei/Shutterstock.com, 7 Ersler Dmitry/Shutterstock.com, 8 GoodMood Photo/Shutterstock.com, 14 Rawpixel.com/Shutterstock.com, 16 Fred Turck/Shutterstock.com, 19 chombosan/Shutterstock.com, 20 Juergen Faelchle/Shutterstock.com, 26 Stefan Schurr/Shutterstock.com, 28 (tl) Petr Toman/Shutterstock.com, (bl) grmarc/Shutterstock.com, 31 Leonard Zhukovsky/Shutterstock.com, 38 Kjeld Friis/Shutterstock.com, 40 Anton_Ivanov/Shutterstock.com, 43 Skreidzeleu/Shutterstock.com, 45 Oscity/Shutterstock.com, 52 WilcoUK/Shutterstock.com, 55 Monkey Business Images/Shutterstock.com, 63 Manu M Nair/Shutterstock.com, 64 Photobac/Shutterstock.com, 67 Juan Aunion/Shutterstock.com, 68 Andrew Sutton/Shutterstock.com, 71 (tl1) TPm13thx/Shutterstock.com, (tl2) Nick Fox/Shutterstock.com, (tl3) Kit Korzun/Shutterstock.com, (tl4) Rich Carey/Shutterstock.com, 76 Tupungato/Shutterstock.com, 79 Svitlana-ua/Shutterstock.com, 81 Golubovy/Shutterstock.com, 87 Kzenon/Shutterstock.com, 88 Thoai/Shutterstock.com, 91 bokehart/Shutterstock.com, 100 (cl) VCG/Visual China Group/Getty Images, (cr) Justin Hobson/Shutterstock.com, 103 Oliver Foerstner/Shutterstock.com, 112 Kleber Cordeiro/Shutterstock.com, 115 wawritto/Shutterstock.com, 117 hxdbzxy/Shutterstock.com, 119 (cr) Tomsickova Tatyana/Shutterstock.com, (br) Antonio Guillem/Shutterstock.com.

Text Credits:
4 "Rescuing an Icon", by A.R. William, National Geographic Magazine, August 2015, p.14., 16 "Big Ideas, Little Packages", by Margaret G. Zackowitz, National Geographic Magazine, November 2010, p.24., 16 "Power to the People", by Chris Costas, National Geographic Traveler, August-September 2015, p.18., 28 "To Greeks We Owe Our Love of Athletics", March 1944, p.315., 40 "Street Dreams: Edinburgh Scotland", by Alexander McCall Smith, National Geographic Traveler, February-March 2015, p.11., 52 "Accents and Perception", by Luna Shyr, National Geographic Magazine, June 2011, p.42., 52 "Curiosity and a Cat", by Steve Boyes, National Geographic Magazine, March 2014, p.42., 64 "Baboon Troop Adapts to Survive in Desert", National Geographic Magazine, February 1992, p4., 67 "Shadow Cats", National Geographic Magazine, February 2017, p.104., 76 "Cities are the Key", by Keith Bellows, National Geographic Traveler, May-June 2011, p.26., 79 "A Thing or Two About Twins", by Peter Miller, National Geographic Magazine, January 2012, p.46., 88 "A World Together", National Geographic Magazine, by Erla Zwingle, August 1999, p.12., 88 "Cultures", text from a National Geographic map, 2014. 100 "Tracking a Tornado's Damage from Every Angle", by Daniel Stone, National Geographic Magazine, October 2016, p.22., 103 "Reader Fixes an African Bridge", National Geographic Magazine, October 2002, p32., 112 "The Art of Recovery", by Susan Goldberg, National Geographic Magazine, February 2015., 115 "A Cure in Sight", by David Dobbs, National Geographic Magazine, September 2016, p.30.

Printed in the United States of America
Print Number: 02   Print Year: 2022

CONTENTS

6 Adapt to Survive

6A Evolution and Conservation

VOCABULARY Endangered species

1 Review Complete the sentences with these words.

drought	environmental	expedition	fishing
route	save	waste	wild

1 Many plant species die during a _____.
2 The world is facing an increasing number of _____ problems.
3 Many charities track illegal _____ boats using technology.
4 Everyone should change their daily routine to help _____ the environment.
5 Campaigners are encouraging restaurants not to _____ food.
6 Illegal hunters catch _____ animals in their habitats.
7 The scientific _____ to Antarctica lasted eight months.
8 The _____ the climbers chose was straight up the mountain.

2 Review Mark each sentence correct (C) or incorrect (I). Then cross out the incorrect words and write the correct ones.

1 The increase in people using cars has led to global cooling. ___ _____
2 A result of the bluehouse effect is the heating up of the Earth's surface. ___ _____
3 Governments need to take action against companies that damage nature. ___ _____
4 Building projects are destroying the nature environment. ___ _____
5 Schools are teaching children about how to protect the environment. ___ _____
6 Climate change is leading to less extreme weather. ___ _____

3 Choose the correct option (a–d) to complete the sentences.

1 The Javan rhino is at risk of ____.
   a endangered   **c** extinction
   b survival   **d** conservation

2 The zoo is running a ____ program for turtles.
   a hunting   **c** species
   b conservation   **d** habitat

3 Parents ____ on their genes to their children.
   a preserve   **c** breed
   b pass   **d** bring

4 Farming is ____ the natural habitat of plants and animals.
   a destroying   **c** losing
   b preserving   **d** improving

5 Scientists are concerned about the long-term ____ of the Western Lowland gorilla.
   a risk   **c** extinction
   b survival   **d** consequence

6 Increased water pollution will have lasting ____ on the area.
   a risks   **c** consequences
   b extinction   **d** species

4 Cross out the phrase that does NOT collocate with the noun.

1 *improve energy / bring a lasting / work in nature* + conservation
2 *discover a new / an endangered / work in nature* + species
3 *lose its natural / destroy the / pass on its* + habitat
4 *leave the / have serious / consider the* + consequences
5 *ensure its / preserve their / its long-term* + survival

5 Complete the phrasal verbs in the sentences with these prepositions.

for	from	on	out	to	to

1 Scientists benefit _____ new technology.
2 We had to adapt _____ the freezing temperatures during our stay.
3 We had to conform _____ the tribe's rules about exploring the area.
4 My parents passed _____ their love of bees to me.
5 Many species have died _____ in the last century.
6 We had to stop them hunting _____ the elephants.

A Namib Desert Darkling Beetle

6 Complete the text with these words.

adapted	endangered	extinct	habitat
risk	species	store	survive

Everyone knows that if your (1) _____ is the desert, there is one thing you lack: water. The Namib Desert Beetle may look ancient, but it is not (2) _____ or even (3) _____. How does this insect (4) _____? This (5) _____ of beetle has (6) _____ to its surroundings. Its back has bumps on it. The bumps contain something that attracts water. Once a day, these bumps collect moisture from the cool morning breeze and (7) _____ it on the beetle's back. When the bumps have collected enough, the water runs down into the beetle's mouth.

Now, using the same idea, a company is trying to make a self-filling water bottle for people and animals at (8) _____ of dehydration in the desert.

7 Listen to the descriptions. Match each description with the item it describes. 🎧 **43**

1 _____ **a** an animal that has adapted for survival in a
2 _____   difficult habitat
3 _____ **b** a species that was saved by conservation
4 _____   efforts
5 _____ **c** a species that is extinct
6 _____ **d** an insect that is beneficial to people
        e a species whose habitat is being destroyed
        f a species that is endangered by hunting

8 **Extension** Complete the table. Use a dictionary if necessary.

Noun	Adjective	Verb
conformity	conforming	
	modified	
	threatened	
habit		habituate
sustenance	sustaining, sustained	

9 **Extension** Complete the crossword.

Across
2 to obey a rule or law
3 the ability to do something unpleasant for a long time
6 a small change
7 a danger or risk
8 the chance or hope that something will happen

Down
1 protection from heat or cold, etc.
4 well known to you
5 a place that is safe from danger

PRONUNCIATION

10 Listen to the sentences. Is the underlined *have* or *been* pronounced in its weak or strong form? Practice saying the sentences. 🎧 **44**

1 Those animals should <u>have</u> been protected.
   a weak   **b** strong

2 That article must <u>have</u> been fake.
   a weak   **b** strong

3 How have the gorillas <u>been</u> doing?
   a weak   **b** strong

4 He's <u>been</u> working with endangered species all his life.
   a weak   **b** strong

5 <u>Have</u> they benefited from the conservation efforts?
   a weak   **b** strong

6 Most of their habitat has <u>been</u> destroyed.
   a weak   **b** strong

7 What has <u>been</u> most rewarding about the work?
   a weak   **b** strong

8 I think we all might <u>have</u> done more.
   a weak   **b** strong

LISTENING

11 Listen to the conversation. Complete the collocations that you hear. 🎧 **45**

1 consider _____
2 an endangered _____
3 destroying _____
4 risk of _____
5 involved in a conservation _____
6 ensure the _____
7 pass on their _____
8 a potential _____

a crocodile bag

12 Listen again and answer the questions. 🎧 **45**

1 How did Janice react to what Laura showed her?
   a She was disappointed.
   b She wasn't interested.
   c She was a bit jealous.
   d She was very curious.

2 What did Janice criticize Laura for not considering?
   a how expensive the bag was
   b which country the bag came from

   c what the bag was made of
   d who actually made the bag

3 What did Janice tell Laura she was doing to crocodiles?
   a destroying their only habitat
   b ensuring their final extinction
   c not considering their rights
   d adding to the threat to them

4 How did the man describe Janice?
   a patronizing   **c** pessimistic
   b passionate   **d** perplexed

5 What was one of Janice's arguments in favor of conservation?
   a the possible benefits to humankind
   b stopping unnecessary cruelty to animals
   c reducing the amount of consumerism
   d ensuring the survival of the human race

6 In the end, how would you describe Laura's attitude?
   a She was even more offended.
   b She was a bit upset with the man.
   c She was rethinking her position.
   d She was finished with Janice.

13 Listen to the lecture. Match these scientific terms with their definitions. 🎧 **46**

1	species	**a**	the usual weather conditions in an area
2	habitat	**b**	a group of particular animals
3	troop	**c**	the ways in which a person or animal acts
4	climate	**d**	continuing to live despite difficult circumstances
5	adapt	**e**	an animal's natural home or environment
6	behavior	**f**	to change because of new or different conditions
7	primatologist	**g**	a group of similar individuals capable of breeding
8	survival	**h**	an expert in the study of primates

14 Listen again. Are the statements true (T) or false (F)? Practice saying the true sentences. 🎧 **46**

1 Male chacma baboons generally weigh more than 88 pounds. _____
2 Chacmas do not usually live in desert areas. _____
3 Long periods without water affects the baboons' behavior. _____
4 The baboons get water from the Kuiseb River all year round. _____
5 Chacmas in the Namib will sometimes sleep during the day. _____
6 Temperatures in the Namib are often higher than 113 degrees Fahrenheit. _____

GRAMMAR Modals and meaning

15 Choose the best option to complete the sentences.

1 The Korowai people in southeastern Papua, Indonesia, *can / may* disappear in the next generation because the young people are moving to nearby towns.

2 A drought in Kenya *shall / might* make life even more difficult for the Samburu people who travel across northern Kenya looking for water and food for their animals.

3 The Awa people in Brazil *can / should* be protected from the farmers and loggers who are coming into their homeland and destroying the habitat.

4 If the Tsaatan people in Mongolia *could / would* get help from the government, their culture and their reindeer, on which they depend, could survive.

5 Help from the Indian government *may / must* help the Ladakhis in the state of Jammu and Kashmir as their culture modernizes and changes very quickly.

16 Choose the best options to complete the text.

Even though we (1) *shall not / may not* realize it, language is always changing. It changes so slowly that we (usually) don't notice it. Some people (2) *may / must not* assume that language change is bad and the result of laziness or mistakes, but in truth, language change is neither good nor bad. It just *is*.

Language evolution (3) *shall / can* include changes in vocabulary, grammar, and pronunciation. Because it reflects the needs of its speakers, a language (4) *could / will* require new words if the needs of its speakers change, due to new technology, new products, or unique experiences.

Languages (5) *can / should* adapt by borrowing words (for example, *sushi*), by shortening words or phrases (*text messaging* has become *texting*), or by combining words to create a new word (*breakfast + lunch = brunch*).

Geography (6) *should / can* lead to language change, too. If a group of speakers is separated from other people who speak the same language, their language (7) *will / must* change differently or at a different speed than the other people. British and American English are an example of this.

If languages didn't change, we (8) *couldn't / wouldn't* have any words for the digital technologies that have appeared in the 21st century so far. Language (9) *must / could* change to keep up with the lives of its speakers.

17 Complete the sentences with these words. You may use the words more than once. There is more than one correct answer for some items.

can	could	may	might	must

1 In the plains and grasslands of North America, we _____ not interfere with the habitat of the bison or they, too, will become extinct.

2 The blue whale _____ die out if we don't stop polluting the Gulf of California.

3 Building roads in the jungle _____ destroy the habitat of the endangered bonobos in the Congo Basin.

4 We _____ protect the Galapagos Islands in order to save the giant tortoise.

5 You _____ borrow the binoculars, but please be careful with them.

6 In order for animals to survive, they _____ evolve along with their changing habitats.

18 Complete the sentences with these phrases.

can expect	couldn't connect	might even be
must call	must rely	should know

1 Reading a map is a disappearing skill. Now, we _____ on the sat nav on our smartphones.

2 Changing a car tire is a disappearing skill. Because no one can do it now, we _____ for help when we have a flat tire.

3 Knowing correct spelling and grammar is a disappearing skill. People these days _____ their computers, tablets, and smartphones to fix mistakes.

4 In the 21st century, people _____ how to use a smartphone.

5 It would be practically unthinkable if someone _____ to Wi-Fi these days.

6 It _____ dangerous if people didn't understand how online privacy settings work.

19 Choose the correct option to complete the sentences.

1 In the future, it's unlikely that people *will / would / must* wear watches to know what time it is.

2 People probably *should / shall / will* not have DVD players because they will stream movies from the internet.

3 People *shall / can / might* get by with just a cell phone these days so there's no need to have a landline.

4 Because their smartphones have built-in music players, people *might / can / must* not need stereo equipment in the future.

5 And because their phones have built-in cameras, fewer people *will / could / must* want digital cameras.

6 Email is such a popular way to communicate now, so I doubt anyone *might / would / must* need a fax machine.

6B The Lynx Returns

VOCABULARY BUILDING Compound nouns

1 Match the words to form compound nouns.

1	social media	**a**	creatures
2	sea	**b**	products
3	science	**c**	shop
4	animal	**d**	age
5	rain	**e**	campaign
6	ice	**f**	teacher
7	book	**g**	house
8	farm	**h**	drop

READING

2 Read the article and choose the best summary (a–d).

a Without more European rabbits, the survival of the Iberian lynx is in question.

b Spanish pride in their native cat, the Iberian lynx, has never been higher.

c While still endangered, the Iberian lynx population is steadily recovering.

d Like many small cats, the Iberian lynx is able to blend in with its environment.

3 Choose the correct option according to the information in the article.

1 What can we infer from the first paragraph?
 a Iberian lynx like to live in and around olive trees.
 b It is usual for Iberian lynx to have two babies.
 c The cat is wearing some kind of electronic device.
 d Iberian lynx like to be around loud noises.

2 What has surprised Germán Garrote about the Iberian lynx?
 a their ability to survive without any rabbits to eat
 b their ability to adapt to strange environments
 c their devotion and caring for their newborns
 d their incredible strength for such a small size

3 What kind of fur does the Iberian lynx have?
 a striped
 b bushy
 c amber
 d spotted

4 How many Iberian lynx were there when the Iberlince project started?
 a less than 100
 b more than 2,000
 c approximately 176
 d around 60

5 Why have scientists been able to reintroduce so many lynx into the wild?
 a They know how to hide extremely well.
 b They can eat things other than rabbits.
 c They always have at least two babies.
 d They breed well, even when confined.

6 What is the current status of the lynx?
 a critically endangered
 b almost extinct
 c endangered
 d surviving in captivity

7 What are Simón and his team providing in order to save more lynx?
 a public information
 b underpasses
 c native cats
 d road crossings

4 Sentences a–g have been removed from the article. Decide which sentence belongs in each place (1–6). There is one extra sentence that you do not need to use.

1 _____		**4** _____
2 _____		**5** _____
3 _____		**6** _____

a Four breeding centers and one zoo raised most of the cats, all of which were fitted with radio collars.

b Of the world's 38 wildcat species, 31 are considered small cats.

c Lynx are more adaptable than we thought, he explains.

d He says it's a beloved national figure.

e The team works closely with private landowners to earn their trust and persuade them to welcome lynx on their property.

f If it weren't for her radio collar, we'd never know that one of the world's rarest cats is hiding among the neat rows of trees.

g The lynx population was so small that it was suffering from dangerously low genetic diversity, making it vulnerable to disease and birth defects.

The Iberian Lynx 🎧 47

1 "She's very close," whispers Germán Garrote, pointing to a handheld receiver picking up Helena's signal. Somewhere in this olive grove* beside a busy highway in southern Spain, the Iberian lynx and her two cubs are probably watching us. (1) Helena has learned to blend into the human landscape, even hiding with her newborn cubs in a vacant house during a loud festival.

2 "Ten years ago we couldn't imagine that the lynx would be breeding in a habitat like this," says Garrote, a biologist with the Life+Iberlince project, a government-led group of more than 20 organizations working to help protect the Iberian lynx. The area where Helena lives is very hot for about five months of the year, and has heavy traffic on the roads. Garrote says that the spotted cat's future is to live in fragmented* areas. (2)

3 After many years of decline, the lynx population has started to increase. When Iberlince stepped in to rescue the lynx in 2002, fewer than a hundred of the cats were scattered throughout southern Spain. The numbers were drastically reduced by hunting and a virus that nearly killed all the region's European rabbits, the lynx's main food. (3)

4 Luckily for scientists, lynx breed well in captivity, and 176 have been reintroduced* into carefully selected habitats since 2010. (4) Sixty percent of the reintroduced cats have survived and some have done extremely well.

5 Two lynx traveled across the Iberian peninsula, each walking more than 1,500 miles to new territory, says biologist Miguel Simón, director of the reintroduction program. (5) In 2012, when the population hit 313—about half of which were old enough to breed—the International Union for Conservation of Nature upgraded the lynx's status from critically endangered to endangered.

6 Cars and trucks are the leading killers of lynx, so Simón and his team are working with the government to create wildlife underpasses* so the animals can cross beneath the roads. Simón says that everyone knows about the Iberian lynx and the Spanish are very proud of their native cat. (6) With Simón's and others' help, the remarkable feline should continue to inhabit the peninsula for which it is named.

grove *an area in which a certain kind of tree grows*
fragmented *broken up; not connected*

reintroduced *when an animal goes to live in the wild*
underpasses *walkways under roads*

6C Mysterious Changes

GRAMMAR Modals and infinitive forms

Blue whale

1 Choose the correct option to complete the sentences.

1 Today there _____ only between 10,000 to 25,000 blue whales left.
   a be
   b have been
   c being
   d are

2 Blue whales can _____ from 82 to 105 feet and weigh up to 200 tonnes.
   a be ranging
   b ranged
   c range
   d have been ranged

3 Every day, the blue whale must _____ about 4.5 tons of food.
   a have eaten
   b be eating
   c eating
   d eat

4 Blue whales can _____ in every ocean.
   a being found
   b be found
   c find
   d found

5 Climate change could _____ the survival of blue whales.
   a being threat
   b threaten
   c have been threatened
   d threat

6 We should _____ into consideration the effects of pollution on blue whales' habitats.
   a be taking
   b have take
   c took
   d taking

7 More must _____ to help blue whales by preserving their environments.
   a be
   b have been
   c being done
   d be done

2 Listen and complete the sentences. 🎧 48

1 The pizza _____ cooked too long.
2 We _____ left earlier.
3 You _____ studying all night.
4 I don't know where they are. They _____ gone to the museum.
5 It _____ mattered if we had made more coffee.
6 They _____ set up the tent by now.
7 You _____ talking during class.

3 Choose the correct option to complete the sentences logically.

1 Paleontologists have discovered feather imprints in many dinosaur fossils. They now believe that most dinosaurs must *be / were / have been* covered in feathers.

2 The Carolina parakeet, the only parrot native to the United States, was extinct by 1904 as a result of hunting, deforestation, and disease. People *should / may / won't* have protected them.

3 NASA has found some interesting mineral deposits on Mars. Similar formations on Earth were formed by ancient bacteria. This means that life *can't / could / should* have existed on Mars.

4 Every year, people report seeing a yeti, Bigfoot, or Sasquatch—all large, hairy, human-like creatures from local legends. However, there is no scientific evidence that these creatures actually exist. They may *see / be seeing / be seen* an ape, a bear, or another animal.

5 The black-footed ferret was almost extinct, but biologists have been working hard to save the species. In fact, they are hoping that by 2020, the black-footed ferret *will have / will have been, / would have been* removed from the endangered species list.

6 The Amazon Rainforest is home to 10% of plant and animal species in the world. Unfortunately, humans are cutting down the forest at an alarming rate. We *wouldn't be / can't have been / shouldn't be* destroying this precious natural resource.

4 Complete the sentences with these phrases.

as you can see	could have been done
could have come	have to study
must have been	need I explain
should have seen	wouldn't have come

1 _____ how your new phone works?

2 We _____ for the final exam.

3 _____, the climate is getting warmer.

4 You _____ to the party.

5 I _____ to the party if I'd known Dominic would be here.

6 We _____ many more birds on our hike.

7 More _____ to clean up the river.

8 The book _____ really interesting. She was up until at least midnight reading.

5 Match the related sentences.

1 I didn't invite my friends on the camping trip last weekend.

2 The students all finished the test in less than 20 minutes.

3 The documentary wasn't great.

4 They went on a trip to Antarctica last year.

5 Friday is the last day for us to turn in our science projects.

6 Ten o'clock is definitely too late for us to arrive at the dinner party.

7 The students have a big test tomorrow.

8 Wait. Don't call the neighbors right now.

a It could have been better.

b It must have been exciting!

c It can't have been very difficult.

d They should be studying now.

e They will have finished eating by then.

f They might be eating dinner.

g They must be finished by then.

h They wouldn't have come.

6 Which option is closer in meaning to the original sentence?

1 You can't have cooked the rice long enough.
a You didn't cook the rice long enough.
b Next time you may want to cook the rice longer.

2 We must make more spaghetti next time.
a We might want more spaghetti next time.
b Next time we make spaghetti, we need to make more.

3 He can't drive his friend to the movies on Friday.
a He won't be able to drive his friend to the movies on Friday.
b On Friday, he may be able to drive his friend to the movies.

4 I can't believe how long it took to hike to the waterfall.
a It took longer than I thought it would to hike to the waterfall.
b The hike to the waterfall was really long.

5 We should set up our tents before we eat.
a We might set up our tents before we eat.
b It would be a good idea for us to set up our tents before we eat.

6 I shouldn't have taken five classes this semester.
a I wish I had taken fewer classes this semester.
b I shall take fewer classes next semester.

7 Put the words in the correct order to make sentences.

1 see / I / can / on / movie / Saturday / the / .

_____

2 studying / be / you / every / should / at / library / the / day / .

_____

3 Madagascar / summer / he / go / to / this / might / .

_____

4 she / new / need / bike / to / may / buy / a / .

_____

5 have / you / read / that / can't / book / entire / !

_____

6 he / the / might / more / have / beach / enjoyed / weather / better / in / .

_____

7 should / before / went / have / you / told / me / I / !

_____

8 Complete the sentences with the correct form of the verbs in parentheses.

1 An Amur tiger can also _____ (call) a Siberian tiger.

2 In the past, Amur tigers could _____ (find) in eastern Russia, northern China, and the Korean peninsula.

3 Experts say there might _____ (be) only 540 Amur tigers left in the world today.

4 In the 1940s, there may _____ (be) only 40 Amur tigers left because of hunting.

5 A reason these numbers could _____ (be) higher today is because the Russian government was the first to grant these tigers full protection.

6 There might not _____ (be) such an increase in numbers if the government hadn't stepped in to protect them.

7 We must _____ (encourage) industries such as logging, agriculture, and mining to consider the Amur tiger's habitat as they make business plans.

6D You Have no Idea Where Camels Actually Come From

TEDTALKS

AUTHENTIC LISTENING SKILLS

1 Listen and complete each extract from the TED Talk with one, two, or three words. 🎧 49

1 She's a paleobiologist, which means she specializes in _____ really old dead stuff.

2 … maybe I'm looking _____ more closely and realizing it doesn't quite look like this has tree rings.

3 … and eventually collected 30 fragments of that exact same bone, _____ really tiny.

4 Having hit a wall, she showed one of the fragments to some colleagues of hers in Colorado, and they _____.

5 And usually, after so many _____, it breaks down.

6 And he processed it, and compared it to 37 known and modern-day mammal species. And _____ a match.

7 Well, scientists have known for _____, turns out, even before Natalia's discovery, that camels are actually originally American.

8 It went from being this ridiculously niche creature suited only to this one _____ environment…

WATCH ▶

2 Complete the sentences with a word or short phrase.

1 The Fyles Leaf Bed is located near the _____ Pole.

2 Over the years, Rybczynski collected 30 _____ of the same bone.

3 Eventually, Rybczynski used a 3D surface _____ to complete her work.

4 Collagen is what gives _____ to our bones.

5 The bone belonged to a camel that would have been _____ feet tall.

6 Camels are originally _____.

7 Camels' humps are filled with _____.

8 Llamas and alpacas are relatives of camels that live in _____.

3 Number these events from the talk in chronological order.

_____ Eventually, the North American camels went extinct.

_____ In 2006, Natalia Rybczynski discovered ancient camel bones in the Arctic.

_____ Camels first evolved in North America, where there were around 20 species.

_____ Now scientists are questioning whether camels may have evolved for cold climates, instead of the desert.

_____ For a long time, people assumed camels originated in the desert.

_____ Around 7 million years ago, camels migrated to South America and to Asia.

VOCABULARY IN CONTEXT

4 Match the words and phrases to the sentences that illustrate their meaning.

1 spot _____   **4** surface _____

2 willingness _____   **5** proof _____

3 hit a wall _____   **6** camp _____

a The scientists knew they had to dig deeper than **the top layer of land** to find the oldest artifacts.

b They chose a quiet **place to set up their tents** and spend the night.

c Natalia went back to the same **place** to look for more bone fragments.

d She tried hundreds of different ideas, but eventually, she **reached a point where she couldn't make any more progress**.

e One of the key things we look for is **evidence** that our hypotheses are true.

f I was impressed by Natalia's **desire to keep trying** to find the answer even though it was a difficult challenge.

6E Finding a Solution

SPEAKING

1 Look at the photos. Match the anecdotes with the pictures. Write the correct letter in the space provided.

a    c

b    d

1 Last year, I had the opportunity to go scuba diving in the Red Sea. I felt a little frightened when I first got into the water, but I forgot all about my fear when I started seeing beautiful fish. _____

2 For their thirtieth wedding anniversary, my parents went whale watching. Seeing whales in their natural environment had always been their dream. _____

3 When I graduated from high school, my parents surprised me with plane tickets to South Africa. They'd made plans for us to visit an elephant sanctuary. _____

4 Over the summer, I went on a safari. It was an unforgettable experience. _____

2 Complete the conversation using these words and phrases. Some items may have more than one answer.

How amazing!   Really?
So, what did you do?   That must have been wonderful!
What happened?

A: Last year my family and I decided to visit a nature reserve.

B: (1) _____ I've always wanted to do that.

A: So had I! Anyway, we weren't quite sure where to go, but after considering several options, we decided to travel to Tanzania.

B: Wow. (2) _____

A: Yes, that's what I thought, but for the first few days we didn't see any animals.

B: Oh, no. How disappointing!

A: My parents were sure that eventually we would see something. After all, we were in the animals' natural habitat.

B: (3) _____

A: Well, on our last day, we were really lucky.

B: (4) _____

A: Well, very early in the morning we came across a herd of zebras. They were grazing by the side of the road and it was just beautiful.

B: (5) _____ Were you able to take any photos?

Now answer the following questions.

1 Which photo are the two friends speaking about?

_____

2 How would you feel if you were in Speaker A's situation?

_____

3 What other questions could Speaker B ask to find out more information?

_____

3 Choose one of the photos in Activity 1 and write your own anecdote. You can begin with one of these prompts or a sentence in Activity 1. Make notes below.

Last year, my family and I decided to…
Ever since I was a child, I had always wanted to…
Once, I had the opportunity to…
It had always been my dream to…
On my last vacation, my family and I…

4 Listen to an anecdote. Then write a list of questions you could ask to find out more. Use these expressions.
🎧 **50**

How did you feel when…?   What did you do when…?
What happened after…?   Who else…?
Why do you think…?

Now, write the ending to the story. Include some of the details you asked about in your questions.

5 Read the following questions. Make notes on how you would answer them. Listen and compare your ideas to the sample answers. 🎧 **51**

1 Would you like to go on a safari? Why? / Why not?

2 Does whale watching appeal to you? Why? / Why not?

3 Would you enjoy scuba diving? Why? / Why not?

4 What do you think is the best way to protect endangered species? Why?

5 What are the advantages of nature reserves compared to zoos?

WRITING A problem-solution essay

6 **Put the steps for writing a problem-solution essay into the correct order, 1–7.**

a Also, try to start each new paragraph with a topic sentence. _____

b Begin the essay by outlining the problems and saying you will suggest solutions. _____

c First, read the essay topic carefully. _____

d Finally, if you have time, write a brief conclusion to sum up. _____

e Next, plan your essay. Make notes on your ideas and main points. _____

f Write about one problem and solution in each new paragraph. _____

g As you plan, do some research if possible. To give your main points greater authority, refer to other sources. _____

7 **Complete the problem-solution essay with sentences a–h.**

(1) _____

(2) _____ Apart from loss of habitat, these animals are also hunted for their meat. The worst issue of all, though, is frequent poaching, that is, they are illegally hunted for their horn. (3) _____

(4) _____ One of the greatest of these is deforestation (cutting down trees). (5) _____ Conservation groups such as Save the Rhino relocate, or move, the rhino to safer areas, and also run various projects to protect the animals.

People in developing countries often don't have enough to eat. This is not a new problem. (6) _____ I agree with the solution proposed by experts from Stirling and Oregon State universities to have local governments encourage their people to switch to alternative food sources.

(7) _____ In some countries, the horn is believed to provide medical benefits, although there is no scientific evidence for this. In recent years, some conservationists have been using chemicals to dye rhino horns pink, so that they become less valuable to poachers. (8) _____ It is not yet clear whether or not this solution is working, but it's certainly an interesting approach.

a Large animals, such as rhino, can provide meat for entire villages in some areas.

b Loss of habitat happens for a number of reasons.

c According to the Rhino Rescue Project, humans who consume these chemicals would become ill.

d How can we protect the world's rhino?

e In this essay, I will suggest solutions to these three problems.

f Being poached for their horn is the greatest threat the rhinos face.

g Today, most species of rhinoceros in the world are critically endangered.

h This forces the rhino to move to more open areas where they may not have enough food, and where they are more vulnerable to other threats.

8 **Read the essay in Activity 7 again. Then match the questions (1–8) with the answers (a–k). Three answers are not used.**

1 What are the three problems faced by the rhino? _____

2 Which of the problems is the worst? _____

3 What is one solution to the loss of habitat problem? _____

4 Why are rhino hunted for their meat in some areas? _____

5 Why are rhino poached for their horn? _____

6 What are some conservationists doing to the rhino horn? _____

7 What source claims that the dye could make people sick? _____

8 Is the dye and chemicals solution a success? _____

a moving the rhino to safer areas

b applying chemicals and pink dye to it

c it isn't yet known

d loss of habitat

e loss of habitat, being hunted for their meat, and being poached for their horn

f yes, it's very successful

g it's used as medicine in some countries

h poaching

i experts from Stirling and Oregon State universities

j the people in those villages are very hungry

k the Rhino Rescue Project

9 **Read the text below and follow the instructions.**

A number of zoos around the world are important centers for research and conservation of certain species. The animals in zoos may be well cared for, but they don't have freedom and aren't in their natural environment.

There are numerous benefits from having animals in zoos.

Do you agree or disagree? Write an essay giving your thoughts on this topic.

Review

1 Rewrite the sentences. Complete the sentences using the words in capital letters. Use between two and five words.

1 The Madagascan dwarf hippopotamus has become extinct.

The Madagascan dwarf hippopotamus _____ _____. OUT

2 Sea turtles are endangered.

Sea turtles _____. RISK

3 The animals haven't been able to live in the new environment.

The animals _____ the new environment. ADAPTED

4 We are concerned that many birds won't survive for long.

We are concerned about the _____ of many birds. TERM

5 The Amur tiger hasn't become extinct yet.

The Amur tiger has _____. SAVE

6 I got my red hair from my mother.

My mother _____ her red-hair gene to me. PASS

2 Complete the sentences with one word.

1 Tropical forests are the natural _____ of millions of species.

2 Conservation programs breed animals at _____ of extinction.

3 The Canarian oystercatcher was a _____ of bird.

4 We need to ensure the _____ of as many species as possible for future generations.

5 Your _____ can even determine the length of your life.

6 Millions of species have _____ to life in the rainforests.

3 Choose the correct option to complete the sentences. There may be more than one correct answer.

1 Scientists have plenty of ideas of how to rescue the elephants and they _____ need any more.

a must not   **b** may not   **c** should not

2 If the government promises to protect our traditional way of life, it _____ survive for future generations.

a must   **b** will   **c** can

3 The loggerhead turtles in the Mediterranean _____ be saved because several countries are working together.

a could   **b** shall   **c** need

4 Stopping people from cutting down the trees in their habitat _____ help save the endangered bonobos.

a should   **b** would   **c** must

5 The red panda _____ be protected because its forest habitat is being destroyed.

a must   **b** can   **c** should

6 Habitat loss _____ be the most dangerous factor faced by snow leopards today.

a should   **b** might   **c** must

4 Match the two parts of the sentences.

1 More money must _____

2 Now we should _____

3 I can't _____

4 As you can _____

5 You should _____

6 I don't think we could _____

7 Nicaragua must _____

8 If the Amur tiger hadn't been given protection, they would _____

a have been even more beautiful before so many of its trees were cut down.

b see, protecting the forest elephant's habitat is vital.

c have done more to protect Australia's Great Barrier reef.

d have died out.

e be spent on protecting the environment.

f be doing more to protect the environment.

g see why people hunt endangered species.

h have told us more about how Amur tigers protect their young.

5 Choose the correct option to complete the sentences.

1 A: Did Sasha have a lot of interesting things to say about the reading assignment?

B: She didn't have much to say about the book in class. She *can't have / may have* read it very thoroughly.

2 A: Do you think we're lost?

B: Yes, we *can have / must have* turned the wrong way.

3 A: I can't believe we're still going to be on the train at midnight.

B: I know! Normally, I *shall be going / would be going* to bed by 10 o'clock.

4 A: Why didn't you take the early train?

B: I *should've / wouldn't have* made it on time, even if I'd taken the early train.

5 A: We had such a great time on our trip to Puerto Rico.

B: It *must have been / can have been* fun to explore the island and the old city.

6 A: Why didn't you study more for your exam?

B: Studying more *would helped / wouldn't have helped* me do better on the exam.

7 A: But what can we do to help the environment?

B: More animals *can't have lived / could live* here if we planted more trees and cleaned up the river.

7A Rules of Creativity

VOCABULARY Breaking the mold

1 Review Rewrite the sentences. Complete the sentences using the word in capital letters. You may use between one and four other words in your answer.

1 Kate Robinson works as a photographer in New York.

Kate Robinson _____ as a photographer. LIVING

2 I always do a lot with my time.

I _____ of my time. MAKE

3 Many people don't understand abstract art.

Abstract art _____ to a lot of people. SENSE

4 Please decide in the next few minutes.

Please _____ in the next few minutes. MIND

5 The public loved Banksy's artwork in Calais.

Banksy's artwork _____ in Calais. SPLASH

6 The movies *Planet Ocean* had a big effect on the viewers.

The movies *Planet Ocean* _____ on the viewers. MADE

2 Review Cross out the mistake in each sentence. Write the correct words.

1 I'm sorry, but I really can make up my mind. I don't know what I want. _____

2 The mural will make a big different to the hospital. _____

3 Let's make the most for our gallery visit. _____

4 Supermarkets should make way to small, independent shops. _____

5 He makes a good live as an actor. _____

6 The documentary did quite a splash—people loved it. _____

7 Her novels don't make many sense to me. _____

8 Your photographs are going to make a big impressive. _____

3 Match the two parts of the sentences.

1 I'm going to create   a person.
2 He's made   b creatively.
3 She's a very creative   c to the problem.
4 He's an artist who breaks   d up some lyrics for the song.
5 We need a new approach   e something new to wear.
6 She thinks   f the rules.

4 Complete the sentences with these verbs.

adapt	create	follow	has	kill	make	score	work

1 Jazz musicians don't _____ traditional rules.

2 New Bollywood movies always _____ a lot of excitement.

3 Less money means we need to _____ existing ways of doing things.

4 Teaching more grammar in schools might _____ creativity.

5 Artists generally _____ high on intelligence tests.

6 I always _____ up new words in my poems.

7 He _____ an interesting approach to problem-solving.

8 The marketing team _____ very creatively together.

5 Choose the correct option to complete the sentences.

1 We couldn't come ___ with a solution.
   a up
   b down
   c in
   d out

2 I go to ___ writing classes twice a week.
   a create
   b creativity
   c creative
   d creatively

3 Street artists usually ___ the rules of traditional art.

  a obey

  b follow

  c solve

  d break

4 Let's ___ up a cool name for our band.

  a give

  b make

  c write

  d do

5 The team had a wide variety of ___ to the problem.

  a approaches

  b rules

  c creations

  d ways

6 He had to ___ his way of working when he moved to a new country.

  a follow

  b invent

  c break

  d adapt

6 Cross out the mistake in each sentence. Write the correct word.

1 We're going to creatively a storytelling group in our local library. _____

2 Boredom actually encourages creation in children.

_____

3 The festival led to the create of a lot of opportunities for young people. _____

4 World leaders need to think more creative about solutions. _____

5 It's difficult to come up to a solution.

_____

6 She made out a new way of singing. _____

7 **Extension** Circle the option that does not form a collocation.

1 create + *a scene / an email account / a bank account*

2 break + *the law / a deadline / someone's heart*

3 come up with + *an emotion / a plan / a theory*

4 follow + *your heart / your instinct / your resume*

5 *wealth / disease / job* + creation

6 *destroy / stifle / find out* + creativity

8 **Extension** Complete the sentences with these words.

gift	imagination	ingenious
innovative	originality	vision

1 Mozart had a creative _____ .

2 It was an _____ piece of work that showed skill and intelligence.

3 The play didn't have any new ideas and lacked

_____ .

4 Creating storybooks is great for sparking children's

_____ .

5 _____ artists experiment with forms and materials.

6 Any great project starts with its creator's

_____

PRONUNCIATION

9 Listen to the sentences. Underline the words where the final consonant disappears. Then practice saying the sentences. 🎧 **52**

1 I'd rather you didn't take all the same classes as me.
2 My teacher says I should try to be more creative.
3 She still couldn't decide how to tell her parents.
4 Creativity doesn't mean the same thing to everybody.
5 I wish I could design my own house.
6 If only I hadn't stayed up all night.
7 He wishes he had a year off so he could travel.
8 I really can't believe how creative she is.

LISTENING

10 Listen to six different people talking. Match the speakers (1–6) with the statements (a–h). There are two extra statements. 🎧 **53**

Speaker 1
Speaker 2
Speaker 3
Speaker 4
Speaker 5
Speaker 6

a He wishes the classes weren't mandatory.
b If only she weren't so busy all the time.
c If only he had listened to his friend.
d He would rather have joined the other group.
e She wishes they could understand how she really feels.
f If only she'd been more serious about her studies.
g He wishes that he could have played basketball instead.
h She'd rather focus on less creative subjects.

11 Listen to part of an interview with Professor Richard Florida. What seems to be the main point of his theories? 🎧 **54**

a the loss of sense of community in our cities and the resulting damage
b the exploding populations of our cities and our inability to support this
c the increasing concentration of creativity and innovation in our cities
d decreasing innovation because of people and firms clustering together

12 Listen to some of Professor Florida's statements. Decide if they are fact (F) or opinion (O). 🎧 **55**

1 ___   2 ___   3 ___   4 ___
5 ___   6 ___   7 ___   8 ___

13 Listen to the interview again and answer the questions. 🎧 **54**

1 What does the professor say increasingly determines a person's prosperity?
   a location   **b** economic trends   **c** education
2 What word is in the title of both of Professor Florida's books?
   a economy   **b** city   **c** creative
3 How many world centers of innovation does the professor mention?
   a 3   **b** 4   **c** 5
4 What does the professor say is the downside to all of this innovation and development?
   a growing concentration
   b growing inequality
   c growing prosperity
5 What percentage of the population does the professor say now lives in cities?
   a less than 20 percent
   b more than 40 percent
   c more than 50 percent
6 How many of our new innovations does the professor say come from mega-regions?
   a less than 20 percent
   b 2/3
   c 90 percent
7 Why does the professor say that sense of community is so important?
   a because so many people have been dislocated
   b because so many people have anchors
   c because so many people want to live alone
8 What does the professor say he is attracted to?
   a a remade suburb
   b a place with a soul
   c a livable city

GRAMMAR First, second, third, and mixed conditionals

14 Choose the correct option to complete the sentences.

1 If teachers *had allowed / allow* creative students to daydream, they would be better prepared for their future.

2 Students *would have / will have* difficulty in the future if education doesn't include creativity because we are going to need workers who can think creatively.

3 How can we expect students to be creative if their assignments *have / would have had* very specific instructions?

4 If students *are / were* taught that there's only one solution to a problem, they won't be able to imagine creative solutions.

5 Students *are / would be* better prepared to be scientists or musicians if we didn't expect them to focus on memorizing facts and formulas.

6 If students *have been / were* able to decide what they want to learn about, they would be more interested in the subject.

15 Choose the correct option to complete the sentences.

1 If we *hadn't played / didn't play* the video game, we *aren't / wouldn't have been* in such a good mood, which often makes us more creative.

2 If you *would meditate / meditate*, you *will be able to think / could think* about a problem differently and perhaps come up with a new solution.

3 If you *had exercised / exercised* more often, your body— and mind—*are / would feel* more relaxed, which makes it easier to have creative ideas.

4 If you *look / would look* at something blue, you *had thought / might think* more clearly. (According to researchers, we associate blue with the sea, sky, and openness.)

5 If you *had taken / took* a walk outdoors, you *could think / thought* more creatively. (Being outdoors stimulates all five of your senses, which can stimulate creativity.)

6 We *hadn't been / might not have been* distracted by the background noise if we *had gone / went* to a cafe to do our work.

7 If I *hadn't taken / haven't taken* a nap, I *can think / wouldn't have been able to* tackle the problem in a creative way.

16 Correct the verb forms in bold. Sometimes there is more than one correct answer.

1 If creative people daydream, or let their minds wander, sometimes new ideas **came** into their minds while they are thinking about something else. _____

2 There would probably be fewer distractions if you **would work** late at night or early in the morning, like Benjamin Franklin or Ernest Hemmingway. _____

3 Creative people **were able to plan** their days more effectively if they know when they do their best work. _____

4 If they **hadn't taken** failure personally, creative people could learn from their mistakes and not be afraid of taking risks. _____

5 If J.K. Rowling hadn't been able to work anywhere, at any time, she **hadn't written** the *Harry Potter* books. _____

6 Beethoven and Tchaikovsky might not have been such brilliant composers if they **didn't walk** every day for exercise. _____

7 If creative people **are** motivated by money or awards, they might not find challenges so exciting. _____

17 Complete the sentences with the correct forms of the verbs in parentheses.

1 If she _____ (know) how other people solved similar problems, she _____ (find) a way to solve this problem.

2 You _____ (understand) the problem differently if you _____ (think) about it in a more creative way.

3 If I _____ (not start) listening to how other people solved their problems, I _____ (not learn) so many different ways of solving the problems I've been having.

4 She _____ (be) inspired to be more creative if she _____ (surround) herself with creative people when she starts university next month.

5 If he _____ (try) to solve his problem backwards, he _____ (understand) the problem differently, but he doesn't see that.

6 He _____ (not start) listening to what other people have to say if he _____ (not realize) how important it is.

7 If we _____ (not draw) a picture representing our problem, we _____ (not find) this amazing solution!

8 You _____ (realize) how similar these problems are if you _____ (research) different problems.

7B Testing Times

VOCABULARY BUILDING Noun forms

1 Complete the chart by forming nouns from the verbs and adjectives.

Verb	Noun	Adjective	Noun
vary		useful	
publish		logical	
know		fluent	
conclude		flexible	
assess		intelligent	
analyze		concerned	

READING

2 Read the article. Match these words from the article with the definitions. Use the context to help you.

1 nurture ___
2 DNA ___
3 vulnerability ___
4 heredity ___
5 indistinguishable ___
6 IQ ___

a being unprotected from harm, either physically or emotionally
b a measure of intelligence, usually with a number score
c unable to identify as different
d the process of taking care of someone, for example, a baby
e the passing of mental or physical characteristics from parents to children
f the carrier of genetic information

3 The paragraphs in the article are numbered 1–6. Choose the most correct heading (a–g) for each paragraph. There is one extra heading.

Paragraph 1
Paragraph 2
Paragraph 3
Paragraph 4
Paragraph 5
Paragraph 6

a Separated at birth
b What is the role of DNA?
c Early research
d Human diversity
e Understanding identical twins
f Answering the questions
g Two areas of research

4 Complete the statements with one or two words from the article.

1 Twins that look the same are _____.
2 Twins that do not look the same are

_____.

3 Comparing both kinds of twins help us understand the role of nature and _____.
4 Research on twins who had been separated _____ began in the 1980s.
5 People found the way the two Jims spoke to be

_____.

6 Research at the University of Minnesota tried to answer some of the mysteries of _____.
7 Bouchard concluded that heredity was more important in determining _____ than education.
8 Everywhere scientists look, they find _____ shaping who we are.

A Thing or Two About Twins

1 To scientists, twins offer a special opportunity to understand the influence of genes and the environment—of nature and nurture. Identical twins share virtually the same genetic code. Any differences between them—one twin having younger-looking skin, for example—must be due to environmental factors such as less time spent in the sun.

2 Alternatively, by comparing the experiences of identical twins with those of fraternal twins, who share about half their DNA, researchers can measure the degree to which genes affect our lives. If identical twins are more likely to both have an illness than fraternal twins are, then vulnerability to the disease must come at least in part from heredity.

3 These two lines of research—studying the differences between identical twins to identify the influence of environment, and comparing identical twins with fraternal ones to measure the role of heredity—have been crucial to understanding the role of nature and nurture in determining our personalities, creativity, behavior, and vulnerability to disease.

4 The idea of using twins to measure heredity dates back to 1875, when the English scientist Francis Galton first suggested the approach (and came up with the phrase "nature and nurture"). But twin studies took a surprising turn in the 1980s, following the discovery of a number of identical twins who had been separated at birth.

5 The story began with the famous case of two brothers, both named Jim. Born in the US state of Ohio in 1939, Jim Springer and Jim Lewis were put up for adoption as babies and raised by different parents, who gave them the same first name by chance. When Jim Springer reconnected with his brother at age 39 in 1979, they uncovered many similarities. Both men were six feet tall and weighed 180 pounds. Growing up, they both had dogs named Toy and had taken family vacations in St. Pete Beach in Florida. As young men, they'd both married women named Linda, and then divorced them. Their second wives were both named Betty. They named their sons James Alan and James Allan. They'd both worked as part-time sheriffs, enjoyed home carpentry projects and suffered severe headaches. Although they wore their hair differently, their voices were indistinguishable.

6 Over the next two decades, the Jim twins and hundreds of other twins were studied by Thomas Bouchard Jr., a psychologist at the University of Minnesota. Bouchard and his colleagues tried to answer some of the mysteries of human nature: Why are some people happy and others sad? Why are some outgoing and others shy? Where does general intelligence come from? Bouchard's team reached a controversial conclusion: IQ depended more on heredity than on training or education. Until this time, most scientists thought that our brains were shaped more by experience. It was as if it didn't matter in which family the twins had been raised. They concluded that IQ scores were influenced more by genetics than parenting. Other studies found that heredity could predict criminal behavior and religious beliefs. Wherever scientists looked, they found genetic influence helping to shape our lives.

7C *If only...*

GRAMMAR *Wish, if only, would rather*

1 **Choose the correct option to complete the sentences.**

1 I wish I _____ play the guitar. I tried to learn when I was younger, but I wasn't very good.
  a would
  b had
  c could
  d was

2 I'm not a very creative person. If only I _____ been taught more about art at school.
  a have
  b could
  c would
  d had

3 I have never liked art galleries. I wish I _____ had to visit them when I was young, but my parents were really into art.
  a had
  b hadn't
  c wouldn't
  d could have

4 I am not a fan of modern art. I wish I _____ understand what the artist was trying to say.
  a could
  b would
  c were
  d can

5 I would _____ study a subject like media at college, but my parents really want me to do business.
  a prefer
  b like
  c rather
  d enjoy

6 If I _____ so shy, I would love to try acting.
  a was
  b would
  c wasn't
  d couldn't be

7 If only we _____ that movie, it was terrible. There are so many other movies we could have chosen.
  a had chosen
  b didn't choose
  c would choose
  d hadn't chosen

8 I wish he _____ talking about galleries and museums. I'm just not interested.
  a would stop
  b could stop
  c did stop
  d had stopped

2 **Complete the conversation using *was*, *would*, or *could*. Then listen and check your answers.** 🎧 **57**

A: Hi Julia, what are you doing?

B: Oh hi, Stephen. I'm just watching a short video about making videos to put online. I wish I (1) _____ creative like that.

A: Yeah, I know what you mean. If only we (2) _____ learn things like that at university. I wish they (3) _____ focus on things like that a little more.

B: Exactly, these kinds of skills are really important in the modern world. Ah, anyway. Are you going to come to the lecture tonight? It's on the future of creative marketing.

A: I wish I (4) _____ but I really have to do some work on my project.

B: That's a shame. I'm going with a few friends, but they will probably show up late. I wish they (5) _____ check their watches a little more often.

A: Ha ha. Yeah, we all have friends a bit like that. Well, I should get back to my project. I wish I (6) _____ coming tonight. Have fun.

B: I wish you (7) _____ come. Oh well. See you tomorrow.

A: Yeah, see you tomorrow.

3 **Choose the correct option to complete the sentences.**

1 I wish I *would / could* think like a child.
2 If only I *had / have* studied design at school.
3 I would *prefer / rather* listen to classical music.
4 I wish I *am / was* good at art.
5 I wish he *would / could* stop telling everyone how creative he is.
6 If only I *listened / had listened* to my parents. They told me to study media.
7 I wish advertisers *would stop / had stopped* making such abstract advertisements these days.
8 I would rather *go / gone* to the old town. There is a bit more culture in that part.

4 **Read the sentences below and decide if they are correct or incorrect. Correct the incorrect sentences.**

1 A lot of people say that creativity is about breaking the rules. Sometimes I wish I would be braver.

_____

2 I wish I'd had more time to play at school. Scientists say play is really important for making us more creative.

_____

3 I wish you could stop talking. You are really annoying me.

_____

4 If only I haven't chosen this approach for my project. There's so much work to do and I think the presentation is going to be really detailed.

_____

5 I wish we didn't have to go to the exhibition.

_____

6 I would rather to go to the theater than to the movies.
_____

7 I wish they give additional marks in exams for original ideas. _____

8 If only I had more time for my hobbies. I'd love to spend more time painting. _____

⑤ Rewrite the second sentence so that it has the same meaning as the first using the word in parenthesis.

1 It would be amazing to be a fashion designer.
(wish) _____

2 I would prefer to be at the beach right now.
(rather) _____

3 My parents made me learn the violin. I hated it.
(hadn't) _____

4 I have to practice for the concert but I don't want to.
(wish) _____

5 He always tells me how to finish my writing. It's annoying.
(would) _____

6 I did not finish my project on time. I really regret that now.
(only) _____

7 I want to be like my brother.
(was) _____

⑥ Complete the email with these phrases.

I wish I could go	I wish I'd chosen	I wish I'd signed
I wish you were	I'd rather make	I'd rather she had
If only I'd paid		

Hey Sara,

How are you? Well, I hope. You'll never believe what I did last weekend! Do you remember I signed up to that pottery course? Well, it started on Saturday and (1) _____ up ages ago—it was amazing! (2) _____ in the class too though—you would have loved it!

At first, the teacher told us about how to treat the clay. To be honest, this part of the class was a bit boring. (3) _____ let us start making things

immediately, but I think it was an important thing to know. (4) _____ more attention, the next part of the class might have been better! Next, she showed us how to turn the wheel and I was pretty good at that.

Finally, we got to use the clay. We could choose to make a bowl or a cup. I said (5) _____ a cup, but now (6) _____ a bowl. My cup wasn't very good, but the teacher said I was very creative ☺

(7) _____ every day—it is so much fun!

You should come next time. The classes are on Saturday morning.

See you soon,

Yeon-soo

⑦ Put the words in the correct order to make sentences.

1 encouraged / me / my / had / play / to / wish / instrument / I / an / parents / .
_____

2 only / his / he / if / wasted / talent / hadn't / .
_____

3 neighbor / wish / practicing / drums / stop / all / day / I / my / would / .
_____

4 rather / I / in the book / the / was / more / likeable / would / main character / .
_____

5 open / I / the / was / really / wish / gallery / .
_____

6 didn't / I / have / to / invent / I / wish / solutions / all the time / .
_____

7 could / paint / only / like / Picasso / if / I / .
_____

8 teacher / freedom / would / the / more / gave / rather / us / I / .
_____

⑧ Complete the sentences so they are true for you.

1 I wish I could _____
_____

2 I wish my parents would _____
_____

3 I wish I had _____
_____

4 If only I hadn't _____
_____

5 I'd rather go to _____
_____

6 I'd rather my family _____
_____

7D Go Ahead, Make up New Words!

TEDTALKS

AUTHENTIC LISTENING SKILLS

1 Listen to these extracts from Erin McKean's TED Talk, and repeat the sentences. Listen especially to the speed of her speech, and try to match her pace and intonation. 🎧 58

1 Every language is just a group of people who agree to understand each other.
2 That rule lives in your brain. You never had to be taught this rule, you just understand it.
3 So we've been talking about this for a long time.
4 And I think that is, well, stupid.
5 "Motel" is a blend of "motor" and "hotel."

WATCH ▶

2 Choose the best options.

1 What is the main topic of this TED Talk?
   a Dictionaries are useful tools.
   b English grammar is so complicated it's easy to make mistakes.
   c It's OK to be creative with language.
   d A lot of English words come from Japanese.
2 According to McKean, what are the two types of rules language has?
   a old-fashioned rules and modern rules
   b formal rules and informal rules
   c rules based on Latin and rules based on German
   d unconscious rules and learned rules
3 What is McKean's attitude towards grammar rules?
   a They shouldn't stop people from inventing words.
   b They help you decide whether a word is acceptable.
   c They explain confusing patterns.
   d They are the only rules we should follow.
4 According to McKean, how are words like hats?
   a Both words and hats come in many forms.
   b Both words and hats are used by humans.
   c Both words and hats have "natural" and "learned" rules associated with them.
   d You can find the word "hat" in the dictionary.
5 How does McKean organize her recommendations about creating new words?
   a She begins by telling a story.
   b She describes six ways to form new words and gives examples.

c She compares and contrasts word formation in English with other languages.
d She starts with simple words and ends with complex words.

6 Why does McKean say, "OMG"?
   a to give a humorous example of a word formed with the first letters of a phrase.
   b to show shock that the audience likes NASA.
   c to emphasize her point that anyone can create new words.
   d to demonstrate that she disagrees with formal grammar rules.

3 Choose the correct option to complete the sentences.

1 If you look at the word NASA, *you'll / you would* notice that the letters come from "National Aeronautics and Space Administration".
2 If we didn't borrow words from other languages, we *don't have / wouldn't have* the word "kumquat" in English.
3 If the word "brunch" did not exist, what *do we call / would we call* a late breakfast?
4 If you want a job making dictionaries, you *should / should have* become a lexicographer.
5 If you hadn't been taught what a "wug" was, you *would still know / will still know* how to form the plural, "wugs".
6 If you learn a language as a child, you *understand / would understand* some grammar rules unconsciously.
7 If you use unusual words when you speak, people *will pay / paid* more attention to what you say.
8 If we didn't create new words in English, how *do we name / would we name* new technologies?

VOCABULARY IN CONTEXT

4 Match the words (1–6) with the sentences that show their meaning (a–f).

1 get your meaning across ___   4 heartbroken ___
2 manners ___   5 edit ___
3 grab ___   6 electrocute ___

a It's always a good idea to use **polite behavior.**
b Miguel was **very sad** when his team didn't win the basketball tournament.
c During the storm, the electricity company warned people that fallen power lines could **seriously injure** them.
d Lily works for her school newspaper; she **decides what information should be included** in each issue.
e When you know more words, you have more ways to **explain your ideas**.
f When you say something surprising or unexpected, you can **attract** people's attention.

7E Creative Solutions

SPEAKING

1 Read the sentences. Match each one with its function: Raising concerns (C), Making suggestions (S), or Giving reasons (R).

1 That way we will be sure to finish on time. ___
2 If we do that, we can save time and money. ___
3 Wouldn't that approach lead to other problems? ___
4 I can't see how that would work. ___
5 If you ask me, we should do it a different way. ___
6 This approach will enable us to be more efficient. ___
7 I propose doing it differently. ___
8 What do you think about this idea? ___
9 I can see several issues with that. ___
10 Wouldn't it be better to consider an alternative? ___
11 That will allow us to complete the project faster. ___

2 Choose the correct response to each question or statement.

1 How do you feel about the plan?
  a Personally, I can't see how it would work.
  b It allowed us to make progress more quickly.
2 Do you agree with the approach we're taking?
  a On the other hand, I can't think of any alternatives.
  b If you ask me, we should consider an alternative.
3 What is the main advantage?
  a Doing it this way will allow us to save money.
  b Wouldn't it be better to do it a different way?
4 Can you see any problems with this strategy?
  a I can think of three main issues.
  b If we do that, it will definitely work.
5 I think we should work on it as a group.
  a If you ask me, we should do it that way.
  b If we do that, won't it take longer?
6 Why do you think that?
  a Well, it will enable us to get better results.
  b The thing is, I can't see how that would work.

3 Complete the conversation with these words and phrases.

if we do that, won't it	my only issue is
it would allow us	that way we could
maybe we should	what do you think about

A: I'm worried we're not going to be able to finish the project on time. You know, we only have two days left.
B: I agree. (1) _____ asking for an extension?
A: Hmm… (2) _____ affect our final grade?
B: Yes, maybe. But on the other hand, (3) _____ to put in some extra time this weekend.

A: Yes, and (4) _____ go to the library this afternoon to do more research.
B: Exactly.
A: (5) _____, I asked for an extension a couple of months ago.
B: Oh, I see. I didn't realize that.
A: (6) _____ see how much we get done this evening, and think about it again tomorrow.
B: That's a good idea.

4 Choose one of the situations below and suggest a better approach. Make notes about your ideas in the space provided. Use these expressions to help you.

I'd suggest…
If you ask me, I think you should…
My recommendation would be to…
Perhaps it would be better to…
That way, you would/could…
That would enable/allow you to…
Wouldn't it be better to…?

a Your friend is considering running a half marathon, but he hasn't done very much training.
b Two of your classmates have had an argument, but they need to work together on a school assignment.
c Your sister doesn't like her part-time job and she is considering leaving it.

5 Read the following text and listen to the conversation that follows it. 🎧 59

Public Bikes in Stoney Bridge

Town leaders in Stoney Bridge are thinking about implementing a public bicycle system. They want to install thirty stations around the town, each of which will have ten bikes. For a monthly fee, anyone will be able to borrow a bike and use it to get from place to place. Several neighboring towns recently put similar systems in place and research has shown that they are an effective way to reduce congestion and improve air quality. In addition, cycling is a good way to promote a healthy lifestyle and encourage exercise.

Make notes on what you would say to answer the question below. Then listen to the sample answer and compare your ideas. 🎧 60

Question: Why does the mayor want to install the bike system now? What is the council member's concern?

WRITING A report

6 Read the sentences from various reports. Underline those that make recommendations.

1 We might consider adding an extra five minutes to the school lunch break.
2 In order to represent everyone, we interviewed both students and teachers.
3 This report will also explain what the background issues are.
4 I would strongly recommend revising the rules for cell phone use at school.
5 We explored a range of possible solutions before completing our report.
6 It is clear that many students are unhappy with the "no jewelry" policy at school.
7 We would suggest making more space available for students' bicycles.
8 I propose giving senior students the opportunity to design part of the curriculum.

7 Complete the report with these words and phrases.

Background	Findings
Methods of investigation	Purpose
Recommendations	This report will
We might consider	We then surveyed

Creating a gardening section on school grounds

Introduction

(1) _____

The aim of this report is to establish how we could create a new gardening area at school. (2) _____ make recommendations on the best location for the garden, as well as on how to get students involved in the project.

(3) _____

Our principal, Mr. Barboza, introduced a suggestion box for students to share their ideas about what improvements could be made at school. A number of students expressed an interest in having a dedicated area at school for growing vegetables, herbs, fruit, and flowers.

(4) _____

In order to approach this from an informed perspective, a team of us carried out some research on other schools that have gardening areas. This gave us a realistic sense of how much space would be required for the project. (5) _____ the school grounds carefully and considered a number of possible locations before agreeing on the best spot for our purposes.

(6) _____

Although there is a good-sized green area outside the assembly hall, it is frequently in the shade, and therefore not ideal for planting and growing. The best space appears to be outside the library, but there is one issue to be overcome: the entire area is paved in concrete.

(7) _____

To solve this problem, we would recommend keeping the paved area, and creating a garden using plant pots of various sizes. (8) _____ recycling containers brought in from home by students. This would enable us to use our ideal location, while also getting students to contribute materials to the new garden.

8 Read the report in Activity 7 again. Then choose the correct option to complete the statements.

1 The main aim of the report was to establish the *right spot / best schedule / overall costs* for the new school garden.
2 The idea for a school garden was suggested by *the principal / students / teachers*.
3 *One student / Two students / A group of students* worked on the report.
4 One method of investigation was *improving / researching / recommending* other school gardens.
5 The first decision was about the amount of *space / soil / vegetables* the garden would need.
6 Several possible *plants / perspectives / places* were considered before a decision was reached.
7 A possible green area was not selected because of not getting enough *rain / sunlight / interest*.
8 The problem with the area selected is that it's covered in *soil / concrete / shade*.
9 The proposed solution is to plant everything *indoors / in the library / in containers*.
10 An added advantage is that it provides a way to get other students *involved / surveyed / informed*.

9 Your head teacher has asked you to write a report on the school cafeteria. You should include an overview of what the cafeteria currently offers, comment on any recent dissatisfaction, and make some recommendations.

Write your report in 140–190 words in an appropriate style.

Review

1 Complete each sentence with a word based on the root word *create*. You can use the same word more than once.

1 The exercises encourage _____ thinking.
2 We don't have time to _____ anything new today.
3 The government is discussing job _____ .
4 Children should have more time for _____ play.
5 He cooks _____ with the ingredients.
6 The writing course encouraged his _____ .

2 Read the phrases. Underline those that describe something creative.

1 adapt existing ways of doing things
2 break the rules
3 come up with new ways of doing things
4 follow sets of rules
5 invent things
6 make up words
7 obey the rules
8 write definitions

3 Are the words in bold correct or incorrect? Correct those that are incorrect.

1 If we **would want** technology to help students, we need to see computers as creative tools, not as televisions to entertain us or machines for finding information.
_____

2 If we believe that all children are born with creativity, we **should use** technology to keep that creativity alive.
_____

3 If teachers **encouraged** students to create comics to explain concepts or describe historical figures, they will be more engaged with the topics. _____

4 Students **feel** more responsible for their own learning if they were encouraged to write blog posts for their friends and family to read. _____

5 If students **won't use** mind maps or brainstorming in class, they probably wouldn't try thinking outside the box. _____

6 If the school hadn't encouraged us to make videos, we **wouldn't develop** our creative skills.
_____

7 Students **wouldn't be able** to try any of these techniques if they didn't have access to computers.
_____

4 Choose the correct option to complete the sentences.

1 If you like broccoli, I imagine _____ like cauliflower as well.
  a you'll   c she will
  b you want to   d she'd

2 I _____ forgotten all about Sibran's birthday if you hadn't reminded me.
  a will have   c would have
  b had   d might

3 My mother _____ I wanted to study abroad.
  a wish   c wishes
  b is wishing   d had been wish

4 He might take his classes more seriously _____ he understood how important good grades are.
  a if   c through
  b when   d how

5 She'd _____ text than call someone.
  a wish   c would
  b only   d rather

6 _____ I didn't have so much homework, I could go for a walk.
  a Rather   c Wish
  b If   d So

7 _____ I were more interested in the theatre.
  a Rather   c If wish
  b If   d If only

5 Match each trait shared by many creative people to the statement someone with that trait might say.

1 They take time to be alone sometimes.
2 They daydream.
3 They take advantage of new experiences.
4 They sometimes take risks.
5 They look for beauty in their everyday lives.
6 They look for the good in bad situations.

a I'd rather try something new, even if I'm not sure it will work.
b If only I hadn't failed that test. Now I know I need to study a lot more for the next one.
c I'd rather spend time by myself this afternoon.
d I wish I had seen the sunset with you. It must have been gorgeous!
e I'd rather travel to new places and meet the people who live there.
f I wish I had more time to just sit back and let my mind wander.

8A Cultural Crossings

VOCABULARY Identity and communication

1 Review Complete the sentences with these words.

connect	get	have	join
make	pay	respond	share

1 Drivers _____ distracted by their cell phones.
2 The project is encouraging older people to _____ on social media.
3 Why don't you ever _____ to texts?
4 Users need to sign in to _____ photos from the album.
5 What point was he trying to _____ ?
6 You need to _____ attention during the debate.
7 Teachers regularly _____ in on professional online forums.
8 People complain when doctors don't _____ very good interpersonal skills.

2 Review Circle the option that does not form a collocation.

1 get   my message out / distracted / a chat
2 connect   online / a message / on social media
3 make   photos / connections / a point
4 post   on social media / photos / texts
5 face-to-face conversation / on the phone / skills
6 share   my message out / photos / posts

3 Match the sentence halves.

1 We need to sort ___
2 The best ___
3 They've had a ___
4 I feel really ___
5 He's made a negative ___
6 She didn't mean ___

a awkward about it.
b to offend you.
c misunderstanding.
d it out.
e comment.
f response is to walk away.

4 Are the phrases associated with positive or negative ways of communicating? Complete the table.

avoid discrimination	be offended
create an awkward silence	discriminate against
have a misunderstanding	pay a compliment
sort something out	stereotype people

Positive association	Negative association

5 Choose the correct option to complete the sentences.

1 The rules _____ against foreign workers.
  a discourage   c discriminate
  b offend   d stereotype
2 The teacher _____ me a compliment about my work.
  a said   c felt
  b had   d paid
3 He _____ we should go home.
  a avoided   c discouraged
  b hinted   d reacted
4 People are more _____ of racism nowadays.
  a reaction   c conscious
  b awkward   d offended
5 She hasn't spoken to me since we had our _____.
  a misunderstanding c compliment
  b reaction   d response
6 The teacher's negative comments are _____ him.
  a responding   c sorting
  b discouraging   d hinting

7 The best _____ is to ignore him.
    a comment   **c** response
    b hint   **d** compliment

8 I didn't know what to say and there was
_____ silence.
    a a negative   **c** a conscious
    b a positive   **d** an awkward

6 Cross out the mistake in each sentence and write the correct word.

1 We tried to discourage him for going.
_____

2 He always takes offend at what I say.
_____

3 My initial react was to laugh.
_____

4 I'm consciously of the situation.
_____

5 She was very compliment about my artwork.
_____

6 He's a stereotype actor.
_____

7 **Extension** Are the statements true (T) or false (F)?

1 If you praise somebody, you are paying that person a compliment. ___
2 A flattering comment will cause offense. ___
3 We pay tribute to people we admire. ___
4 An insult is a positive comment. ___
5 If you put someone off doing something, you're encouraging them. ___
6 If someone compliments you and then you return the compliment, you say the same thing. ___
7 A back-handed compliment is offensive. ___

8 **Extension** Complete the sentences with these words.

enthusiasm	flatter	insult	pay
praise	put	reaction	swallowed

1 They always _____ tribute to well-respected actors at the Oscars.
2 Sportspeople shouldn't _____ their opponents during a game.
3 I tried to _____ him off leaving the country.
4 Fans of *Star Wars* have so much _____ for the movies.
5 She wanted to _____ him for his hard work.
6 People will often _____ you with false praise when they want something.
7 I _____ the insult and kept silent.
8 I had a delayed _____ to his insult. I got angry the next day.

PRONUNCIATION

9 Listen to the conversations. Underline the word or phrase that is stressed for clarification. Then practise saying that sentence. 🎧 61

1 A: There must be hundreds of different languages in the world.
  B: Actually, there are thousands of different languages.

2 A: We should get going. The movie starts at seven.
  B: What? I thought you said that it started at eight.

3 A: I'm driving up to see my sister this weekend.
  B: By yourself? Didn't you tell me that you're not allowed to drive alone?

4 A: She has to move to Europe with her parents.
  B: And leave college? I thought she didn't have to go with them.

5 A: My mother just turned 58.
  B: Oh, that makes sense. At first I thought you said 98.

6 A: I've decided to start studying Mandarin.
  B: That's a surprise. I'm sure you told me that you weren't interested in Chinese.

LISTENING

10 Listen to the lecture on cultural globalization. Match the words and phrases you hear. 🎧 62

1 developing		**a** marketplace
2 experiencing		**b** change
3 global		**c** societies
4 human		**d** communication
5 barriers		**e** entertainment
6 cross-border		**f** global culture
7 worldwide		**g** and connections

11 Listen again to the lecture and complete the sentences. There are no more than three words for each answer. 🎧 62

1 There's no doubt that we are experiencing change at an ever _____.

2 The term *globalization* is most often used to describe the _____.

3 Cultures leave behind _____ that can be studied and tracked over time.

4 The thousands of _____ are coming together on just a handful of global languages.

5 What is lost and what is gained in each case _____ us personally and globally.

Languages depend on older generations passing them on to younger generations.

12 Listen to the lecture on languages. What is the main idea of the talk? 🎧 63

a language provides insight into cultures
b the variety of languages under threat
c linguists don't all agree on what language is
d some countries don't have a variety of languages

13 Now listen to the lecture again and answer the questions. 🎧 63

1 How do linguists classify languages?
  a by narrow classifications
  b by age of the language
  c by location and features

2 What determines higher-level family groupings of languages?
  a particular spoken features
  b ancient linguistic origins
  c geographical locations

3 How does the speaker describe language use today?
  a there are many people who speak many languages
  b there are few people who speak few languages
  c there are many people who speak few languages

4 What does the speaker say should happen next?
  a rare languages should be brought back
  b new film and audio technologies should be developed
  c less common languages should be recorded

5 What does the speaker say helped create some multi-cultural countries?
  a a wide variety of languages
  b trade and cultural exchange
  c people of the same culture

6 How many countries does the speaker mention as having multiple surviving ethnic groups?
  a 3   **b** 4   **c** 5

7 What determines when a language dies?
  a every 14 days
  b no recording for posterity
  c its last speaker

8 How is language usually passed on?
  a within family groups
  b by cultural identity
  c recordings for posterity

GRAMMAR Reported speech

14 Read the statements. Choose the correct option to complete the sentences.

1 Caitlin: "Americans are very, very friendly; sometimes it seems that they're *too* friendly."

She answered that Americans *were / are / will be* very friendly and that sometimes they're *too* friendly.

2 Yui: "There is public transportation in most American cities but not in smaller towns."

She advised that most American cities *have / have had / would had* public transportation but not smaller towns.

3 Natalia: "Americans eat dinner kind of early: 6 o'clock."

She complained that Americans *eat / have eaten / would eat* dinner too early.

4 Ye-jun: "There's a special relationship between Americans and their cars."

He confirmed that Americans *are having / has / have* a special relationship with their cars.

5 Nora: "Soft drinks and water are served with ice, so you need to tell the server if you don't want ice."

She reminded us that soft drinks and water are always *served / serve / serving* with ice in the US.

6 James: "Americans are usually on time and appreciate it if you are, too."

He repeated that Americans *like / would liked / have liked* it when you are on time.

15 Complete the sentences with the correct forms of the verbs in parentheses.

Read these travelers' comments on visiting Peru.

- museumlover commented that while in Lima he (1) _____ (visit) a lot of great museums.
- foodie67 added that the Inca ruins (2) _____ (be) the most interesting he'd ever seen.
- iloveperu explained that ceviche (3) _____ (be) the most popular dish in Peru.
- inkaking02 told us that the Norte Chico people (4) _____ (build) a civilization in Peru more than 5,000 years ago, long before the Inca.
- travelismylife confirmed that it (5) _____ (take) her a while to get used to the high altitude in the Sacred Valley, and she (6) _____ (warn) that the sun is very strong there.
- limaismyhome announced that he (7) _____ (think) the dry season (May to October) was the best time to visit Peru.
- pacificsurfer said she (8) _____ (be) able to see Machu Picchu because she didn't buy tickets in advance.

16 Put the words in the correct order to create reported speech questions.

1 **Jens asked if** / was / funny / for making / there / a championship / faces / .

_____

_____

2 **Monika asked whether** / Turkey / camel wrestling / in / there / was / .

_____

_____

3 **Chen asked what** / to celebrate /weddings / Germans / did / .

_____

_____

4 **Wilma asked how** / China and Japan / business cards / exchanged / people / in / .

_____

_____

5 **Hasan asked if** / a monkey festival / was / Thailand / there / in / .

_____

_____

6 **Petra asked whether** / unusual / to close / was / is / it / while another / person / speaking / for people / their eyes / .

_____

_____

7 **Ana asked where** / in the world / took / tomato fight / place / the biggest / .

_____

_____

8B The Third Wave

VOCABULARY BUILDING Compound adjectives

1 Match the adjectives with the nouns to form compound adjectives. Note that one of the compound adjectives is not hyphenated (-).

1 well-		**a** faced
2 long-		**b** effective
3 heart		**c** minded
4 two-		**d** respected
5 like-		**e** broken
6 deep-		**f** wide
7 world-		**g** mannered
8 open-		**h** rooted
9 highly-		**i** minded
10 cost-		**j** lasting

READING

2 Read the article and choose the best summary.

a The "cultural assault" of Western influences will severely weaken other cultures.

b Globalization continues a long tradition of cultural connections, but at a faster pace.

c Countries like Brazil that have a mix of civilizations will dominate world culture.

d Many cultures will be unrecognizable as a new "global culture" gets more powerful.

3 Complete the statements with one or two words from the article.

1 Changes in politics, business, health and entertainment all fall under the umbrella of _____.

2 Teenagers all over the world are one of the _____ driving the new global culture.

3 Commercial and _____ are nothing new. Humans have been making them for centuries.

4 A _____ is that goods, people and ideas move. At the same time, cultures change.

5 Alvin Toffler's first book, _____, was a best-seller and very influential around the world.

6 Toffler says that in our current world, _____ economies will dominate the others.

7 Toffler is optimistic that countries can still have a _____ based on their core culture.

4 Read the article again and answer the questions.

1 In paragraph 1, the word "merging" is closest in meaning to
a coming together
b moving forward
c going backward
d changing into

2 Which of the following can be inferred from the statement in paragraph 2 that globalization is a reality, not a choice?
a Globalization has already happened and now we have to find a better way.
b There was actually more globalization in the past than what we're seeing now.
c Even with globalization, the reality is that we still have a great deal of choice.
d People opposed to globalization need to accept its reality and deal with it.

3 According to paragraph 2, what is one example given of change in the 1800s?
a radio   **c** newspapers
b television   **d** air transport

4 In paragraph 4, what do some social scientists fear could result from globalization?
a more Western companies
b English replacing other languages
c the weakening of all cultures
d a kind of cultural cloning

5 In paragraph 4, the word "wave" is closest in meaning to
a movement   **c** signal
b flood   **d** crashing

6 What word does Toffler use in paragraph 4 to describe industrial economies?
a knowledge-based   **c** agrarian
b smokestack   **d** trisection

7 Which of the following can be inferred from Toffler's comment that "You can have a unique culture made of your core culture. But you'll be the Chinese of the future, not of the past."?
a the global culture of the future will include all cultures
b the cultures of the past will be replaced by new modern ones
c unique cultures will survive based on their central values
d Chinese culture will take over the new global culture

The Third Wave 🎧 64

1 Today we are in the middle of a worldwide reorganization of cultures, a change in habits and dreams that social scientists call *globalization*. It's a broad term for sweeping changes in politics, business, health and entertainment. The huge number of teenagers—800 million in the world—with time and money to spend is one of the powerful engines of merging global cultures. Kids travel, they hang out, and above all, they buy stuff.

2 How people feel about all this depends a great deal on where they live and how much money they have. Yet globalization, as one report stated, "is a reality, not a choice". Humans have been creating commercial and cultural connections for centuries. In the 19th century the postal service, newspapers, transcontinental railroads and great steam-powered ships brought huge changes. Telegraph, telephone, radio and television made further connections between individuals and the wider world. Now computers, the internet, smartphones, social media, cable TV and cheaper air transportation have made these connections both easier and more complicated.

3 Still one basic truth remains the same: Goods move. People move. Ideas move. And cultures change. The difference now is the speed of these changes. It took television 13 years to get 50 million users; the internet took only five.

4 Alvin Toffler is an author whose book *Future Shock* was published in 1970. He also wrote *The Third Wave* with his wife, Heidi. Waves, he explains, are major changes in civilization. The first wave came with the development of agriculture, the second with industry. Today we are in the middle of the third wave, which he says is based on information. "What's happening now is the trisection of world power," he says. "Agrarian nations on the bottom, smokestack countries in between, and knowledge-based economies on top." There are a number of countries—Brazil, for example—where all three civilizations are present.

5 "Culturally we'll see big changes," Toffler says. "You're going to turn on your TV and get Nigerian TV and Fijian TV in your own language. People ask, "Can we become third wave and still remain Chinese?" "Yes," Toffler says. "You can have a unique culture made of your core culture. But you'll be the Chinese of the future, not of the past."

8C That's What They Told Me

GRAMMAR Patterns after reporting verbs

1 **Choose the correct option to complete the sentences.**

1 My parents *suggested / convinced* me to go on the exchange trip when I was at school.
2 My pen pal *reminded / claimed* me to take warm clothes when I visited her.
3 My school *assured / arranged* for me to go abroad for my work experience.
4 My sister *admitted / promised* to take photographs of her travels.
5 I *suggested / persuaded* that we should try new restaurants to experience different foods.
6 Doctors have *claimed / confessed* that new experiences make us happier.
7 I *persuaded / pretend* my friends to watch more international movies.
8 I was lucky because my school *recommended / encouraged* us to learn about different cultures.

2 **Complete the sentences with these prepositions. Some sentences do not need a preposition.**

for (x2)	of	on	to

1 She accused her friend _____ copying her style.
2 My host family insisted _____ collecting me from the airport.
3 My parents forced _____ me to read about different cultures as a child.
4 I have always blamed my brother _____ writing in my favorite books.
5 We were talking about fashion and I admitted _____ being a goth when I was young.
6 I used to imagine _____ traveling all around the world.
7 I decided _____ study languages so I could have a year abroad.
8 It is important to forgive people _____ their mistakes.

3 **Read the interview with Yasmin about her trip to London and choose the correct option to complete each sentence. Sometimes both words may be correct.**

A: So Yasmin, you are just back from your trip. How was it?
B: Oh, it was all so amazing. At first I was worried as my friends and family had (1) *explained / warned* me that London was going to be very cold. They all (2) *suggested / advised* me to take lots of warm clothes, but it wasn't

so bad. I will (3) *confess / consider* that I wore a lot of sweaters for the first few days though.
A: What do you think you learned most from the experience?
B: Well, that is hard to say, I feel as if I learned so much. When I went I had (4) *claimed / intended* to try to visit as many places as I could. I would definitely (5) *suggest / recommend* going to the museums and what is amazing is that most of them are free! Also, my host family (6) *persuaded / decided* me to go and visit some other places like the Lake District, which was so beautiful.
A: Yes, people always say that. Do you have any advice for people going on a similar trip?
B: Hmmm, well, I would (7) *tell / recommend* that people try to plan what they really want to see. Oh, and don't be afraid to (8) *ask / offer* people to help you. The people were helpful. One last thing, I would (9) *consider / invite* trying to stay a bit longer next time.

4 **Read the sentences below and decide if they are correct or incorrect. Correct the incorrect sentences.**

1 A lot of people claim to me that modern technology makes the world smaller. _____
2 Katarina warned us for avoiding the city center on Saturday as it was busy. _____
3 Michael urged us to visit him in the summer for their local festival. _____
4 When I was younger, I used to pretend being an explorer. _____
5 The government declared that companies should pay men and women equally. _____
6 Schools should avoid to make some subjects like woodwork only for boys. _____
7 Clement thanked Makie to the advice she gave him. _____
8 Denise asked to help her choose traditional local gifts for her family. _____

5 **A word is missing in each sentence. Choose the two correct options to complete each sentence.**

1 The presentation _____ me to do more to fight discrimination.
   a suggested   **c** recommended
   b persuaded   **d** convinced
2 My parents always _____ me not to believe stereotypes.
   a warned   **b** suggested   **c** advised   **d** insisted
3 My colleague _____ to forgetting to update the company's website.
   a confessed   **b** declared   **c** promised   **d** admitted

4 She _____ him for using offensive language and upsetting the guests.
   a blamed **b** criticized **c** refused **d** told

5 Max advised my brother to _____ working abroad as it was good for his resume.
   a offer   **c** carry on
   b consider   **d** claim

6 A family friend _____ that I learn to ignore people who make negative comments.
   a thanked   **c** recommended
   b suggested   **d** avoided

7 The news report _____ that Iceland was the best place to live if you were female.
   a claimed   **c** assured
   b told   **d** announced

8 My sister _____ to help me with my project on international co-operation.
   a encouraged   **c** insisted
   b offered   **d** promised

6 Rewrite the second sentence so that it has the same meaning as the first using the word in capital letters. Use between two and five words.

1 "You should be careful of believing stereotypes," he said.
He _____
stereotypes. WARNED

2 The speaker put forward the idea that we could learn from other cultures.
In the talk it _____
we could learn from other cultures. ARGUED

3 My parents didn't let me dye my hair when I was younger.
My parents _____
my hair when I was younger. REFUSED

4 Most modern companies want to employ people with good intercultural communication skills.
Most modern companies _____
people with good intercultural communication skills. INSIST

5 "You should go to a place if you want to understand the people," she said.
She _____ a
place to understand the people. SUGGESTED

6 Society should make companies react strongly to any discrimination in the workplace.
Companies should _____
strongly to any discrimination in the workplace. FORCED

7 Challenging social norms is a normal part of teenage years, scientists have said.
Scientists have _____
social norms is a normal part of teenage years. STATED

7 Put the words in order to make sentences.

1 threatened to / more cost-effective / dismiss workers / The company / to be / .
_____

2 I / to make / urge everyone / like-minded / would / friends / .
_____

3 notified us that / by email / the tickets / The company / had been sent / .
_____

4 discriminated against / He denied that / anyone / he had / .
_____

5 being called / She / a goth / resented / .
_____

6 for being / He thanked / well-mannered / the audience / so / .
_____

7 always asked / My / my clothes / to borrow / sister / .
_____

8 people / I / staying away from / would recommend / two-faced / .
_____

8 Complete the paragraph with these words.

announced	claimed	confess
deny	insist	persuade

Writers have recently (1) _____ that there is a new subculture among the country's youth: meet Seapunk, which is (2) _____ to be a mix of punk and pirates, and features the use of lots of marine colors. The followers of this new trend (3) _____ that it is completely original and (4) _____ being influenced by anyone. Instead they try to (5) _____ us that this new subculture grew from online sites. There is no denying that the movement is humorous and doesn't take itself too seriously. But, I must (6) _____ that it will be a while before I am brave enough to experiment with this new fashion.

9 Complete the sentences so they are true for you.

1 My parents warned me not to
_____

2 When people ask me about where to go in my hometown, I always advise them
_____

3 I was lucky my parents encouraged me
_____

4 When I was younger, I always tried to avoid
_____

5 Last week I asked
_____

6 I think it is wrong to criticize someone for
_____

8D Why I Keep Speaking up, Even When People Mock My Accent

TEDTALKS

AUTHENTIC LISTENING SKILLS

1 Listen to the extracts from Safwat Saleem's TED Talk and select which meaning of *just* he uses in each statement. 🎧 65

1 I just had to grunt a lot for that one.
   a soon   **b** simply   **c** exactly

2 I just sat there on the computer, hitting "refresh."
   a simply   **b** recently   **c** soon

3 This was just the first of a two-part video.
   a exactly   **b** only   **c** recently

4 I just could not do it.
   a exactly   **b** soon   **c** simply

5 if I stutter along the way, I just go back in and fix it.
   a simply   **b** soon   **c** only

6 And just the year before, that number was about eight percent.
   a soon   **b** exactly   **c** only

7 Just like the colour blue for Ancient Greeks, minorities are not a part of what we consider normal.
   a recently   **b** exactly   **c** only

WATCH ▶

2 Are the following statements true (T) or false (F)?

1 Saleem was self-conscious about his accent when he was a boy. ___

2 Saleem uses very different accents for each of his animated characters. ___

3 Saleem realized that people were reacting to his accent because they didn't think it was normal for an editor to have an accent. ___

4 At first, Saleem took the comments about his accent very personally. ___

5 Historical texts include more reference to colours than do modern texts. ___

6 Studies show that people are treated differently because of the expectations that we have. ___

7 Saleem says that it isn't enough to tell children they can do anything; we have to show them examples of people like them who have been successful. ___

8 Saleem says it is easy for him to be on stage. ___

3 Read the sentence and paragraph. Look at the places in the text marked by a, b, c, and d. In which place could the sentence be added to the paragraph? Choose a, b, c, or d.

And the most popular theory for why that might be the case is that cultures begin to recognize a colour only once they have the ability to make that colour.

Let me give you an example. I came across this story about the Ancient Greek writer, Homer. Now, Homer mentions very few colours in his writing. **(a)** And even when he does, he seems to get them quite a bit wrong. For example, the sea is described as wine red, people's faces are sometimes green and sheep are purple. But it's just not Homer. If you look at all of the ancient literature—Ancient Chinese, Icelandic, Greek, Indian, and even the original Hebrew Bible—they all mention very few colours. **(b)** So basically, if you can make a colour, only then can you see it. A colour like red, which was fairly easy for many cultures to make—they began to see that colour fairly early on. **(c)** But a colour like blue, which was much harder to make—many cultures didn't begin to learn how to make that colour until much later. They didn't begin to see it until much later as well. So, until then, even though a colour might be all around them, they simply did not have the ability to see it. **(d)** It was invisible. It was not a part of their normal.

VOCABULARY IN CONTEXT

4 Match each word with the sentence that shows its meaning.

1 somewhat constructive ___
2 breakdown ___
3 around ___
4 humorous ___
5 huge step ___
6 self-conscious ___

a Sometimes misunderstandings can lead to **funny** situations.

b Saleem has always felt a little **embarrassed** about the way he speaks.

c The comments people made about Saleem's accent were **a little helpful**, but also a little offensive.

d When I arrived at school, I was surprised not to see anyone **in the building or nearby**.

e Getting positive feedback from people who didn't know him was **a very important event** for Saleem to increase his self-confidence.

f Sometimes people have so many problems all at the same time that they get **anxious and upset and can't do anything**.

8E Agreeing, Disagreeing, and Challenging

SPEAKING

1 Match the expressions (1–8) with the explanations (a–h).

1 I'm in favour of the idea.
2 That's crazy.
3 I'm against the idea.
4 I'm totally for it.
5 I don't get what you mean.
6 From my point of view…
7 I mean…
8 Are we supposed to…

a I completely support that.
b What I think is…
c I don't agree.
d What I want to say is…
e I strongly disagree.
f Do we have to…
g I agree with that.
h I don't understand.

2 Complete the sentences with these words. Two options will not be used.

as a	for	from
I mean	I think	I'm in
it doesn't mean	it's crazy	just because
point of view	speaking as	totally supports

1 _____ that's how it was done in the past, _____ we have to do it that way now.
2 If you look at it _____ your parents' _____, you might see the matter differently.
3 _____ someone who has done it before, I don't think it's a good idea.
4 Everyone else _____ the proposal, but personally, I think _____.
5 _____ young person, _____ doing it this way has a lot of advantages.
6 There are a lot of reasons I'm for the idea. _____, first of all, it will help us save time.

3 Read the statements. Do you agree or disagree? Write your response and use these expressions.

I don't get that.	I totally support that.
I'm against the idea.	I'm in favour.
I'm totally for the idea.	That's crazy.

1 More people should adopt a vegetarian diet.
_____

2 Driving should be taught in schools.
_____

3 All universities should be free.
_____

4 Standardized tests should be eliminated.
_____

5 All schools should be bilingual.
_____

6 Art and music should be required subjects.
_____

4 Complete the conversation. Use one word in each space. Then listen and check your answers. 🎧 66

Kim: I was thinking of going to the cinema tonight.

Carlos: I'd be in (1) _____ of that.

Kim: Yeah…

Carlos: You sound a little uncertain. (2) _____ wrong?

Kim: Well, I suggested the idea to Adam, and he told me he doesn't want to come.

Carlos: Oh, I see. But (3) _____ because he's not into the idea, that (4) _____ mean we can't go, does it?

Kim: No, I suppose you're right.

Carlos: If you look at it (5) _____ his point of (6) _____, it makes sense. He's had quite a long week.

Kim: Yes, he has.

Carlos: I (7) _____, he must be pretty tired.

Kim: Well, even if he doesn't want to join us, (8) _____ you still want to go?

Carlos: Sure. I'm all (9) _____ it. What do you want to see?

Kim: How about watching a thriller?

Carlos: I (10) _____ support that idea. I love movies with a lot of suspense.

5 Choose one of the topics below. Think about how you would answer and make notes. Practice saying your response out loud. You should speak for one to two minutes and record yourself. Then listen to the sample responses. 🎧 67

1 Your best friend wants to go on a road trip this summer. You should say:
   • Whether you like this idea
   • Why you are in favour or against it
   • Where you would like to go

2 Your parents want you to get a part-time job. You should say:
   • Whether you like this idea
   • Why you are for or against it
   • What type of job you would like to get
   • What you will do if you don't get a job

WRITING A complaint

6 Match the sentence halves.

1 I am writing to complain about an offensive term ___
2 This is a matter that ___
3 Your article implied that most women are ___
4 While I value freedom of expression, ___
5 I realize it was meant as a joke, ___
6 As a student myself, I was very upset ___
7 I feel it is highly inappropriate ___
8 I would like you to ___

a should be taken very seriously.
b however, I feel it was irresponsible.
c publish a formal apology as soon as possible.
d I believe it is important to remain respectful.
e used in last night's broadcast.
f by your implication that all students are lazy.
g mean to each other, which is simply untrue.
h to make a claim such as this on a popular website.

7 Complete the complaint with these words and phrases.

as it suggests	however
I am writing to complain	I suggest
I would like you to	problems
stereotype	the attitude
There is a risk	While

Dear Sir/Madam,

1 _____ about an article on the issue of homelessness, which was published in your magazine last week. This article is extremely insulting to homeless people, _____ they are deliberately trying to ruin our towns and cities. It also implies that their _____ are entirely their fault and, furthermore, that they could easily improve their situation if they wanted to.

2 I was very distressed by _____ expressed in this article. With some students from my school, I was recently involved in a fundraising event for the homeless, and I learned how difficult their lives really are. _____ it might make us uncomfortable to see homeless people sleeping on our streets, it is important to remember that they are human beings, and many of their stories are heartbreaking.

3 I understand that this was an opinion piece, _____ , I feel it is irresponsible and dangerous to _____ homeless people in this way. _____ that it could make other readers lose sympathy for these disadvantaged people who need our help. In fact, it could even make residents angry towards the homeless.

4 _____ publish a revised version of the article, this time offering a more balanced view. In addition, _____ you make a donation to a homeless shelter to show your support for those in our society who are vulnerable.

Yours faithfully,
Kasia Baran

8 Read the complaint in Activity 7 again, paying attention to the paragraph numbers. Then read the list of points mentioned, and highlight the paragraph or paragraphs they appear in.

a where the article appeared   1 2 3 4
b the reason for complaining   1 2 3 4
c helping the homeless   1 2 3 4
d the effects the article could have 1 2 3 4
e specific problems with the article 1 2 3 4
f how the article made the writer feel 1 2 3 4
g what action the writer expects 1 2 3 4
h how the article represents the homeless 1 2 3 4

9 The chart below gives information about a survey carried out in one high school in Mexico, in Germany, and in Korea over a 30-year period. The survey shows how many students identified themselves with a sub-culture.

Summarize the information by selecting and reporting the main features, and make comparisons where relevant.

You should spend about 20 minutes on this task. Write at least 150 words.

Percentage of students who identified themselves with a sub-culture

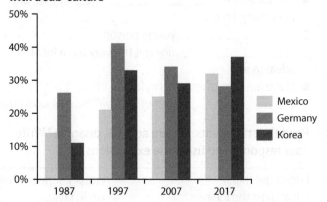

Review

1 Rewrite the sentences. Complete the sentences using the words in capital letters. Use between two and five words.

1 They need to resolve their differences.

They need to _____ . SORT

2 Your words upset me very much.

I _____ by your words. OFFENDED

3 She made a nice comment about my hair.

She _____ my hair. PAID

4 It's better to say that you're busy that day.

The _____ to say that you're busy that day. RESPONSE

5 They don't want me to go abroad.

They're trying to _____ abroad. DISCOURAGE

6 I didn't feel comfortable talking to the manager.

I _____ talking to the manager. AWKWARD

2 Complete the crossword.

Across

4 The children were quiet and polite. They were well-_____.

6 It is _____ to hire only people under age 50.

7 When she broke up with him, he was _____.

8 There is no _____ medicine against the common cold.

Down

1 We agree about everything. We are like-_____.

2 She told me one thing and my friend the opposite. She is very two-_____.

3 She said she liked my new dress and my shoes. She was very _____.

5 Not so long ago, women were _____ as housewives on TV.

3 Complete the reported statements with the verbs in parentheses. Some sentences have more than one correct answer.

1 Chul asked if I _____ (take) offence when he asked how old I was.

2 Chailai answered that it _____ (seem) unusual for no one to be at home.

3 Apo announced that he _____ (make) plans to visit his grandparents.

4 Anurak asked how the tourists _____ (react) when they saw the whale.

5 Ja-kyung observed that some people _____ (clap) to get his attention.

6 Wayna explained that she _____ (expect) everyone to help plan the trip.

4 Rewrite the sentences with the words in parentheses.

1 I avoid studying at the weekends.

_____

(*tell / you*)

2 I convinced her that seeing a doctor was a good idea.

_____

(*tell*)

3 He insists that studying in Cairo was a great experience.

_____

(*assure / his parents*)

4 We invited our friends to join us at the poetry reading.

_____

(*insist on*)

5 Did you tell him to study at the library after school?

_____

(*ask*)

5 Which sentence is closest in meaning to the original sentence?

1 He admitted telling her my secret.
  a He admitted that he had been telling her my secret.
  b He admitted that he told her my secret.

2 She denied that she had eaten all the cake.
  a She denied eating all the cake.
  b After eating all the cake, she wanted to deny it.

3 He reported that he had passed the test.
  a He told he passed the test.
  b He reported passing the test.

4 I propose that we take the train to Mumbai.
  a Perhaps we may take the train to Mumbai.
  b I propose taking the train to Mumbai.

9A In Times of Crisis

VOCABULARY Dealing with disaster

1 **Review** Read the email. Complete the sentences with these words.

disastrous	flooded	impact	level
rescued	saved	shelter	

Hi Nicole,

I just wanted to let you know that we're safe, but we've had a (1) _____ few days here. On Saturday, the sea (2) _____ just kept getting higher and higher. Eventually it (3) _____ the railway line. By noon the water had reached our house and we had to be (4) _____ in boats. We went to a (5) _____ and we spent the night there. However, the water has completely ruined the furniture in our house downstairs. The flood has had a terrible (6) _____ on the community. There are a dozen families whose homes couldn't be (7) _____ .

—Mark

2 **Review** Cross out the mistake in each sentence and write the correct word(s). One sentence has two mistakes.

1 Being an aid worker is a very challenge job.

_____

2 The work hours are sometimes longer.

_____

3 The job can be stress and demanding.

_____

4 You have to be flexibility and creative.

_____

5 If you feel a responsible to help people in need, this job might be reward for you. _____

3 Put the words in the correct order to make sentences.

1 The / destroyed / infrastructure / completely / was / city's / .

_____

_____

2 roads / The / blocked / main / were / .

_____

_____

3 The / struck / earthquake / center / the / city / .

_____

_____

4 a / gas / shortage / of / There / was / .

_____

_____

5 had / Volunteers / the / of / rebuilding / task / .

_____

_____

6 They / flee / tried / the / area / to / .

_____

_____

4 Choose the correct option to complete the sentences.

1 The earthquake led to widespread _____.
  a infrastructure
  b crisis
  c devastation
  d impact

2 The government evacuated _____.
  a the people
  b the debris
  c the food
  d the water

3 It is a serious _____.
  a aid
  b debris
  c strike
  d crisis

4 The charity _____ to the public for money.
  a asked
  b responded
  c reacted
  d appealed

5 The drought led to food _____.
  a limits
  b shortages
  c blocks
  d supplies

6 The government agreed to send _____ to the area.
   a charity
   b debris
   c aid
   d relief effort

7 People started to flee the _____ zones.
   a humanitarian
   b disaster
   c blocked
   d rescue

8 There was a _____ in the number of homeless people after the second earthquake.
   a shortage
   b strike
   c rise
   d drop

5 Match the sentence halves.

1 Helicopters dropped food	**a** international community.
2 There were food	**b** debris.
3 They had to first clear the	**c** relief effort.
4 The charity launched a	**d** supplies.
5 It damaged the	**e** infrastructure.
6 They asked for help from the	**f** shortages.

6 Circle the option that does not form a collocation.

1 The earthquake *fled / struck / devastated* the region.
2 The war led to a humanitarian *crisis / infrastructure / disaster*.
3 There were shortages of *roads / water / food*.
4 Helicopters dropped *debris / food / aid*.
5 The government launched *an appeal / a relief effort / an aid*.
6 There was widespread *infrastructure / destruction / devastation*.

7 **Extension** Complete the table.

Noun	Verb
devastation	
	destroy
	appeal
supplies	
	provide
	evacuate

8 **Extension** How many types of extreme weather and natural disaster do you know? Complete the crossword.

Across

4 A very large and destructive wave in the ocean
5 A sudden violent movement of the Earth's surface
6 A period of time when the weather is much hotter than is normal
7 When a large amount of water covers an area that should be dry

Down

1 A long period of very dry weather
2 A time when the electricity supply to an area is cut off
3 A storm with strong winds and heavy rain
6 Frozen rain

PRONUNCIATION

9 Listen to the sentences. Write the *-ing* word that you hear. Then practice saying the sentences. 🎧 68

1 _____
2 _____
3 _____
4 _____
5 _____
6 _____
7 _____

LISTENING

10 Listen to part of an interview at a disaster scene and answer the questions. 🎧 69

1 What does the captain say about the storm?
  a The strongest part of the storm is approaching.
  b The strongest part of the storm is happening now.
  c The strongest part of the storm is over.

2 What seems to be the biggest continuing problem?
  a flooding   **b** high winds   **c** casualties

3 What is the captain's advice for residents?
  a Get to a rescue centre quickly.
  b Stay in place if you're safe.
  c Go to the hospital for food and water.

4 Are there any rescue centres operating?
  a Yes, there are three.
  b None have opened yet.
  c So far, only the hospital.

5 What is the situation with casualties?
  a there are many life-threatening injuries
  b no injuries that she has heard of
  c no deaths have been reported

6 How is the hospital doing?
  a Luckily, it never lost power.
  b It's operating with a generator.
  c It's overwhelmed with injuries.

7 What does the captain say about the community?
  a It's pulling together.
  b It's restoring power.
  c It's clearing roads.

11 Listen to the talk about a tornado. Match the phrases you hear. 🎧 70

1 cost of the   **a** frame by frame
2 the loss   **b** and path
3 more questions   **c** was personal
4 destroyed everything **d** in its path
5 turn his grief   **e** damage
6 a storm's strength   **f** day and age
7 revealed   **g** into action
8 in this   **h** than answers

12 Listen to the talk again. From what you've heard, how would you best describe Anton Seimon? 🎧 70

a fatalistic and discouraged
b overwhelmed and overworked
c resilient and determined
d defeatist and dispirited

13 Listen again. Are the statements true (T) or false (F)? 🎧 70

1 It was the widest tornado ever recorded. ___
2 Seimon's vehicle was carried nearly a mile. ___
3 Seimon left the area because of his grief. ___
4 He decided to create a visual representation of the storm. ___
5 Seimon put the videos in order by time. ___
6 Seimon focused on the storm's strength and path. ___
7 Seimon hoped to inspire engineers with his work. ___
8 Seimon believes that deaths caused by tornados are inevitable. ___

GRAMMAR Relative clauses

14 Choose the correct relative pronoun to complete the sentences. Choose *x* if no pronoun is needed.

1 The students, *who / whose / who's / whom* were happy about missing a day of school, celebrated the news that a blizzard was expected last night.
2 The wind inside a tornado, *who / which / x* normally moves from southwest to northeast, blows in the opposite direction in the Northern Hemisphere.
3 The waves of a tsunami, *which / who / x* are caused by an underwater earthquake, can be as tall as 98 feet.
4 The blizzard *who / whom / x* they predicted dropped about three feet of snow and stranded people in their homes.
5 Hurricanes, like the one *that / who / x* hit New Orleans, can be more than 590 miles across.
6 Most of the survivors, *who / whose / who's / whom* homes were destroyed by the tornado, are now homeless.
7 More than 216,000 people in fourteen different countries died in the 2004 tsunami *that / who / x* occurred in the Indian Ocean.
8 We went to the parade for the rescuers, *who / whose / who's / whom* the president called heroes.

15 Choose the correct relative pronoun to complete the sentences.

1 The oil *whom / that* leaks into the environment is poisonous to both animals and plants.
2 The oil covers birds' feathers, *who / which* makes it difficult for them to maintain their body heat.
3 Animals *that / whom* accidently swallow the oil soon die from poisoning.
4 The animals *whom / that* are most affected by oil spills live on or near the shoreline.
5 Seabirds, *whom / which* are the most common victims of oil spills, can be washed and often survive oil spills.
6 Volunteers *which / who / whom* haven't been properly trained should not try to wash birds.

16 Combine the sentences into one sentence using a relative pronoun.

1 There is new technology. It was designed for use in disaster zones.

_____

2 Dr. Paul Gardner-Stephen is a computer researcher at a university in Australia. He developed a way for people to communicate after a natural disaster.

_____

3 He designed a new technology that lets people communicate by cell phone where there is no wireless network or the wireless network has been destroyed. It is called "mesh networking."

_____

4 In mesh networking, each phone sends and receives data for the whole network. The data could be text messages, phone calls, or files.

_____

5 Google started a drone program. The drones could deliver aid to hard-to-reach places.

_____

6 Google also developed project Loon. It is a way to provide internet connections to remote places with a network of high-altitude balloons.

_____

17 Put the words in the correct order to create sentences with relative clauses.

1 which / created / solar generator / Michael and Kenny Ham / is / the All Terrain Solar Trailer, / a / .

_____

2 that / in disaster areas / cameras and software / OpenRelief / a drone / will use / to identify and locate / people / is developing / .

_____

3 which / allows / The PLOTS spectrometer, / costs / people / about $10 / their drinking water, / to test / .

_____

4 which / can / terrain / carry / was invented / The Aid Necessities Transporter (ANT), / by Brian Lee, / supplies / over rough / .

_____

5 which / disaster aid / Anna Stork and Andrea Sreshta / makes / it / a solar-powered light, / easier / to distribute / created /.

_____

18 Cross out the mistake in each sentence and write the correct word. Each sentence contains one mistake.

1 Every eight minutes, the Red Cross, who responds to more than 60,000 disasters each year, responds to an emergency somewhere in the world.

_____

2 In 2013, the Red Cross, that has 97 million volunteers worldwide, helped 100 million people.

_____

3 When a disaster strikes, the Red Cross, which it opens shelters in disaster areas, ensures that people have somewhere to stay. _____
4 Red Cross health volunteers go to disaster areas to help people which need first aid, shelter and medical care.

_____

5 People whose volunteer with the Red Cross provide hot meals, snacks and water as part of emergency response.

_____

6 The Red Cross reunites families whom have been separated by natural disasters. _____

9B Bridges to Prosperity

VOCABULARY BUILDING *the + adjective*

1 Complete each sentence with *the* + one of these adjectives.

best	brave	old	poor
rich	traumatized	young	worst

1 Mental health experts were on the scene to help _____.

2 Many would argue that _____ have a moral responsibility to help _____.

3 Only _____ would dare enter such a disaster scene to rescue others.

4 The old saying goes, "Youth is wasted on _____."

5 In a real crisis you will encounter _____ and _____.

6 It was especially difficult for _____, who had lived there all their lives.

READING

2 Read the article and choose the best headings for paragraphs 1–4 from the list of headings below. You will not use all the headings.

Paragraph 1 ___
Paragraph 2 ___
Paragraph 3 ___
Paragraph 4 ___

a Destroying a Bridge
b An Organization Is Born
c Bridges Around the World
d It All Started with a Photo
e Donkeys Can Do It
f Innovate, Educate, Inspire

3 Answer the questions below. Use one word and/or one number from the article for each answer.

1 What word describes the way Ken thinks of himself? _____

2 What were the Ethiopians using to cross the river before Ken arrived? _____

3 What does Ken hope to create for people with his organization? _____

4 What kind of steel design was chosen for the bridge? _____

5 How were the bridge supplies transported to the site? _____

6 How many thousands of dollars did the first bridge cost? _____

7 What word describes the third part of the organization's strategy? _____

8 What kind of bridge did the organization construct in Indonesia? _____

4 Sentences a–g below have been removed from the article. Decide which sentence belongs in each gap. One sentence is extra.

1 ___
2 ___
3 ___
4 ___
5 ___
6 ___

a Being appropriate to the community is key—one size does not fit all.

b Ten men would stand on either side of the broken span and pull themselves across.

c In addition to local governments, it also works with other charitable organizations.

d Rural, isolated areas almost always have higher levels of poverty and disease.

e Happily, this "boy" owns a construction company.

f Additionally, both farming productivity and labour rates increase by more than 30%.

g "Now they can trade, get to hospitals and schools on the other side, and see family members they haven't seen for years."

Bridges to Prosperity

A suspension bridge in Nepal

1 Ken Frantz decided to fix an Ethiopian bridge because, he says, "I'm a boy, and boys love bridges." (1) Ken, 52 at the time, was waiting for mechanics to service a truck in his hometown of Gloucester, Virginia in the US, when he picked up an issue of *National Geographic* magazine. He saw a photo of Ethiopians being hauled on a rope across the Blue Nile river. (2) The 360-year-old bridge located there had been destroyed during the Italian occupation of 1935–1941. "I looked at the photo once, twice, three times," Ken recalls, "and it came to me: What I want to do is repair that bridge."

2 Having made his decision, Ken helped launch Bridges to Prosperity, an organization dedicated to building bridges to help create wealth in developing nations. The group surveyed the site, won backing from tribal elders, and chose a lightweight steel design. Donkeys carried in 25,000 pounds of supplies, and Ken, his crew, and Ethiopian volunteers rebuilt the bridge in ten days at a cost of $108,000, largely donated by the organization's founders. "Half a million people live near the bridge," he says. (3)

3 Bridges to Prosperity has three main strategies that determine where and how they build. First, build to innovate: Using local knowledge and materials, the bridges must be cost-effective and appropriate for the community. (4) Second, build to educate: Each project has to involve the community and local labourers to increase their knowledge of bridge building. Finally, build to inspire: Community members must take responsibility for the project, including providing volunteers for construction, and maintenance of the bridge after completion.

4 Bridges to Prosperity is a non-profit organization that works at the local level. (5) Since its founding, Bridges to Prosperity has built more than 200 footbridges in countries across Africa, Southeast Asia, and Central and South America—cableways in Nepal, a suspension bridge in Indonesia, and a second Ethiopian bridge. A study conducted by the University of Notre Dame found that bridge connectivity has a huge effect on rural communities and the people that live there. For example, the study concluded that each family's income increases by an average of 32%.
(6) The organization's central goal is the same today as when it started: to reduce poverty by eliminating rural isolation.

9C Ready to Help

GRAMMAR Participle clauses

1 Choose the correct option to complete the sentences.

1 Countries *affecting* / *affected* by disasters often need international aid.
2 Students *wanting* / *wanted* to help raise money for the appeal should meet in the library at 2pm.
3 I find it hard to watch news of disasters *including* / *included* images of children.
4 Donations *making* / *made* by the public will be sent to the victims of the earthquake.
5 Many countries give development aid to countries *damaging* / *damaged* by war.
6 The headquarters of the U.N., *basing* / *based* in New York, was set up in 1945.
7 There has been an increase in companies *investing* / *invested* in green technologies.
8 There has been a series of natural disasters *leading* / *led* to a food shortage.

2 Rewrite the sentences from Activity 1 using a full relative clause.

1 _____
_____
2 _____
_____
3 _____
_____
4 _____
_____
5 _____
_____
6 _____
_____
7 _____
_____
8 _____
_____

3 Read the article and then change the relative clauses in bold into reduced relative clauses.

Torrey Canyon

The *Torrey Canyon* was one of the largest oil tankers of its day when it was first built in 1959. It had a capacity of 66,000 tons, (1) **which was enlarged** to 132,000 tons in Japan. The ship, (2) **which was traveling** to Milford Haven, was full of oil, when it hit rocks off the coast of Britain. As soon as the ship started to break up, there was an attempt to prevent the oil escaping,

(3) **which included** the use of detergent. When this was unsuccessful the government decided to try to set fire to the oil. Jets from the air force dropped bombs (4) **that were filled** with fuel to start the blaze. These all failed because of the weather. Eventually the ship sank, but the oil damaged a lot of the coastal areas of the UK and northern France.

The chemicals (5) **that were used** often did more harm than good and the government was criticized. However, the disaster did lead to changes in the law and the mistakes (6) **that were made** did mean countries were better prepared for future disasters.

1 _____
2 _____
3 _____
4 _____
5 _____
6 _____

4 Read the sentences below and decide if they are correct or incorrect. Correct the sentences that are wrong.

1 Attending the UNICEF conference, the other students asked me all about it. _____
2 Wanted to remain neutral, the UN works with many countries and charities. _____
3 Providing role models to children globally, the youth assembly is an important project. _____
4 Having fleeing the disaster zone, many people find themselves homeless. _____
5 Watching the terrible news reports, people began sending donations. _____
6 Making money, the rich have a responsibility to give assistance when appeals are launched.
_____
7 Facing with an earthquake, I would leave my home.
_____
8 Working in a disaster zone, the rescuers were in danger. _____

5 Rewrite the second sentence so that it has the same meaning as the first using the word in capital letters. The answer will be between two and five words.

Example: He attended the conference, then returned to his university.
Having attended the conference, he returned to his university. HAVING

1 If I was forced to flee my home, I would take my diary with me.

_____,
I would take my diary with me. FORCED

104 Unit 9

2 They were totally exhausted so they had to abandon the search for survivors.

_____,
they had to abandon the search for survivors. EXHAUSTED

3 Because she was in an unfamiliar place, she felt nervous.

_____,
she felt nervous. BEING

4 He realized he had forgotten his conference notes after he left the room.

_____,
he realized he had forgotten his conference notes. LEFT

5 He took notes while he listened to the other delegates.
He took notes _____.
LISTENING

6 Because he lacked money, he decided to get a part-time job.

_____,
he decided to get a part-time job. LACKING

6 Read about a group of school friends who decided to become involved in charity. Complete the text with these phrases. Capitalize words as necessary.

after appointing	asking them to make donations
having decided	having done so
having met	raising half of the required funds
recently destroyed by fire	

(1) _____ in their first year at school, a group of students decided to do something to restore their local community center. The center, which had been (2) _____, was the home of many local groups. It was especially important to the older members of the community who used it as a place to meet. (3) _____ to try to raise money to rebuild the center, they began by holding a sponsored silence.
(4) _____, the event was a success. However, they then decided to become more serious. (5) _____ a committee, they tried to involve local businesses,
(6) _____. This proved successful and they soon reached their target, but
(7) _____, they decided to continue their work. So far the group has raised money for many projects based in the local area and abroad and it is a reminder to us all that we can all make a difference.

7 Complete these sentences with the correct form of the word in parentheses.

1 International response to disasters, _____ (cause) by extreme weather, is fast.

2 _____ (travel) to the disaster zone, he met other aid workers.

3 _____ (have) headquarters all over the world, it is a global company.

4 The Red Cross, _____ (set up) in 1881, provides emergency assistance to people in need.

5 _____ (join) the NGO, she was sent abroad where she helped to build infrastructure projects.

8 Complete these sentences so they are true for you.

1 Having finished school, I

_____

2 I love watching TV shows based on

_____

3 Studying a new language, I discovered that

_____

4 Using wireless technology, it is easier to

_____

9D (Re)Touching Lives Through Photos

TEDTALKS

AUTHENTIC LISTENING SKILLS

1 Listen to an extract from Becci Manson's TED Talk. Decide whether the intonation on the bold words is rising or falling. Choose the correct answer. 🎧 72

Once a **week** (1) (rising / falling), we would set up our scanning equipment in the temporary photo libraries that had been set up, where people were reclaiming their **photos** (2) (rising / falling). The older **ladies** (3) (rising / falling) sometimes hadn't seen a scanner **before** (4) (rising / falling), but within 10 minutes of them finding their lost **photo** (5) (rising / falling), they could give it to us, have it **scanned** (6) (rising / falling), uploaded to a cloud **server** (7) (rising / falling), it would be downloaded by a **gaijin** (8) (rising / falling), a stranger, somewhere on the other side of the **globe** (9) (rising / falling), and it'd start being **fixed** (10) (rising / falling).

WATCH ▶

2 Listen to the extracts from the TED Talk. Choose the correct answers. 🎧 73

1 What was Mason's profession?
   a a fashion model
   b a photo retoucher
   c a rescue worker

2 What had happened in Ofunato?
   a It had been devastated by the wave.
   b It had a large fish market.
   c 50,000 people had died.

3 What happened at the onsen?
   a People started taking baths at the onsen again.
   b The volunteers prepared a community dinner.
   c The volunteers collected the photos they had found.

4 What is a *gaijin*?
   a a stranger
   b a photo retoucher
   c a computer technician

5 Why does she compare cleaning photos to doing a tattoo?
   a because both are artistic
   b because both are permanent
   c because both use many colours

6 Which is NOT a reason Mason gives to explain the importance of photographs?
   a They are important legal documents.
   b They preserve people's memories.
   c They help people feel connected.

7 What does Manson say she learned from the project?
   a how difficult it is to recover from natural disaster
   b how similar people are in all parts of the world
   c how beautiful Japanese kimonos are

3 Put the statements about the photo retouching process in order.

___ **a** The photo retouchers worked very carefully on the photos—sometimes for weeks or months—to make sure that the photographs were restored to their original state.

___ **b** The volunteers realized that these photos must contain important memories for their owners, so they brought the photos to the onsen, where Manson was collecting them.

___ **c** Once the restoration was complete, the photos were returned to the families.

___ **d** People from the town came to the photo libraries to identify and reclaim their photos.

___ **e** As the volunteers cleaned up the debris from the giant wave, they found photo albums that people had lost when they fled their homes.

___ **f** Once the townspeople had reclaimed their photos, they scanned the photos and sent them to photo retouchers around the world.

___ **g** Very carefully, the team cleaned the photos.

VOCABULARY IN CONTEXT

4 Match the words with the sentences that show their meaning.

1 sirens_____   **4** globe_____
2 give it a go_____   **5** on the ground_____
3 struck a chord_____   **6** unfolded_____

a I'll never forget the events that **developed** that day.
b The police were **at the location of the problems** within 20 minutes.
c Sharon was afraid the problem would be too complex, but she decided to **try**.
d The **loud warning noise** from the ambulance woke the baby.
e People from all over the **world** went to Japan to help out after the tsunami.
f When she looked at the photographs of other people's families, she **felt an emotional connection** to those people.

9E Give It a Try

SPEAKING

1 Circle the option that correctly completes each expression.

1 Now, I know *which / what / about* you might be thinking…
2 I realize *there's / that's / have* a perception that…
3 I'm obviously not *to deny / denial / denying* that…
4 To begin *with / of / about*, consider the fact that…
5 On *above / top / plus* of that…
6 Let's *do not / not / cannot* forget that…
7 And finally, it's important *note / noting / to note* that…

2 Match the sentence halves.

1 Let's not forget that anyone ___
2 Among many people, there's ___
3 I'm obviously not denying the ___
4 To begin with, consider the fact ___

a fact that evacuations are difficult to carry out.
b that there are widespread food shortages.
c can be affected by a natural disaster.
d a perception that aid is mismanaged.

3 Put the story in order. Write the numbers 1–7 in the spaces provided. Use the <u>underlined expressions</u> to help you.

___ **a** <u>Now, I know you're probably thinking</u>, isn't that a difficult line of work?

___ **b** <u>On top of that</u>, I really feel like I'm making a difference. Very often, the people that I meet have lost everything.

___ **c** <u>Two years ago</u>, I decided to look for a job in disaster relief. Even though I didn't have very much experience, I was very motivated.

___ **d** <u>To begin with</u>, I organize food, clothing, transportation, and health services. Later, my team and I help people try to rebuild their lives.

___ **e** <u>It's important to remember that</u> anyone can be affected by a disaster. One day, we might need someone to help us, too.

___ **f** <u>I'm obviously not denying that</u> it's hard. It's very stressful at times. On the other hand, it's also very fulfilling.

___ **g** <u>Now I work as</u> an Emergency Response coordinator. When there is a crisis, my job is to get people the help they need as quickly as possible.

4 Complete the radio program with these expressions. Then listen and check your answers. 🎧 74

Let's not forget that	It's also important to
final points you want to note	I'm obviously not going to deny that
On top of	To begin with
what do you recommend	Now, I know what you
Today I want to speak to you	might be thinking
	it's too late

A: On today's show, we have the opportunity to speak to Angela Park. She is an expert in crisis management. Ms. Park, it's a pleasure to have you with us.

B: Thank you. (1) _____ about an important issue.

A: What's that?

B: The need to be prepared in the event of an emergency. (2) _____. Everyone already knows how important it is to be prepared!

A: Well, (3) _____.

B: The thing is, many people think they know what to do in a crisis, but when the time comes, they realize that they didn't take the necessary steps.

A: I see. And by then, perhaps (4) _____.

B: Exactly.

A: So, (5) _____?

B: (6) _____, all people should have a disaster supplies kit ready in their homes. (7) _____ essentials like food and water, people should stock batteries, flashlights and mobile phone chargers. (8) _____ a first aid kit is also extremely important.

A: I see.

B: (9) _____ keep a list of emergency telephone numbers written down somewhere. Often, people forget to do this, and then they have no way of getting in touch when they need help.

A: That makes a lot of sense. OK, and are there any (10) _____?

5 Read the questions below and make notes for how you would answer them. Then listen to sample answers and compare your ideas with them. 🎧 75

1 Lending a helping hand
   • Describe a time when you helped a friend or family member.
   • What did you learn from the experience?
   • How did the experience make you feel?
2 Community Service and Volunteer Work
   • Have you ever done this type of work?
   • Why did you decide to volunteer?
   • What did you learn from the experience?
3 Responding to Crises
   • What skills do you have that might be useful in a crisis?
   • What is the best way to help when a crisis happens?
   • How can we raise awareness when emergencies happen?

WRITING   A letter of application

6 Read the sentences from a letter of application. Then choose the correct option. Write (I) for Introducing a subject that you want to discuss or (E) for Explaining your suitability.

1 I believe I can make a difference because I'm very enthusiastic and I'm a fast learner. ___
2 With regard to qualifications, I took a first aid course at school last year. ___
3 I feel I would be suitable because I am hardworking and dependable. ___
4 As far as language skills go, my English is quite good, and I am also learning Japanese. ___
5 I'm also prepared to take on extra responsibilities because I believe it is very important to be flexible. ___
6 With regard to my availability, I finish my exams in late June. ___

7 Match the topics with the sentences from a young man's letter of application for a voluntary position.

1 basic information about himself ___
2 his personal traits ___
3 his plans for the future ___
4 his skills and experience ___
5 how he found out about the post ___
6 main reason for writing ___
7 requesting information ___
8 what he is doing now ___

a I'm writing in relation to the opportunity for volunteers to work at this year's film festival in Edinburgh.
b I came across the advertisement on your website today.
c I was wondering if you could send more details about the post, and instructions on how to apply.
d My name is Antonio Conti. I'm 18, and I'm from Naples in the south of Italy.
e I'm currently in my final year of high school.
f I have a positive attitude and I'm very organized. In addition, I have always been passionate about movies.
g In September I'll be starting at college.
h My level of English is very good, and I also worked at our local movie theater last summer.

8 Write the missing words to complete the letter of application for a voluntary post. The first letters have been provided for you.

Hello,
I'm writing in (1) r_____ (8-letter word) to the ad for (2) v_____ (10-letter word) to visit the elderly in our local hospital. I came across your ad on the community website. Please let me know what I need to do to
(3) a_____ (5-letter word).

My name is Lisa Liu. I'm 16, and I'm a student at the international high school in Beijing. As biology is my best subject, I would like to become a doctor in the (4) f_____ (6-letter word). I'm keen to volunteer for two reasons. (5) F_____ (5-letter word), I think this is a very worthwhile program, and I would like to do something nice for the elderly in our community. Second, I would value spending time in a (6) h_____ (8-letter word) environment and observing how patients are cared for. With (7) r_____ (6-letter word) to what I would (8) b_____ (5-letter word) to the program, everyone says I'm a very friendly person, and I believe that would make me a (9) s_____ (8-letter word) volunteer for hospital visits. In addition, I have quite a lot of confidence, so I find it easy to chat to others, and I enjoy hearing their stories. I'm also very reliable.
Although I don't have any formal (10) e_____ (10-letter word), when my aunt broke her leg last year, I visited her at home every day for a month and she said I was really good company.
I hope this convinces you of my suitability for the program, and I look (11) f_____ (7-letter word) to hearing from you soon.
Best wishes,
Lisa

9 Read Lisa Liu's letter of application in Activity 8 again. Is the information true (T), false (F), or not given (NG)?

1 This voluntary program is specifically for visiting old people in the hospital. ___
2 Lisa saw the ad on a community website. ___
3 She requests some information about applying. ___
4 Lisa is in her final year at high school. ___
5 She wants to be a doctor. ___
6 She would like to volunteer for the program because she has lots of free time. ___
7 Lisa spends some time describing her personality. ___
8 She also gives details of her past experiences as a hospital volunteer. ___

10 Write 140–190 words in an appropriate style.

In your English class you have been talking about community action against crime. Now your English teacher has asked you to write an essay.

There is a growing trend in community action against crime, where local residents volunteer to help tackle crime in their community. What are the advantages and disadvantages of community action against crime?

Notes

Write about **(1)** lower crime rates, **(2)** risk to participating residents, and **(3)** _____ (your own idea).

Review

1 Complete the sentences with the correct forms of these verbs.

block	evacuate	flee	flood
launch	rescue	rise	survive

1 Humanitarian aid workers _____ dozens of people in the community.
2 Women and children were _____ first.
3 The organization _____ an appeal for more funds.
4 The risk of disease has started to _____.
5 All of the residents _____ the earthquake.
6 Rising sea levels _____ the coastal area every year.
7 We tried to _____ the danger.
8 The army _____ the roads.

2 Complete the words in the sentences.

1 The earthquake had an i_____ on the whole city.
2 The worst-a _____ areas were by the coast.
3 Bridges and roads are part of a country's i_____.
4 The disaster z_____ was heavily damaged by the floods.
5 Everyone in the building died—there weren't any s_____.
6 There was a s _____ of drinking water.
7 The richer countries sent medical s_____.
8 Falling d_____ from the building made it dangerous.

3 Choose the correct word to complete the text.

For more than 40 years, Save the Whales has worked to educate people about how they can protect the ocean and the animals (1) *who / that* live in it. It was founded in 1977, by a mother and daughter (2) *who / whom* volunteered their time by handing out information about saving whales.

Save the Whales worked with other groups to stop the US Navy from exploding bombs in the Pacific Ocean. This has saved more than 10,000 marine animals, (3) *who / which* include whales, dolphins, and seals. It also supports a rescue boat, (4) *which / who* saves whales, dolphins, seals, and birds (5) *who/ that* are trapped in fishing nets.

Save the Whales is best known for its educational programs.

Scientists (6) *which / who* have studied the habitat and lives of marine animals teach these programs.

They teach students how they can take action to save whales and sea life. Save the Whales programs, (7) *which / who* more than 300,000 students have already participated in, are taught at many schools in California.

In 2015, Save the Whales was awarded the "Best of Seaside Awards for Environmental, Conservation, and Ecological Organizations" for the fourth year in a row, (8) *who / which* means it is now part of the Seaside Business Hall of Fame. In 2017, it was named a "top rated" nonprofit organization.

4 Are the words in bold correct or incorrect? Correct those that are incorrect. Use reduced relative clauses when possible.

1 People **lived** in Australia are called Australians. _____
2 A type of pastry **is calling** a doughnut is often served with coffee. _____
3 Tokyo is a city **who is famous** for its excellent subway and train lines. _____
4 We are grateful for people, **who are willing to help,** after a disaster. _____
5 Cyclones are storms **that** usually occur from late spring to early autumn. _____
6 I love **coffee which** many people in my country drink at breakfast. _____
7 My new shirt, **which I bought online,** fits perfectly! _____

5 Rewrite the sentence with a reduced relative clause.

1 When I was younger, I had a good friend. Her name was Megan.
_____
_____
2 There is a man reading by the pool. He is my father.
_____
_____
3 Many people went to the concert. It was held at the park.
_____
_____
4 Did you see the email? It was sent by Kailash.
_____
_____
5 I love the dress the girl who is walking ahead of us is wearing.
_____
_____
6 The boy who is riding the blue bike isn't looking where he's going.
_____
_____

10A Road to Recovery

VOCABULARY Illness and injury

1 Review Complete the sentences with these verbs.

absorb	beats	breathe	infect
pass	support	tastes	use

1 Veins do not allow substances to _____ through their walls.
2 Our lungs do not _____ all of the oxygen that we breathe in.
3 Over 200 bones _____ the body.
4 Mosquitoes _____ humans with malaria.
5 It is a myth that we only _____ 10% of our brain.
6 We _____ at different rates when we are asleep.
7 A newborn baby's heart _____ very fast.
8 Your tongue _____ food.

2 Review Choose the correct option to complete the sentences.

1 Nutrients are *absorbs / absorbed* from the food we eat.
2 Many types of *bacteria / bacterias* are good for the body.
3 She's got a lung *infection / infected*.
4 Taste, touch, and smell are examples of *sensories / senses*.
5 He had an irregular *heartbeat / heartbeats*.
6 There are three types of *muscular / muscles*.
7 The *digestion / digestive* system absorbs food.
8 The sense of *touch / touching* is extremely important when you can't see.

3 Match the two parts of the phrases.

1	control the	a	normal life
2	a head	b	intensive care
3	be in	c	injury
4	speech	d	therapy
5	be left	e	stomach
6	keep down	f	paralyzed
7	lead a	g	food
8	an upset	h	symptoms

4 Write these words in the correct column in the table.

antibiotics	bleeding	cancer
operation	physical therapy	stroke

Illness	Treatment

5 Choose the correct option to complete the sentences.

1 She's in a wheelchair because she's paralyzed from the *wrist / wheel / waist* down.
2 I've been out of *active / action / the act* since the accident.
3 It's dangerous to play with doors, you may *crash / slam / injury* your finger.
4 The infection cleared *up / out / off* after three weeks.
5 It's vital to detect cancer early before it *cures / prescribes / spreads* to other parts of the body.
6 She's *made / done / had* a full recovery.
7 After a week in the hospital, his chest *damage / infection / bleeding* was much better.
8 He had severe brain *damaged / damaging / damage* after the stroke.

6 Complete the crossword.

Across

2 Don't _____ about the bad things, only the good things.

3 I've broken my leg so I'm out of _____ for six weeks.

5 My grandfather can't walk anymore so he uses a _____.

8 The infection _____ to different parts of his body.

Down

1 They were able to _____ the illness early.

4 After the surgery, she was in _____ care for one week.

6 There is no _____ for the common cold.

7 She complained of _____ pains so she went to the hospital.

7 Extension Choose the correct words to complete the paragraph.

A stroke is a life-threatening medical (1) _____. There is increased risk of a stroke if you suffer from diabetes or high (2) _____ pressure. You should seek urgent treatment if you think someone is having a stroke. What are the main symptoms of stroke? The face, mouth, or eye may be (3) _____ on one side. A person may not be able to (4) _____ both arms. Your fingers, hands, or jaw may feel (5) _____. You might not be able to speak or your speech may be (6) _____. Any delay in seeking treatment will increase the risk of brain injury or a permanent (7) _____. In order to recover from a stroke, people often undergo a long period of (8) _____.

1 a symptom
  b sign
  c condition
  d injury

2 a blood
  b bleed
  c bleeding
  d bloody

3 a droops
  b drooped
  c drooping
  d a droop

4 a lift
  b carry
  c hold
  d hang

5 a normal
  b numb
  c dizzy
  d hurt

6 a slipped
  b stopped
  c slurred
  d paralyzed

7 a disabled
  b disabling
  c disable
  d disability

8 a habitat
  b rehabitat
  c habilitation
  d rehabilitation

8 Extension Put the words in order to make sentences.

1 attacks / disability / can / heart / cause / .

_____

2 the / his / felt / in / legs / numbness / patient / .

_____

3 conditions / from / he / suffers / medical / a range of / .

_____

4 hospital / people / the / rehabilitation / start / in / .

_____

5 became / her / slurred / speech / .

_____

PRONUNCIATION

9 Listen to these exchanges. Underline the auxiliary verb that is stressed for contrast. Then practice saying that sentence. 🎧 76

1 **A:** Are you saying that just so I don't worry?
   B: No, really, I am feeling better.

2 **A:** I'm sorry, but I really think he needs to see a doctor.
   B: But he has seen a doctor.

3 **A:** I think you need to take it slower. You were doing too much.
   B: You're wrong. I was taking it easy.

4 **A:** That's not good. You've been skipping your physical therapy.
   B: No, I haven't. I go every week.

5 **A:** They were insensitive to the situation. Rude, actually.
   B: No, they weren't. They were just upset.

6 **A:** It doesn't look to me like the injury is healing very quickly.
   B: But it is. It's much better than it was.

7 **A:** That store still hasn't installed a ramp for wheelchairs.
   B: No, they have installed it. I saw it yesterday.

8 **A:** Sometimes I think he doesn't even try.
   B: But he has tried. It's just very difficult.

LISTENING

10 Listen and complete the sentences with the missing word or phrase that you hear. Then practice saying the sentences. 🎧 77

1 The doctors believe she is capable of making a full _____.

2 The man was complaining of debilitating _____.

3 He was initially a little _____ to trying art therapy.

4 Rather than _____ more medications, can we try something else?

5 There is a growing _____ of brain injuries.

6 Some traditional doctors can be resistant to new _____.

11 Listen to the talk on brain injuries. What do you think would be the best title for this talk? 🎧 78

a The Art of Recovery
b An Impossible Diagnosis
c Broken Dreams, Lost Lives
d The Brain of an Artist

12 Listen again and choose the correct options. 🎧 78

1 What do these two soldiers have in common?
   a They both suffered arm and leg injuries.
   b They were together when a bomb went off.
   c They are both in the US Air Force.
   d Neither of them suffered visible injuries.

2 How does Major Hall describe himself?
   a injured, but he is still the same man
   b as not the same person he once was
   c not even feeling like a human being
   d able to forget the worst experiences

3 How many wars are mentioned?
   a two
   b three
   c four
   d five

4 What medical condition is not mentioned?
   a sleep disorders
   b headaches
   c seizures
   d stomach aches

5 What kind of treatment is being described here?
   a reading therapy
   b art therapy
   c writing therapy
   d physiotherapy

6 What does Major Hall compare his mask to?
   a painting
   b speaking
   c thinking
   d writing

13 Match the comments with the speakers. You can use the speakers more than once. Listen again if necessary. 🎧 78

1 "Most of my injuries are invisible, and the rest are hidden." _____

2 "I am just not the same human being as I used to be." _____

3 "I was wrong," _____

4 "I don't know why, but that's what needed to come out of me." _____

5 "… The artwork is like a printed page—it is there if you want to read it." _____
   a Staff Sergeant Robert "Bo" Wester
   b Army Staff Sergeant Perry Hopman
   c Army Major Jeff Hall

GRAMMAR Expressing past ability

14 Choose the best option to complete the sentences.

1 Jae-Hwa *could / managed to* lose some weight by eating less and exercising more every day—he looks great now!
2 Lena knew she *could / managed to* eat healthy snacks on her diet.
3 Jae-Hwa *could / managed to* read the nutrition facts labels on food.
4 Lena *could / was able to* choose foods with less sugar.
5 If Jae-Hwa *could / managed to* ride his bike to school instead of taking the bus, he could get more exercise.
6 Lena *was able to / succeeded in* get enough exercise by walking to and from school.
7 Jae-Hwa *could / managed to* get all of his homework done—and still sleep eight hours every night.
8 Lena *was able to / managed* lose 10 pounds thanks to diet and exercise.

15 Choose the correct options to complete the questions.

1 **A** *Could / Was* your friend *able to / manage* go back to school last week?
  B No. She still had a temperature, so her mother made her stay home.
2 **A** *Did / Was* he *able / managed* to play in the football game yesterday?
  B No. He had sprained his ankle, so he just watched the game.
3 **A** *Was / Did* she *able go / manage to go* to the party last night?
  B No, she was still feeling bad, so she decided to stay at home.
4 **A** *Did / Was* he *able / succeed* in talking to his doctor about the prescription?
  B Yes. He left several messages, and the doctor finally called him back.
5 **A** *Were / Did* the doctors *succeeded in / able to* cure his condition?
  B No, not yet. They're still researching new drugs that might be effective.
6 **A** *Could / Was* she *manage to walk / walk* around the school after her surgery?
  B Well, at first she needed to use a wheelchair, but after a while she was fine.
7 **A** *Did / Were* you *managed / able* to visit your grandmother in hospital this morning?
  B No. The nurses asked us to wait until tomorrow because she was very tired this morning.
8 **A** *Did / Was* your cousin *manage / able to* to find a physiotherapist near his house?
  B Yes, eventually. His new physiotherapist isn't that far away.

16 Choose the correct option to make the sentences negative. In some cases, both options are correct.

1 Guilherme _____ raise his arm after his bicycle accident.
  a couldn't   **b** didn't manage
2 Guilherme _____ or write with his left hand after the accident.
  a couldn't draw   **b** wasn't able to draw
3 Luiza _____ take the test on Friday because she was ill.
  a wasn't able to   **b** didn't manage
4 Luiza _____ work as a lifeguard at the pool because she didn't do the first aid course.
  a couldn't   **b** wasn't able to
5 Henrique couldn't focus during the game and _____ in scoring a goal.
  a didn't manage   **b** didn't succeed
6 Henrique _____ to exercise last week because of his sore muscles.
  a didn't manage   **b** couldn't
7 After she fell, Ester _____ to walk to the school nurse's office.
  a wasn't able   **b** didn't manage
8 Ester _____ go on the school trip.
  a didn't manage to   **b** couldn't

17 Complete the questions with the correct form of the verbs in parentheses.

1 **A:** What was the first medicine people _____? (could, buy)
  B: Aspirin was the first medicine you could buy. Felix Hoffman created it from a chemical in willow bark in 1899.
2 **A:** When _____ companies _____ aspirin as tablets? (be able to, manufacture)
  B: The first aspirin was a powder, but they were able to make it into a tablet in 1900.
3 **A:** How many chemical compounds _____ scientists _____ in coffee? (manage to, identify)
  B: Scientists have managed to identify more than 1,000 chemical compounds in a cup of coffee. Together they make up the special flavor of coffee.
4 **A:** How _____ doctors _____ a cure for smallpox in the last century? (succeed in, find)
  B: They didn't cure the disease, but it was eradicated due to the success of vaccinations.
5 **A:** When _____ doctors _____ blood transfusions? (be able to, give)
  B: The first transfusion of human blood was in 1818.

10B Medical Possibilities

VOCABULARY BUILDING Dependent prepositions

1 Complete the sentences with these words. Pay attention to the preposition that follows each of them.

aimed	awareness	capable	chance
devoted	resistant		

1 You're in great shape. I think you have a good _____ of finishing the marathon.

2 She's done a great job of raising _____ of that illness.

3 With all the new technology, who knows what we're _____ of doing.

4 I'm usually _____ to change at first. It takes me a while to get used to things.

5 His life has been _____ to helping those less fortunate.

6 The campaign against smoking is especially _____ at young people.

READING

2 Read the article and choose the correct options.

1 The word "devoted" in paragraph 1 could best be replaced by
  a enthusiastic   **c** dedicated
  b caring   **d** affectionate

2 The word "justify" in paragraph 2 is closest in meaning to
  a support   **c** produce
  b explain   **d** question

3 The word "sightless" in paragraph 2 could best be replaced by
  a eyeless   **c** sighted
  b deaf   **d** blind

4 The word "function" in paragraph 3 could best be replaced by
  a behavior   **c** work
  b performance   **d** service

5 In stating "… the immune system restrains itself…," the author means that the immune system
  a holds back   **c** calls out
  b moves forward   **d** stays on

6 The word "privileged" in paragraph 4 is closest in meaning to
  a unfortunate   **c** private
  b explained   **d** advantaged

7 In stating "Gene therapy offers the promise…," the author means that gene therapy
  a gives hope   **c** provides confirmation
  b guarantees   **d** suggests

3 According to the article, are the following statements true (T), false (F), or not stated (NS)?

1 More than 200 million people on Earth are blind. ____

2 Medical advances in ending blindness are promising. ____

3 The eye acts as a kind of laboratory for the body. ____

4 A "control" gives you valuable perspective on what you're doing. ____

5 If something is "immune privileged" it makes things more complicated. ____

6 Unlike the eye, the brain is not "immune privileged". ____

4 Read the article again. For the following questions, choose the answer that you think fits best according to the text.

1 In the first paragraph, what is the author's main point?
  a the worsening global blindness problem
  b the severe limitations of people who are blind
  c the heavy cost of global vision loss
  d the unfair burden on the relatives of the blind

2 How many new medical treatments does the author mention?
  a two   **c** four
  b three   **d** five

3 What is another way to say "bionic"?
  a implanted   **c** electronic
  b advanced   **d** biomedical

4 What does the author suggest about new treatments for the eye?
  a They are specific to the eye because of its uniqueness.
  b They may lead to treatments for the entire body.
  c Some treatments are promising, but a lot more time is needed.
  d They are limited because it's hard to find a control.

5 We can infer from what the author says that the immune system
  a usually attacks invaders in organs of the body.
  b has a much stronger response in the eyes.
  c attacks inflammation in the organs of the body.
  d makes gene therapy problematic in the eyes.

6 We can infer from the text that neuroscientists' main focus of work is
  a the eyes.   **c** the brain.
  b the organs of the body.   **d** the immune system.

7 What is the promise of biomedical implants?
  a replacing eyes   **c** replacing genes
  b replacing bodies   **d** replacing organs

A Cure in Sight

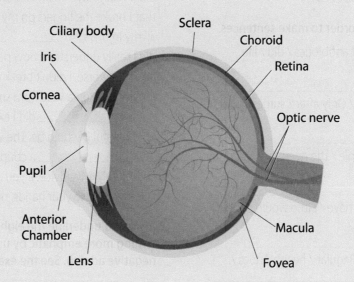

Ciliary body
Sclera
Choroid
Iris
Retina
Cornea
Optic nerve
Pupil
Anterior Chamber
Macula
Lens
Fovea

1   Roughly one in every 200 people on Earth—39 million of us—can't see. Another 246 million have poor vision, which is serious enough that it complicates their lives. Vision loss also affects hundreds of millions more people, often relatives, devoted to helping their family members who can't see.

2   These problems alone justify the search for new treatments. Within roughly the past decade, efforts in gene-replacement, stem cells, and biomedical, or "bionic," implants have given at least some sight to people previously sightless. These advances encourage talk of something unthinkable just 10 or 20 years ago: ending human blindness, and soon.

3   Yet the eye is also getting increased attention because it provides a safe, available place to test treatments that might also be used elsewhere in the body. To start with, researchers can look directly into the eye to see what's wrong and whether a treatment is working. Likewise, the patient can see out of the eye (or not), providing a quick, important measure of function. The eye also offers feedback such as pupil dilation* or electrical activity in the optic nerve. In addition, a researcher running an experimental treatment on one eye can usually use the other as a control. In an experiment, a control is something that doesn't change so you can compare the effects of the treatment against it.

pupil dilation *when the pupil in the eye becomes larger*

4   The eye is also tough. Within the eye's round shelter, the immune system restrains itself in a way that makes the eye "immune privileged." This means that the eye doesn't react with inflammation like other organs. Therefore, it is safer to try a treatment in the eye, such as gene therapy, which might cause major problems elsewhere in the body.

5   Neuroscientists like the eye because "it's the only place you see the brain without drilling a hole," as one put it. The retina, visible through the pupil, is basically a bowl of nerve cells tied to the brain by the optic nerve; the eye as a whole is an "outpouching of the brain," formed as a baby develops, by stretching away from it. Like the eye, the brain enjoys immune privilege, so treatments that work in the eye may readily transfer to the brain or spinal cord.

6   These advantages take on extra importance because experimental strategies now focused on the eye may advance future treatments for the whole human body. Gene therapy offers the promise of fixing faulty genes that cause illnesses of all kinds. Stem cells offer the promise of replacing entire body parts; bionic implants may replace failing organs. The eye is becoming a window to the possibilities—and limits—of healing methods on which medicine's future may depend.

10C Medical Advances

GRAMMAR Emphatic structures

1 Put the words in the correct order to make sentences.

1 increased / The invention of antibiotics / did / life expectancy / lead to /.

_____

2 the invention of antibiotics / Only after / surgery / did / become more common /.

_____

3 new treatments / have people / the need for / Not until recently / realized /.

_____

4 the negative effect / would have / Little would people / fast food / have guessed /.

_____

5 your / exercise / improve / Regular / health / does /.

_____

6 all the improvements / little did / in medicine / As a child, / I imagine /.

_____

7 most diseases / are invented / will we / be able / Not until / to cure / new drugs /.

_____

8 has there been / of penicillin / a luckier accident / Rarely / than the discovery /.

_____

2 Choose the correct option to complete the sentences.

1 Little *did / do* she realize how much exercise would change her life.
2 In no way *was / am* I ready for the news the doctors gave me.
3 Rarely *have / do* I seen such a fast recovery.
4 Only after my leg *had / have* healed could I walk without pain.
5 At no time when I was a child *did / could* I want to be a doctor.
6 Not until I graduated from medical school *was / am* I allowed to diagnose patients.
7 Nowhere in the world *is / are* healthcare so cheap.
8 Only when I found out I was cured *can / could* I relax.

3 Complete the paragraph with these words and phrases.

did	in no way	little
not only	only after (2x)	

I've always been quite a sporty person, but I have also often had accidents while playing sport. (1) _____ have I had bumps and bruises, but I have also had a few breaks. Most of these were fairly minor, for example, when I broke my fingers. While it (2) _____ hurt, (3) _____

did it really have an impact on my everyday life. I was lucky that I broke the fingers on my left hand. In fact, despite all my injuries, (4) _____ breaking my toe did I really understand how painful broken bones could be. Even worse, I didn't break my toe playing sport, I broke it trying to stop a vase from smashing on the floor. (5) _____ did I expect as I stuck out my foot how painful it would be. The vase broke anyway and (6) _____ a couple of months did the pain go completely. My advice: if you are going to try and catch a falling vase, use your hands, not your feet!

4 Read and underline the eight structures that make the writing more emphatic by using either the verb *do* or a negative adverb. See the example.

Cystic Fibrosis

Cystic Fibrosis was first discovered in 1938. It is a disease that affects all sufferers differently, but it has some common symptoms. For example, not only are people with *CF* more likely to get chest infections, but many also cannot digest food without medication.

For many years, being diagnosed with *CF* did mean a shorter life. These days, it is different. Little can they have imagined when it was first discovered the changes that would happen in the next century. Even when I was growing up things were different. Not until I was ten was I allowed to eat chocolate after new drugs were developed. To be honest, when I was younger, I didn't really think much about my illness. Rarely did it make much of a difference to my life. Only after I was sick when I was 16 did I begin to think about it more.

These days, although I have to take a lot of medication, I also know that without CF, I would not be me. So, rarely do I let it get me down. Also, in recent years the treatment has got so much better, and despite there being no cure, the medication does let me lead a pretty normal life.

1 *not only… but also*
2 _____
3 _____
4 _____
5 _____
6 _____
7 _____
8 _____

5 Rewrite the second sentence so that it has the same meaning as the first using the word in capital letters. Use between two and five words including the word given.

1 As he checked the results he didn't expect what he found.
Little _____
found when he checked the results.   DID

2 They only found a cure after testing many plants.
Only _____
they find a cure.   AFTER

3 It is unusual for patients to recover completely.
_____
completely.   RARELY

4 He was not at all to blame for the accident.
In _____
blame for the accident.   WAY

5 I didn't understand anything they were discussing in the program.
At no _____
what they were discussing in the program.   DID

6 People live longer in Japan than anywhere else.
Nowhere _____
in Japan.   DO

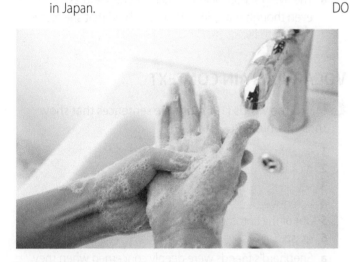

6 Read the paragraph and think about how the numbered sentences could be made more emphatic. Rewrite the emphatic phrases using the words and phrases below.

Clean Hands Stop Disease

(1) Most people don't know what a huge difference washing your hands could make to your health. However, dirty hands have been found to be one of the biggest spreaders of infections. A World Health Organization survey has shown that (2) most people don't wash their hands very often and they also don't use soap. (3) This area of the country seems to be the worst for hygiene. So we are here to tell you to wash, soap, dry. (4) Then we will have improved health.

1 Little _____
_____

2 Not only _____
_____

3 Nowhere in _____
_____

4 Only _____
_____

7 Complete these sentences so they are true for you.

1 Not only do I _____, but I also _____

2 Only after I finished _____, did I _____.

3 Not until I was _____, did my parents let me _____.

4 In no way am I a fan of _____
_____

5 Rarely do I have time to _____
_____

6 Only when I have _____, am I able to _____

10D A Broken Body Isn't a Broken Person

TEDTALKS

AUTHENTIC LISTENING SKILLS

1 Listen to the extract from Janine Shepherd's TED Talk. Write down three key adjectives she uses and three key nouns. 🎧 80

Adjectives:	Nouns:
1 _____	1 _____
2 _____	2 _____
3 _____	3 _____

WATCH ▷

2 Choose the option that best completes the sentences.

1 Before her accident, Shepherd was a competitive
  a cyclist.
  b cross-country skier.
  c pilot.

2 Before her accident, Shepherd had dreamed of
  a becoming a pilot.
  b moving to New York City.
  c competing in the Olympics.

3 The doctors told her that her back
  a had been crushed.
  b would recover completely.
  c was only slightly damaged.

4 In the acute spinal ward, Shepherd
  a became depressed because she had no one to talk to.
  b learned about the possibility of flying school.
  c formed close friendships even though she couldn't see the people she was talking to.

5 When Shepherd went home from hospital, the nurse warned her
  a that she would become depressed.
  b that she would miss her friends in the hospital.
  c that she should be very careful in her wheelchair.

6 Maria was Shepherd's friend in the hospital who
  a had also been a skier.
  b always had a positive attitude.
  c encouraged her to try flying.

7 During her first flying lesson, Shepherd
  a was not allowed to touch the controls.
  b regretted signing up for the lesson.
  c flew over the spot where she'd had her accident.

8 Shepherd's parents
  a also got their pilot's licences.
  b have never been up in the plane with her.
  c told her she should just accept her circumstances.

3 Choose the correct option to complete the sentences and add emphasis to their meaning.

1 When Shepherd started her training ride that day, *little / small* did she know that her life would change.

2 Even though Maria could hardly move, *in no time / at no time* did she lose her positive attitude.

3 While the doctors *did / do* try everything they could, they did not believe Shepherd would walk again.

4 It was *only after / in no way* Shepherd's accident that she decided to learn to fly.

5 *In no way / Not until* Shepherd had received her aerobatics licence was she satisfied with her progress.

6 *Nowhere else / Rarely* had Shepherd been in a situation where she formed deep friendships without ever seeing the people she was talking to.

7 While Shepherd had worked hard in her Olympic training, *never before / little* did she have to overcome emotional obstacles as she did after the accident.

8 The flying school *does / did* accept Shepherd as a student, even though many instructors doubted that she would be able to fly.

VOCABULARY IN CONTEXT

4 Match the words (1–6) with the sentences that show their meaning.

1 superficial _____
2 nickname _____
3 set _____
4 extensive _____
5 out of my comfort zone _____
6 grasp _____

a Shepherd's friends were deeply concerned when they learned about **the large number and different types** of injuries that she had resulting from the accident.

b It took a long time for Shepherd to truly **understand** how much her life had changed.

c Suddenly, the things that used to worry her seemed **silly and unimportant**.

d Shepherd's friends often called her by **a special name** that reflected her strength and perseverance.

e Before the accident, Shepherd's focus and her training were **fixed** on competing in the Olympics.

f Shepherd realized that one of the most important things she could do to help her recovery was to spend time **doing things that were difficult for her in unfamiliar situations**.

10E Developing the Conversation

SPEAKING

1 Choose the correct response to each statement

1 Last week I had a cold, but now I'm much better.
- **a** I'm thinking of you.
- **c** You must be fed up.
- **b** I'm glad to hear that.

2 Sara hasn't been feeling well recently.
- **a** Tell her I'm thinking of her.
- **b** That's really good news.
- **c** Apparently she's not well.

3 The doctor told me that I need physical therapy.
- **a** That's awesome.
- **c** You're kidding!
- **b** Say "hi" from me.

4 The antibiotics are quite expensive.
- **a** Oh no! **b** Wow, that's cool! **c** Amazing!

5 Luckily, the infection hasn't spread.
- **a** Poor you.
- **c** That's good news.
- **b** Are you OK?

6 Julian has been ill for weeks.
- **a** I know. I'm not kidding.
- **b** I heard he was in the hospital.
- **c** Yes, apparently he's been ill.

2 Listen to the conversations. Decide if the second speaker is surprised, sympathetic or if he or she wants to pass on a message. Circle the correct answer. 🎧 81

1 surprised	sympathetic	passing on a message
2 surprised	sympathetic	passing on a message
3 surprised	sympathetic	passing on a message
4 surprised	sympathetic	passing on a message

3 Read the sentences. Write a response in the space provided. Use these expressions to help you.

You're kidding!	Oh no!	Wow, that's great!
Awesome!	Poor guy/girl!	Say "hi" from me.
No, what happened?	Is he/she OK?	

1 Did you hear about Veronica?

_____

2 My wallet was stolen this afternoon.

_____

3 Apparently Yumi has a new job.

_____

4 Did you hear the news? Peter has broken his leg.

_____

5 You'll never guess what happened. I got a raise!

_____

6 I'm seeing Jordan this afternoon.

_____

4 Complete the conversation. Use one word in each space. Then listen and check your answers. 🎧 82

Jack: Have you (1) _____ the news?
Linda: No, I haven't. What (2) _____?
Jack: (3) _____ the class is cancelled.
Linda: You're (4) _____! How come?
Jack: Nobody seems to know.
Linda: I (5) _____ Ms. Davis's dog has been ill. (6) _____ she had to go take care of him.
Jack: (7) _____ Ms. Davis!
Linda: She lives near me. Maybe I'll knock on her door and see if she's (8) _____.
Jack: That's a good idea. If you go, will you (9) _____ her I'm (10) _____ of her?
Linda: Of course.

5 The following photos show people who are ill. Make notes about how you think the people are feeling. Then, speak about the photos, and make comparisons, for one minute. Record yourself.

1

2

Listen to a student compare the photos. 🎧 83

Is this response similar to what you would say? Add to the ideas in your notes if you need to.

Now make notes about the following questions.

- Which person do you think feels worse? Why?
- When you are ill, what do you do to try to make yourself feel better?

Now listen to the sample answers. Add to your answers as necessary. 🎧 84

WRITING A success story

6 Read the sentences. Is this how you felt before succeeding (B) or after succeeding (A)?

1 I'd tried absolutely everything. _____
2 It was a day that changed my life. _____
3 It was a moment I'll never forget. _____
4 It was a truly memorable experience. _____
5 It was the best day of my life! _____
6 I was absolutely terrified. _____
7 I was ready to just give up. _____
8 I was sure I was going to fail. _____

7 Choose the most descriptive verb to complete each sentence.

1 I _____ as quietly as possible from the living room to the front door.
  a crept   **b** walked   **c** ran

2 "Somebody, HELP! I can't swim!" I _____.
  a said   **b** asked   **c** screamed

3 Wasting no time, the firefighters immediately _____ inside the building!
  a went   **b** rushed   **c** walked

4 I _____ the door as hard as I could, and then called the police.
  a shut   **b** closed   **c** slammed

5 Suddenly, a large dog _____ over a garden fence and began to chase me!
  a stepped   **b** leapt   **c** moved

6 I was too frightened to stay there so I _____ my backpack and ran back to town.
  a took   **b** picked up   **c** grabbed

8 Put the missing sentences in the correct places to complete the success story.

> (1) ___ When my friends all went swimming, I'd pretend I didn't feel like it. No one knew I couldn't swim because I was too embarrassed to tell them.
>
> Then, my best friend got an extraordinary graduation present: a boat trip for a full week! Everyone in our group of friends was invited and we were thrilled. (2) ___
>
> I didn't want to miss out, so I secretly started taking swimming lessons. (3) ___ Once, when my feet couldn't touch the bottom, I panicked! (4) ___
>
> My instructor was patient, but after several lessons I was ready to give up, and then a strange thing happened. I got into the pool

> one day and I actually liked how the water felt. (5) ___ It was a moment I'll never forget. It felt amazing! Soon after that, I was able to swim, very slowly at first, but then with more confidence. (6) ___ Our boat trip is next month, and I can't wait!

a The next thing I knew, I was floating.
b The first few times I went to the pool I was terrified.
c Now I love it.
d I've always been scared of water.
e But there was a rule… you had to know how to swim.
f I was screaming, believing I was going to drown.

9 Listen to a lecture. Then read the text. Write an essay summarizing the points made in the lecture you just heard, explaining how they cast doubt on points made in the reading. 🎧 85

If you think we're at our peak in terms of medical science, think again. Thanks to science and technology, we now have driverless cars, space travel, and the internet… but medical developments seem to be moving at a very slow pace indeed.

True, we have better machines than we used to have, but how many people can afford the best medical treatments and procedures, which are usually the most expensive. The true picture in many countries is that health services are struggling to cope due to lack of resources. Hospitals are overcrowded and staff can barely cope with demands. In this day and age, we should have much better systems in place.

And while vaccines have revolutionized modern medicine, how long ago was the last one discovered? And it is well-known that antibiotics are losing their efficiency as we are seeing more and more superbugs that can resist them. So why aren't scientists developing medicines and cures at a faster rate?

With all of today's technology and awareness, we should be the picture of health, but are we? According to the World Health Organization (WHO), heart disease is the number one cause of death worldwide, and that is particularly shocking given that many of those conditions are lifestyle-related. Levels of stress are also rising globally, especially stress in the workplace. And, today, one in four people suffers with a mental health issue.

So, while it may be true that we can now treat many diseases, we are certainly not preventing or curing enough of them.

Review

1 Rewrite the sentences. Complete the sentences using the words in capital letters. Write between two and five words.

1 I'm fit again now.
I'm _____. BACK

2 I've fully recovered.
I've _____. MADE

3 There isn't any permanent damage after the accident.
The accident _____ any permanent damage. LEFT

4 He couldn't do anything for a few weeks.
He _____ for a few weeks. ACTION

5 He's like he was before.
He's _____ now. BACK

2 Complete the sentences with these words.

care	cure	infection	injury
physical therapy	prescribe	stroke	wheelchair

1 Many athletes have _____ following an injury.

2 Scientists are still searching for a _____ for cancer.

3 A _____ is when the blood supply to the brain is damaged.

4 Doctors _____ antibiotics and drugs to patients.

5 She had a chest _____ and couldn't go swimming.

6 Football players with a serious _____ usually come off the field.

7 He was in intensive _____ after the car accident.

8 He lost the use of his legs and needs to use a _____.

3 Find and correct the mistakes in the sentences.

1 My mother is very strong; she managed walk a short distance the day after her surgery. _____

2 The patient made a miraculous recovery and was able leave the hospital after a few days. _____

3 The doctor couldn't found the cause of the infection, so she prescribed antibiotics. _____

4 The doctor succeeded curing the patient with an experimental treatment. _____

5 We couldn't to meet with the doctors because one of them was with another patient. _____

6 The athletes managed to can avoid injuries by stretching and warming up before each race. _____

7 From the x-ray, the doctor could be able to see that her arm was broken. _____

8 I didn't managed to get to the prescription from the pharmacy before it closed. _____

4 Complete the sentences with these words and phrases.

are	can	is
little did we know	must	may be

1 _____ that antibiotics could usher in a new age of superbugs.

2 Patients who _____ infected by a superbug are separated from other patients.

3 People _____ pick up superbugs when they go to hospital for another issue such as a broken leg.

4 Superbugs _____ sometimes found in public areas such as gyms and schools.

5 Superbugs _____ be considered to be a major threat to public health.

6 One strategy that _____ impacting the war on superbugs is educating people about not asking for antibiotics every time they feel ill.

5 Write the words in the correct order to make sentences with negative adverbs and phrases.

1 have / I / last night / a concert / as / much / enjoyed / as / rarely / I / did /.
_____

2 did / he / know / we / little / were / a / surprise party / for / his / sixteenth birthday / planning /.
_____

3 realize / bought / only / couldn't / after / I / the tickets / did / I / I / go / to the movie /.
_____

4 end up / at / no / did / think / I / time / I'd / in / the / hospital / of / a bite from a spider / because /.
_____

5 better / else / in / our / sells / ice cream / nowhere / than / my uncle's shop / town /.
_____

6 underestimate / in / should / way / you / the / of / a good education / importance / no /.
_____

UNIT 6

Review

climate change (n)	/'klaɪmət ˌtʃeɪndʒ/
drought (n)	/draʊt/
environmental (adj)	/ɪnˌvaɪrən'mentəl/
expedition (n)	/ˌɛkspə'dɪʃən/
fishing (n)	/'fɪʃɪŋ/
global warming (n)	/'gloʊbəl 'wɔrmɪŋ/
greenhouse effect (n)	/'grin,haʊs ɪ'fɛkt/
protect (v)	/prə'tɛkt/
route (n)	/rut/
save (v)	/seɪv/
waste (v)	/weɪst/
wild (adj)	/waɪld/

Unit Vocabulary

administration (n)	/ədˌmɪnə'streɪʃən/
agriculture (n)	/'ægrɪˌkʌltʃər/
alarming (adj)	/ə'lɑrmɪŋ/
anger (n)	/'æŋgər/
arise (v)	/ə'raɪz/
assess (v)	/ə'sɛs/
breed (v)	/brid/
capture (v)	/'kæptʃər/
catch on (phr v)	/'kætʃ 'ɒn/
characteristic (n)	/ˌkærɪktə'rɪstɪk/
chase (v)	/tʃeɪs/
clue (n)	/klu/
compensate (v)	/'kɒmpənˌseɪt/
concern (n)	/kən'sɜrn/
consequence (n)	/'kɒnsɪˌkwɛns/
conservation (n)	/ˌkɒnsər'veɪʃən/
constantly (adv)	/'kɒnstəntli/
cure (n)	/kjʊər/
die out (v)	/'daɪ 'aʊt/
diversity (n)	/dɪ'vɜrsɪti/
domestic (adj)	/də'mɛstɪk/
emotion (n)	/ɪ'moʊʃən/
endanger (adj)	/ɛn'deɪndʒər/
ensure (v)	/ɛn'ʃʊər/
equivalent (adj)	/ɪ'kwɪvələnt/
extinct (adj)	/ɪk'stɪŋkt/
fake (adj)	/feɪk/
feature (n)	/'fitʃər/
fox (n)	/fɒks/
gene (n)	/dʒin/
genetic (adj)	/dʒə'nɛtɪk/
growth (n)	/groʊθ/
habitat (n)	/'hæbɪˌtæt/
historian (n)	/hɪ'stɔriən/
hunt (v)	/hʌnt/
indicate (v)	/'ɪndɪˌkeɪt/
influential (adj)	/ˌɪnflu'ɛnʃəl/
inspire (v)	/ɪn'spaɪər/
interfere (v)	/ˌɪntər'fɪər/
mammal (n)	/'mæməl/
mass (adj)	/mæs/
misunderstanding (n)	/ˌmɪsʌndər'stændɪŋ/
mysterious (adj)	/mɪ'stɪəriəs/
overcome (v)	/ˌoʊvər'kʌm/
polar bear (n)	/'poʊlər ˌbɛər/
psychologist (n)	/saɪ'kɒlədʒɪst/
purely (adv)	/'pjʊərli/
put forward (phr v)	/ˌpʊt 'fɔrwərd/
rainfall (n)	/'reɪnˌfɔl/
rate (n)	/reɪt/
rethink (v)	/ri'θɪŋk/
reveal (v)	/rɪ'vil/
revenge (n)	/rɪ'vɛndʒ/
save (v)	/seɪv/
short-term (adj)	/'ʃɔrt'tɜrm/
shorten (v)	/'ʃɔrtn/
significantly (adv)	/sɪg'nɪfɪkəntli/
species (n)	/'spiʃiz/
sponsor (v)	/'spɒnsər/
strengthen (v)	/'strɛŋkθən/
sudden (adj)	/'sʌdn/
surroundings (n)	/sə'raʊndɪŋz/
survival (n)	/sər'vaɪvəl/
survive (v)	/sər'vaɪv/
suspect (v)	/sə'spɛkt/
suspicious (adj)	/sə'spɪʃəs/
take to (phr v)	/'teɪk tu/
unique (adj)	/ju'nik/
unwilling (adj)	/ʌn'wɪlɪŋ/
wipe out (phr v)	/'waɪp 'aʊt/

Extension

conform (v)	/kən'fɔrm/
conforming (adj)	/kən'fɔrmɪŋ/
conformity (n)	/kən'fɔrməti/
endurance (n)	/ɛn'dərəns/
familiar (adj)	/fə'mɪljər/
habit (n)	/'hæbət/
habitual (adj)	/hə'bɪtʃuəl/
habituate (v)	/hə'bɪtʃueɪt/
hazard (n)	/'hæzərd/
insulation (n)	/ˌɪnsə'leɪʃən/
modify (n)(v)	/'mɒdəˌfaɪ/
modification (n)	/ˌmɒdəfə'keɪʃən/
modified (adj)	/'mɒdəˌfaɪd/
prospect (n)	/'prɒspɛkt/
sanctuary (n)	/'sæŋktʃuˌɛri/
sustain (v)	/sə'steɪn/
sustained (adj)	/sə'steɪnd/
sustaining (adj)	/sə'steɪnɪŋ/
sustenance (n)	/'sʌstənəns/

Vocabulary Building

animal product (n)	/'ænəməl ˌprɒdəkt/
book shop (n)	/bʊk ʃɑp/
farm house (n)	/fɑrm haʊs/
ice age (n)	/aɪs eɪdʒ/
rain drop (n)	/reɪn drɒp/
science teacher (n)	/'saɪəns ˌtitʃər/
sea creature (n)	/'si ˌkritʃər/
social media campaign (n)	/'soʊʃəl 'midiə kæmˌpeɪn/

Vocabulary in Context

camp (n)	/kæmp/
hit a wall (idiom)	/'hɪt ə 'wɔl/
proof (n)	/pruf/
spot (n)	/spɒt/
surface (n)	/'sɜrfəs/
willingness (n)	/'wɪlɪŋnɪs/

UNIT 7

Review

make a living (phrase)	/meɪk ə 'lɪvɪŋ/
make a splash (phrase)	/meɪk ə splæʃ/
make an impression (phrase)	/meɪk ən ɪm'prɛʃən/
make sense (phrase)	/meɪk sɛns/
make the most of (phrase)	/meɪk ðə moʊst ʌv/
make up your mind (phrase)	/meɪk ʌp jʊər maɪnd/
make way (phrase)	/meɪk weɪ/

Unit Vocabulary

additional (adj)	/ə'dɪʃənl/
alternative (adj)	/ɔl'tɜrnətɪv/
approach (n)	/ə'proʊtʃ/
assessment (n)	/ə'sɛsmənt/
bacteria (n)	/bæk'tɪəriə/
break (v)	/breɪk/
brick (n)	/brɪk/
combination (n)	/ˌkɒmbɪ'neɪʃən/
commonly (adv)	/'kɒmənli/
contribute (v)	/kən'trɪbjut/
create (v)	/kri'eɪt/
creative (adj)	/kri'eɪtɪv/
creatively (adv)	/kri'eɪtɪvli/
demonstration (n)	/ˌdɛmən'streɪʃən/
desire (v)	/dɪ'zaɪər/
detailed (adj)	/'diteɪld/
displace (v)	/dɪs'pleɪs/
external (adj)	/ɪk'stɜrnəl/
extreme (adj)	/ɪk'strim/
follow (v)	/'fɒloʊ/

format (n)	/'fɔrmæt/
freedom (n)	/'fridəm/
functional (adj)	/'fʌŋkʃənl/
genuine (adj)	/'dʒɛnjuɪn/
imaginary (adj)	/ɪ'mædʒəˌnɛri/
implication (n)	/ˌɪmplɪ'keɪʃən/
integrate (v)	/'ɪntɪˌgreɪt/
learner (n)	/'lɜrnər/
lifestyle (n)	/'laɪfˌstaɪl/
make up (phr v)	/'meɪk 'ʌp/
measure (v)	/'mɛʒər/
needle (n)	/'nidl/
obey (v)	/oʊ'beɪ/
original (adj)	/ə'rɪdʒənl/
outcome (n)	/'aʊtˌkʌm/
preference (n)	/'prɛfərəns/
realistically (adv)	/ˌriə'lɪstɪkli/
recommendation (n)	/ˌrɛkəmən'deɪʃən/
rely on (phr v)	/rɪ'laɪ ɒn/
resolve (v)	/rɪ'zɒlv/
safety (n)	/'seɪfti/
score (n)	/skɔr/
sketch (v)	/skɛtʃ/
solution (n)	/sə'luʃən/
stimulate (v)	/'stɪmjʊˌleɪt/
supervise (v)	/'supərˌvaɪz/
task (n)	/tæsk/
treatment (n)	/'tritmənt/
truly (adv)	/'truli/
usage (n)	/'jusɪdʒ/
variety (n)	/və'raɪəti/

Extension

break someone's heart (phrase)	/breɪk 'sʌmˌwʌnz hɑrt/
break the law (phrase)	/breɪk ðə lɔ/
create a scene (phrase)	/kri'eɪt ə sin/
create an email address (phrase)	/kri'eɪt ən i'meɪl 'æˌdrɛs/
creative gift (phrase)	/kri'eɪtɪv gɪft/
come up with (phr v)	/'kʌm 'ʌp ˌwɪð/
destroy creativity (phrase)	/dɪ'strɔɪ ˌkrieɪ'tɪvəti/
follow your heart (phrase)	/'fɑloʊ jʊər hɑrt/
follow your instinct (phrase)	/'fɑloʊ jʊər 'ɪnstɪŋkt/
imagination (n)	/ɪˌmædʒə'neɪʃən/
innovative (adj)	/'ɪnəˌveɪtɪv/
job creation (phrase)	/dʒɑb kri'eɪʃən/
originality (n)	/əˌrɪdʒə'nælɪti/
stifle creativity (phrase)	/'staɪfəl ˌkrieɪ'tɪvəti/
vision (n)	/'vɪʒən/
wealth creation (phrase)	/wɛlθ kri'eɪʃən/

Vocabulary Building

analysis (n)	/ə'næləsɪs/
analyze (v)	/'ænəˌlaɪz/
assess (v)	/ə'sɛs/
concern (n)	/kən'sɜrn/
concerned (adj)	/kən'sɜrnd/
conclude (v)	/kən'klud/
conclusion (n)	/kən'kluʒən/
fluent (adj)	/'fluənt/
flexibility (n)	/ˌflɛksə'bɪlɪti/
flexible (adj)	/'flɛksəbəl/
fluency (n)	/'fluənsi/
intelligence (n)	/ɪn'tɛləʤəns/
intelligent (adj)	/ɪn'tɛlɪdʒənt/
knowledge (n)	/'nɑlədʒ/
know (v)	/noʊ/
knowledge (n)	/'nɒlɪdʒ/
logic (n)	/'lɒdʒɪk/
logical (adj)	/'lɒdʒɪkəl/
publication (n)	/ˌpʌblɪ'keɪʃən/
publish (v)	/'pʌblɪʃ/
useful (adj)	/'jusfəl/
usefulness (n)	/'jusfəlnɪs/
variation (n)	/ˌvɛri'eɪʃən/

Vocabulary in Context

edit (v)	/'ɛdət/
electrocute (v)	/ɪ'lɛktrəˌkjut/
get (your) meaning across (phrase)	/'gɛt (jər) 'minɪŋ əˌkrɔs/

grab (v) /græb/
heartbroken (adj) /'hɑrt,broʊkən/
manners (n) /'mænərz/

UNIT 8

Review
connect (v) /kə'nɛkt/
face-to-face /feɪs-tu-feɪs
  conversation (phrase) ˌkɑnvər'seɪʃən/
get distracted (v) /gɛt dɪ'stræktəd/
get a message out (phrase) /gɛt ə 'mɛsəʤ aʊt/
interpersonal skills (phrase) /ˌɪntər'pərsənəl skɪlz/
join in (v) /ʤɔɪn ɪn/
make a point (phrase) /meɪk ə pɔɪnt/
make connections (phrase) /meɪk kə'nɛkʃənz/
pay attention (phrase) /peɪ ə'tɛnʃən/
post photos (phrase) /poʊst 'foʊ,toʊz/
respond (v) /rɪ'spɑnd/
share (v) /ʃɛr/

Unit Vocabulary
abuse (n) /ə'bjus/
accuse (v) /ə'kjuz/
acknowledge (v) /æk'nɑlɪʤ/
apparently (adv) /ə'pærəntli/
appropriate (adj) /ə'proʊpriɪt/
associate with (phr v) /ə'soʊʃi,eɪt ,wɪð/
assumption (n) /ə'sʌmpʃən/
assure (v) /ə'ʃʊər/
awkward (adj) /'ɔkwərd/
awkwardness (n) /'ɔkwərdnɪs/
belong (v) /bɪ'lɔŋ/
bully (v) /'bʊli/
campaign (v) /kæm'peɪn/
cardboard (n) /'kɑrd,bɔrd/
citizen (n) /'sɪtəzən/
classic (n) /'klæsɪk/
combine (v) /kəm'baɪn/
compliment (v) /'kɑmplə,mɛnt/
conscious (adj) /'kɑnʃəs/
conservative (adj) /kən'sɜrvətɪv/
criticize (v) /'krɪtɪ,saɪz/
decoration (n) /ˌdɛkə'reɪʃən/
define (v) /dɪ'faɪn/
deliberately (adv) /dɪ'lɪbərɪtli/
deny (v) /dɪ'naɪ/
diplomat (n) /'dɪplə,mæt/
discriminate (v) /dɪ'skrɪmə,neɪt/
dishonest (adj) /dɪs'ɑnɪst/
elect (v) /ɪ'lɛkt/
element (n) /'ɛləmənt/
elsewhere (adv) /ɛls'wɛər/
encounter (v) /ɛn'kaʊntər/
enthusiasm (n) /ɪn'θuzi,æzəm/
equality (n) /ɪ'kwɑlɪti/
experiment (v) /ɛk'spɛrə,mɛnt/
fed up (phr v) /'fɛd ʌp/
fingernail (n) /'fɪŋgər,neɪl/
firmly (adv) /'fɜrmli/
forget (v) /fər'gɛt/
generalization (n) /ˌʤɛnərələ'zeɪʃən/
global (adj) /'gloʊbəl/
identity (n) /aɪ'dɛntɪti/
ignore (v) /ɪg'nɔr/
immigrant (n) /'ɪmɪgrənt/
incident (n) /'ɪnsɪdənt/
insist on (v) /ɪn'sɪst ,ɑn/
intense (adj) /ɪn'tɛns/
interpret (v) /ɪn'tərprɪt/
invisible (n) /ɪn'vɪzəbəl/
make fun (phr v) /'meɪk 'fʌn/
massive (adj) /'mæsɪv/
misbehave (v) /ˌmɪsbɪ'heɪv/
misunderstand (v) /ˌmɪsʌndər'stænd/
modify (v) /'mɒdɪ,faɪ/
norm (n) /nɔrm/
notion (n) /'noʊʃən/
obsession (n) /əb'sɛʃən/
offended (adj) /ə'fɛndɪd/
phenomenon (n) /fə'nɑmɪ,nɑn/
policy (n) /'pɑləsi/
praise (v) /preɪz/
presence (n) /'prɛzəns/
pretend (v) /prɪ'tɛnd/
proportion (n) /prə'pɔrʃən/
protest (n) /'proʊtɛst/

racism (n) /'reɪsɪzəm/
react (v) /ri'ækt/
refresh (v) /rɪ'frɛʃ/
regional (adj) /'riʤənl/
response (n) /rɪ'spɑns/
shopkeeper (n) /'ʃɑp,kipər/
sort (it) out (phr v) /'sɔrt (ɪt) 'aʊt/
statistic (n) /stə'tɪstɪk/
stereotype (n) /'stɛriə,taɪp/
stock (n) /stɑk/

Extension
back-handed /bæk-'hændəd
  compliment (phrase) 'kɑmpləmənt /
flatter (v) /'flætər/
insult (v) /'ɪn,sʌlt/
pay a compliment (phrase) /peɪ ə 'kɑmpləmənt/
pay tribute (col) /peɪ 'trɪbjut/
put someone off (phr v) /pʊt 'sʌm,wʌn ɔf/
reaction (n) /ri'ækʃən/
return a compliment (phrase) /rɪ'tɜrn ə'kɑmpləmənt/

Vocabulary Building
cost-effective (adj) /'kɔst ɪ,fɛktɪv/
deep-rooted (adj) /'dip'rutɪd/
heartbroken (adj) /'hɑrt,broʊkən/
highly-respected (adj) /'haɪli rɪs'pɛktɪd/
like-minded (adj) /'laɪk'maɪndɪd/
long-lasting (adj) /'lɔŋ'læstɪŋ/
open-minded (adj) /'oʊpən'maɪndɪd/
two-faced (adj) /'tu,feɪst/
well-mannered (adj) /'wɛl'mænərd/
worldwide (adj) /'wɜrl'dwaɪd/

Vocabulary in Context
around (prep) /ə'raʊnd/
breakdown (n) /'breɪk,daʊn/
huge step (phrase) /hjuʤ stɛp/
humorous (adj) /'hjumərəs/
self-conscious (adj) /'sɛlf'kɑnʃəs/
somewhat /'sʌm'wʌt kən'strʌktɪv/
  constructive (phrase)

UNIT 9

Review
aid worker (n) /eɪd 'wɜrkər/
demanding (adj) /dɪ'mændɪŋ/
disastrous (adj) /dɪ'zæstrəs/
flood (n) /flʌd/
impact (n) /'ɪmpækt/
rescue (v) /'rɛskju/
save (v) /seɪv/
shelter (n) /'ʃɛltər/
sea level (n) /si 'lɛvəl/
stressful (adj) /'strɛsfəl/

Unit Vocabulary
absence (n) /'æbsəns/
affect (v) /ə'fɛkt/
aid (n) /eɪd/
ally (n) /'ælaɪ/
appeal (v) /ə'pil/
assistance (n) /ə'sɪstəns/
block (v) /blɑk/
care for (phr v) /'kɛər ,fɔr/
coastal (adj) /'koʊstl/
convention (n) /kən'vɛnʃən/
cope (v) /koʊp/
corrupt (adj) /kə'rʌpt/
crisis (n) /'kraɪsɪs/
debris (n) /də'bri/
delegate (n) /'dɛlɪgɪt/
devastation (n) /ˌdɛvə'steɪʃən/
disaster (n) /dɪ'zæstər/
donation (n) /doʊ'neɪʃən/
earthquake (n) /'ɜrθ,kweɪk/
edit (n) /'ɛdɪt/
evacuate (v) /ɪ'vækju,eɪt/
flee (v) /fli/
frustrate (v) /'frʌstreɪt/
global warming (n) /'gloʊbəl 'wɔrmɪŋ/
graduate (n) /'græʤuɪt/
greed (n) /grid/
headquarters (n) /'hɛd,kwɔrtərz/
homeless (adj) /'hoʊmlɪs/

housing (n) /'haʊzɪŋ/
humanity (n) /hju'mænɪti/
imprison (v) /ɪm'prɪzən/
inclusive (adj) /ɪn'klusɪv/
infrastructure (n) /'ɪnfrə,strʌktʃər/
initiative (n) /ɪ'nɪʃətɪv/
interactive (adj) /ˌɪntər'æktɪv/
joy (n) /ʤɔɪ/
launch (v) /lɔntʃ/
limited (adj) /'lɪmɪtɪd/
neutral (adj) /'nutrəl/
on behalf of (phr v) /ˌɑn bɪ'hæf əv/
overlook (v) /ˌoʊvər'lʊk/
panel (n) /'pænl/
portrait (n) /'pɔrtrɪt/
precious (adj) /'prɛʃəs/
programmer (n) /'proʊgræmər/
psychological (adj) /ˌsaɪkə'lɑʤɪkəl/
realization (n) /ˌriələ'zeɪʃən/
reconstruction (n) /ˌrikən'strʌkʃən/
recovery (n) /rɪ'kʌvəri/
relief (n) /rɪ'lif/
reminder (n) /rɪ'maɪndər/
remote (adj) /rɪ'moʊt/
representative (n) /ˌrɛprɪ'zɛntətɪv/
restore (v) /rɪ'stɔr/
right (n) /raɪt/
rise (v) /raɪz/
satellite (n) /'sætl,aɪt/
scale (n) /skeɪl/
senior (adj) /'sinjər/
shelter (n) /'ʃɛltər/
shortage (n) /'ʃɔrtɪʤ/
skip (v) /skɪp/
staggering (adj) /'stægərɪŋ/
supply (n) /sə'plaɪ/
survivor (n) /sər'vaɪvər/
sustainable (n) /sə'steɪnəbəl/
the loud (n) /ðə 'laʊd/
the outgoing (n) /ði 'aʊt,goʊɪŋ/
the stupid (n) /ðə 'stupɪd/
trap (v) /træp/
unfamiliar (adj) /ˌʌnfə'mɪljər/

Extension
blackout (n) /'blæ,kaʊt/
destroy (v) /dɪ'strɔɪ/
devastate (v) /'dɛvə,steɪt/
drought (n) /draʊt/
hail (n) /heɪl/
heatwave (n) /hit weɪv/
hurricane (n) /'hɜrə,keɪn/
provide (v) /prə'vaɪd/
tsunami (n) /tsu'nɑmi/

Vocabulary Building
the best (n) /ðə 'bɛst/
the brave (n) /ðə 'breɪv/
the old (n) /ði 'oʊld/
the poor (n) /ðə 'pʊər/
the rich (n) /ðə 'rɪtʃ/
the traumatized (n) /ðə 'trɔmə,taɪzd/
the young (n) /ðə jʌŋ/
the worst (n) /ðə wɜrst/

Vocabulary in Context
give (something) /'gɪv ə 'goʊ/
  a go (phr v)
globe (n) /gloʊb/
on the ground (phrase) /'ɑn ðə 'graʊnd/
siren (n) /'saɪrən/
strike a chord (phr v) /'straɪk ə 'kɔrd/
unfold (v) /ʌn'foʊld/

UNIT 10

Review
absorb (v) /əb'zɔrb/
bacteria (n) /bæk'tɪria/
digestion (n) /daɪ'ʤɛstʃən/
heartbeat (n) /'hɑrt,bit/
infect (v) /ɪn'fɛkt/
muscle (n) /'mʌsəl/
sense (n) /sɛns/
touch (n) /tʌtʃ/

Unit Vocabulary

actively (adj)	/'æktɪvli/
address (v)	/ə'drɛs/
aim (v)	/eɪm/
allergic (adj)	/ə'lɝdʒɪk/
amazement (n)	/ə'meɪzmənt/
antibiotics (n)	/ˌæntibaɪ'ɒtɪks/
apocalypse (n)	/ə'pɒkəˌlɪps/
award (v)	/ə'wɔrd/
bench (n)	/bɛntʃ/
bestseller (n)	/'bɛst'sɛlər/
blindness (n)	/'blaɪndnɪs/
blink (v)	/blɪŋk/
cast (n)	/kæst/
category (n)	/'kætɪˌgɔri/
cell (n)	/sɛl/
chance (n)	/tʃæns/
cheer (v)	/tʃɪər/
chest (n)	/tʃɛst/
clarify (v)	/'klærəˌfaɪ/
clear up (phr v)	/'klɪər 'ʌp/
close down (v)	/'kloʊz 'daʊn/
combine (v)	/kəm'baɪn/
concentration (n)	/ˌkɒnsən'treɪʃən/
consciousness (n)	/'kɒnʃəsnɪs/
considerable (adj)	/kən'sɪdərəbəl/
contribute (v)	/kən'trɪbjut/
convert (v)	/kən'vɝt/
darkness (n)	/'dɑrknɪs/
deadly (adj)	/'dɛdli/
dependent (adj)	/dɪ'pɛndənt/
design (v)	/dɪ'zaɪn/
determined (adj)	/dɪ'tɝmɪnd/
device (n)	/dɪ'vaɪs/
devote (v)	/dɪ'voʊt/
diagnose (v)	/'daɪəgˌnoʊs/
dictate (v)	/'dɪkteɪt/
disgust (n)	/dɪs'gʌst/
disturbing (adj)	/dɪ'stɝbɪŋ/
dose (n)	/doʊs/
drug (n)	/drʌg/
editor (n)	/'ɛdɪtər/
efficiently (adv)	/ɪ'fɪʃəntli/
expose (v)	/ɪk'spoʊz/
express (v)	/ɪk'sprɛs/
extract (n)	/ɪk'strækt/
fascinated (adj)	/'fæsəˌneɪtɪd/
flash (n)	/flæʃ/
force (v)	/fɔrs/
get out (phr v)	/'gɛt 'aʊt/
gripping (adj)	/'grɪpɪŋ/
heath care (n)	/'hɛlθ ˌkɛər/
helmet (n)	/'hɛlmɪt/
honor (n)	/'ɒnər/
house (v)	/haʊz/
inability (n)	/ˌɪnə'bɪlɪti/
inevitable (adj)	/ɪn'ɛvɪtəbəl/
infection (n)	/ɪn'fɛkʃən/
insufficient (adj)	/ˌɪnsə'fɪʃənt/
intensive (adj)	/ɪn'tɛnsɪv/
keep down (phr v)	/'kip 'daʊn/
lead (n)	/lid/
lung (n)	/lʌŋ/
make the most of (phrase)	/'meɪk ðə 'moʊst əv/
misery (n)	/'mɪzəri/
optimistic (adj)	/ˌɒptə'mɪstɪk/
partial (adj)	/'pɑrʃəl/
peer (v)	/pɪər/
portion (n)	/'pɔrʃən/
precisely (adv)	/prɪ'saɪsli/
prescribe (v)	/prɪ'skraɪb/
prescription (n)	/prɪ'skrɪpʃən/
procedure (n)	/prə'sidʒər/
punishment (n)	/'pʌnɪʃmənt/
rapid (adj)	/'ræpɪd/
resistant (adj)	/rɪ'zɪstənt/
respond (v)	/rɪ'spɒnd/
risk (n)	/rɪsk/
run away (v)	/'rʌn ə'weɪ/
slam (v)	/slæm/
slide (v)	/slaɪd/
slow (v)	/sloʊ/
stroke (n)	/stroʊk/
sweat (n)	/swɛt/
symptom (n)	/'sɪmptəm/
thankfully (adv)	/'θæŋkfəli/
therapist (n)	/'θɛrəpɪst/
therapy (n)	/'θɛrəpi/
think through (phr v)	/'θɪŋk 'θru/
threatening (adj)	/'θrɛtnɪŋ/
treat (v)	/trit/
turn to (phr v)	/'tɝn tu/
vision (n)	/'vɪʒən/
visual (adj)	/'vɪʒuəl/
waist (n)	/weɪst/
ward (n)	/wɔrd/
watch out (phr v)	/'wɒtʃ 'aʊt/

Extension

blood pressure (n)	/blʌd 'prɛʃər/
disability (n)	/ˌdɪsə'bɪlɪti/
heart attack (n)	/hɑrt ə'tæk/
medical condition (n)	/'mɛdəkəl kən'dɪʃən/
numb (adj)	/nʌm/
rehabilitation (n)	/ˌrihəˌbɪlə'teɪʃən/
slur (v)	/slɝ/

Vocabulary Building

aim at (phr v)	/eɪm æt/
chance of (phr v)	/tʃæns ʌv/
devoted to (phr v)	/dɪ'voʊtəd tu/
raise awareness of (phrase)	/reɪz ə'wɛrnəs ʌv/
resistant to (phr v)	/rɪ'zɪstənt tu/

Vocabulary in Context

comfort zone (n)	/'kʌmfərt ˌzoʊn/
extensive (adj)	/ɪk'stɛnsɪv/
grasp (v)	/græsp/
nickname (n)	/'nɪkˌneɪm/
set (n)	/sɛt/
superficial (adj)	/ˌsupər'fɪʃəl/